# PARTICIPATORY FOREST POLICIES
# AND POLITICS IN INDIA

*This book is dedicated to Asharfi, Jawahir, Hari, Pinchu ki maa, Shambhuji, Graeme Wallace, the head porter at Sidney Sussex College, and Janet Raymer, our bedmaker at Herne Lodge, Cambridge.*

# Participatory Forest Policies and Politics in India

Joint Forest Management Institutions in Jharkhand
and West Bengal

MANISH TIWARY

Routledge
Taylor & Francis Group

LONDON AND NEW YORK

First published 2004 by Ashgate Publishing

Reissued 2019 by Routledge
2 Park Square, Milton Park, Abingdon, Oxon, OX14 4RN
52 Vanderbilt Avenue, New York, NY 10017

*Routledge is an imprint of the Taylor & Francis Group, an informa business*

Publisher's Note
The publisher has gone to great lengths to ensure the quality of this reprint but points out that some imperfections in the original copies may be apparent.

Disclaimer
The publisher has made every effort to trace copyright holders and welcomes correspondence from those they have been unable to contact.

A Library of Congress record exists under LC control number:

ISBN 13: 978-0-8153-9103-6 (hbk)
ISBN 13: 978-1-138-62014-8 (pbk)
ISBN 13: 978-1-351-15184-9 (ebk)

# Contents

**Chapter 8  Conclusion: The Role of Ecological Institutions in Participatory Forest Management**

# List of Tables, Graphs, Figures and Maps

# Preface

This monograph looks into issues of effective and sustainable forest management and associated rural development in India. In 1990, the government of India announced a forest policy resolution called Joint Forest Management (JFM) that promises several managerial and usufruct concessions (including cash profit) to forest citizens in exchange for management of state-owned forests. I investigate four institutions – village-based forest protection groups, the Forest Department, *panchayat* (village council) and non-governmental organizations (NGOs) – across the States of Jharkhand and West Bengal.

**Main findings:** I challenge notions of assumed virtues of moral economy and romanticized views of indigenous knowledge and practices. I argue that the shift in management paradigm, from custodial forestry to participation, is as much a consequence of the popular rhetoric on equity and welfare as it is the realization that forests next to habitation cannot be protected without seeking participation from villagers who live nearby. Although the formal grip of the state on both the tenure of forest land and managerial aspects of Joint Forest Management remains strong, the impact of Joint Forest Management at the village-level is evident in several ways. It is demonstrated that the members of the Forest Protection Committee (FPC), an institution formed on the JFM initiative, and the self-initiated forest protection groups are playing active roles in negotiating transactions of forest usufruct within and outside their communities. This includes creating 'zones of exclusion' where local forests are made out of bounds for outsiders while they approve customary extractive methods of resident villagers. The key incentive for participation in forest management, however, lies in being able to secure forest usufruct for routine homestead and agriculture needs. In doing so, the villagers show little remorse in breaking the JFM rules and agreement with the state. The cash share from the timber harvest, on the other hand, is often a paltry sum, and is made available by the Forest Department at irregular intervals, if at all.

The Forest Department in West Bengal has taken several steps, such as policy initiatives and restructuring the department to solicit participation from the forest citizens. Jharkhand's Forest Department, on the other hand, needs to remedy its infrastructure failings and alter what remains as an essentially top-down management to gain the trust of the villagers and engage them in Joint Forest Management. At the village-level, the junior-level forest officials in both States, in spite of lack of explicit instructions or autonomy in JFM resolution, have made adjustments that acknowledge community forestry practices. They prove useful in giving legitimacy to the methods that villagers adopt for managing local forests and resolving intervillage disputes over forest resources.

Although the village-based forest committees do not have the executive powers or the political base of *panchayats*, they have often asserted themselves against this traditional village institution to secure forest usufruct for their members against villagers who are often from the same *panchayat*. The role of NGOs is unclear in the JFM resolution. I contend that NGOs that include a rural development agenda within their projects and provide a sustained presence in villages provide forums that can be used for forestry management as well. This contrasts with the failure of those NGOs that try to foster 'participatory' values through infrequent visits and using superficial participatory rural appraisal tools.

**Policy implications:** Joint Forest Management provides a useful model to equitably manage the state-owned forests. However, rural development incentives need to be put into place in order to sustain this state-citizen partnership. The silvicultural decisions and harvest operations should also acknowledge the immediate goals of the villagers while recognizing market realities and opportunities, and returns for the individual labour that is put into management of the forest. The book recommends more autonomy for both the village-based forest management committees and the lower-level forest officials. It is recommended that the forest management committees be left not as a mere subsidiary of the *panchayat* system. The book also calls for provisions that can allow new surveys and reclassification of forest lands. An ideal participatory forest management should be able to maintain a symmetrical dialogue with local actors and institutions and keep an eye on the equitable distribution of forest usufruct, generation of revenue, conservation, and overall development. However, each goal does not necessarily need to be fulfilled from the same patch of forest land.

**Manish Tiwary**
Rome/ New Delhi, 2004

# Acknowledgements

Heartfelt thanks to the respondents and hosts at Annagarha and Ranchi in Jharkhand, and Arabari, Bankura, Gopegarh, and Kolkata in West Bengal, India. I also wish to thank the staff members of the Forest Departments, NGOs, and *panchayats* in Jharkhand and West Bengal who provided insights, logistical support, and permitted me to view their records.

In West Bengal, my thanks to: Amitabh Singh Deb (and family), Narendra Pandey, Ajoy Biswas, Sidhartha Brari, Sudipto Maiti, Dr. Tapan Mishra, Prof. S. N. Chattopadhyay, Ganesh Yadav, and Subramaniam Palit. Also, Dr. Nita Mitra, Dr. Subrata Ray (and family), Dr. Anjali Basu (and family), Bibha *di*, and Abhay Kumar.

In Jharkhand, my thanks to: Sanjay Kumar (and family), Krishna Kumar Shah (and family), Manikant Jha, H.S. Prasad, Sharuf Khan, Bhupendra Mishra, and Sandeep Kumar.

At the University of Cambridge, I am indebted to: Dr. Bhaskar Vira, Shiraz Vira, Dr. M. Satish Kumar, Diana Mellows, Anthea Ansell, Jeremy Wilson, Niall Johnson, Mark Russell, Rie Tsutsumi, Laura Cameron, Kohei Watanabe, Julian Green, Shwang-ye Wu, Arno Hammann, Jon Bray, and (most certainly) Bipasha Chatterjee.

In Tokyo, Japan, I thank: Marta Bania, Kimberly Bayer, Dr. Makoto Inoue, and Dr. Awais Latif Piracha.

At Yale University I am grateful for assistance from: Prof. Arun Agrawal, Prof. James Scott, Prof. Michael Dove, Prof. Harry Blair, Dr. Brian Carter, Dr. David Schmidt, Uzma Khan, Mukhtar Mohamed, and Kay Mansfield.

At Ashgate, I thank: Valerie Rose for publishing this monograph, Donna Hamer in administration, Bibi Stoute in production for help with redrawing the maps and Pauline Beavers for editing and getting my book to production.

I acknowledge my debt to the staff of libraries at the University of Cambridge, the United Nations University, and Yale University.

The following funds and fellowships helped both financially and intellectually: Fox International Fellowship, The Yale Center for International and Area Studies, Yale University (U.S.A.); Institute of Advanced Studies/United Nations University Fellowship (Tokyo, Japan); J.N. Tata Scholarship, (Mumbai, India); Smuts

Memorial Scholarship, University of Cambridge; Malaysian Commonwealth Scholarship, Commonwealth Trust, Cambridge; Philip Lake Scholarship, Department of Geography, Cambridge; Sidney Sussex College Graduate Fund Scholarship, Sidney Sussex College, Cambridge. Special thanks are due to Prof. Stuart Corbridge, Dr. Bhaskar Vira, and Dr. M. Satish Kumar for their support with the fellowship applications.

Heartfelt thanks must go to Prof. Stuart Corbridge, for bringing me *home* to Bihar. Over the period, my thoughts, for good or bad, have had important influences from him. I fear I may end up owing too much to Stuart. I acknowledge that moment, one hot day in Muzaffarpur at the dining table, when I had given up, and Papa decided to *step in*.

# List of Abbreviations

| | |
|---|---|
| AFO | Assistant Forest Officer |
| ADFO | Assistant Divisional Forest Officer |
| ASEP | Arabari Socio-Economic Project |
| BDO | Block Development Officer |
| BJP | Bharatiya Janta Party |
| CPI (M) | Communist Party of India (Marxist) |
| CPR | Common Property Resource |
| DANIDA | The Danish Agency for Development Assistance |
| DFID | The Department for International Development |
| DFO | Divisional Forest Officer |
| DLLRO | District Land and Land Reforms Office |
| FD | Forest Department |
| FDA | Forest Development Agency |
| FDC | Forest Development Corporation |
| FPC | Forest Protection Committee |
| FSI | Forest Survey of India |
| GIS | Geographic Information System |
| GOB | Government of Bihar |
| GOI | Government of India |
| GOWB | Government of West Bengal |
| HYV | High Yield Variety |
| IBRAD | Indian Institute of Bio-Social Research and Development |
| ICAR | Indian Council for Agricultural Research |
| IFS | Indian Forest Service |
| IIT | Indian Institute of Technology |
| IRDP | Integrated Rural Development Project |
| ITDP | Integrated Tribal Development Programme |
| JD | Janata Dal |
| JFM | Joint Forest Management |
| JFMC | Joint Forest Management Committee |
| JRY | Jawahar Rozgar Yojana |
| KVK | Krishi Vikas Kendra |
| LAMPS | Large Area Multi-Purpose Society |
| NABARD | National Bank for Agriculture and Rural Development |
| NAP | National Afforestation Programme |
| NGO | Non-governmental Organization |
| NTFP | Non-timber Forest Product |
| OECF | Overseas Economic Cooperation Fund |

PCCF        Principal Chief Conservator of Forest
PF          Protected Forest
PFM         Participatory Forest Management
PRA         Participatory Rural Appraisal
PRI         Panchayati Raj Institution
RDC         Rural Development Centre
RF          Reserved Forest
RJD         Rashtriya Janta Dal
RKM         Ram Krishna Mission
RKM-LP      Ram Krishna Mission-Lokasiksha Parishad
RLEGP       Rural Landless Employment Guarantee Programme
SC          Scheduled Caste
SF          Social Forestry
SIDA        Swedish International Development Agency
SPWD        Society for Promotion of Wastelands Development
SRI         Society for Rural Industrialization
ST          Scheduled Tribe
TMC         Trinamaool Mamta Congress
TRIFED      Tribal Cooperative Development Federation of India
USAID       The United States Agency for International Development
VA          Voluntary Agency
VBS         Van Bachao Samiti
VFMPC       Village Forest Management and Protection Committees
VRS         Van Raksha Samiti
VSS         Vivekanand Seva Sangh

Chapter 1

# Political Ecology
# and India's Forests

## 1.1 Introduction

Forest land occupies nearly one fifth of the Indian landmass, the tenurial right of which rests with the state.[1] The villagers who live next to these state-owned lands depend on forests in varying degrees for subsistence and to support the household economy. Since the nineteenth century and up to the 1970s, indigenous rights and access to forests were progressively contested by state agencies claiming to act in the best national interest. Of late, however, there has been a growing realization that problems such as deforestation cannot be arrested without seeking support from forest citizens. There is also an acceptance that forest land must meet the subsistence needs of rural people. The state, alive to these concerns and although it has shown no sign of relinquishing its right over the tenure of forest land, announced in 1990 a policy resolution called Joint Forest Management (JFM). JFM is a radical breakaway from earlier policies that were based on centralized, revenue-orientated control of forests and promises several managerial and usufruct concessions to forest citizens.

This monograph addresses the Joint Forest Management system and its institutional arrangement and evaluates the extent to which decentralized forest

---

[1] Of its total geographical area of 328.8 million hectares (m ha), India's forest land covers 67.4 m ha (Agrawal 1985). According to the Forest Department's statistics, however, the area of forests in 1976 stood at 74.9 m ha (GOI 1980). (It is possible that areas classified as forests by the Forest Departments have been considered under other categories by the Revenue Department or the Ministry of Agriculture [Agrawal 1985, 6]). Of the total forest area of 74.9 m ha, 50.8 % is declared reserved, about 32 % is protected, whereas 16.9 % is unclassed. Again, since independence, 95.2 % of this is state owned. Joint Forest Management is proposed mainly on protected category forests (also see Appendix II for the ownership pattern of forests in India).

The difference between forest land and forested land: A land registered with the government as forest land may not necessarily have sufficient or any forest cover, as is the case with many such lands in Jharkhand and Bengal. On the other hand, a land with good forest cover may not be registered as forest land.

management can be fostered in varying political environments with marked contrasts among the stakeholders. It examines four institutions – village-based forest protection committees, the Forest Department, *panchayats*, and NGOs – in two Indian States, Jharkhand and West Bengal.[2] I have selected West Bengal and Jharkand because on the one hand, these two States share a comparable ecology and history of forest and management infrastructure, and on the other hand, they present a clear contrast on institutional and community characteristics that are under examination here. West Bengal is a pioneer in the attempt to address the failures of Social Forestry and, later, improvise its own JFM rules. Jharkhand, on the other hand, remains tied to top-down forest management and is plagued by problems, such as lack of funds. Additionally, the manner in which the forest community and peripheral ecological institutions (*panchayats* and NGOs) have organized themselves around management of local forests in Jharkhand and Bengal presents both contrasting and analogous features that provide definitive insights into the workings of JFM. The selection of these two States helps illustrate not only how the actual implementation of Joint Forest Management differs from one province to another but also how they differ, given a similar set of community and institutional characteristics, at microlevels. I have taken a political ecology[3] approach to probe the sociopolitical foundations of these institutions and communicative systems (local democracy, gender relations, charismatic leaders) and address areas that might reasonably be assumed to give life to village-based ecological institutions.

This chapter provides a theoretical and policy context for the research. The first part reviews the directions political ecology studies have taken in the past three decades. The next section, using relevant literature, identifies key perceptions of the nature of state control and community dependence on forests in India. At least two schools of thought are found discernibly opposed to each other: one that finds the Forest Department an extension of exploitative colonial bureaucracy demands nothing short of reverting the forest lands to indigenous management, and another that challenges these key findings and seeks the involvement of the state in the

---

[2] In this book, the term institutions is not meant in its broadest sense, but to represent mainly four kinds of organizations – the Forest Department, community forest protection groups, *panchayats* (village councils), and non-governmental organizations (NGOs) – each of which has its own set of rules, actors, and is located in a certain spatial and temporal context.

Also, 'State', when it means a province, has been capitalized to distinguish it from the nation-state.

[3] Blaikie and Brookfield (1987, 17) offer a useful definition: 'The phrase political ecology combines the concerns of ecology and a broadly defined political economy. Together this encompasses the constantly shifting dialectic between society and land-based resources, and also within classes and groups within society itself.'

issues of rural development forestry.[4] The next section discusses the evolution of the control of the Indian state on the forested land and assesses how colonial and postcolonial forestry policies have shaped the management of forests. The final section of this chapter discusses participatory forestry programmes in India. It argues that Social Forestry programmes, despite many failures, held positive lessons for Joint Forest Management. Despite certain constraints, JFM, on the other hand, shows good potential in addressing decentralized forest management and rural development forestry. The section also introduces the institutional design of JFM and points out inconsistencies that continue to exist in the participatory forestry framework.

## 1.2 The Third World's Political Ecology: Moral Economy at its Core

In the last three decades, research has examined extensively, if somewhat unevenly, the contextual sources of environmental change in developing countries. Scholars from diverse academic and institutional backgrounds have examined links between natural resources and political activities in parts of Asia, Africa, and Latin America. Analyses of historical material have also combined cultural and social perspectives. Consequently, a body of work that might be termed third-world political ecology (Bryant 1992) has emerged. Peluso (1992) and Peet and Watts (1996) have stated that the discipline can, however, hardly be considered to be providing any set of theories; if anything, political ecology lacks coherence.[5] Nonetheless, the directions that political ecology studies have taken have been assured. To begin with, there has been a clear shift in the focus of research towards attempting to understand deforestation, land degradation, and other problematic environmental issues in developing countries. The most compelling models to explain disrepairs in natural systems in recent decades have come not from pure (physical) sciences but from factors that are embedded in historicity, social structures, and sociopolitical forces, the very tenets of political ecology. Adams (1990), for example, views environment management (and development) as a political process where the core of green planning lies 'not in its concern with ecology or environment per se, but in its concern with control, power and self-determination'. In a much quoted work, Blaikie and Brookfield (1987) suggest the causes of environmental problems lie in the societal infrastructure and inequalities. Bryant (1992), in an exhaustive literature review of the third world's political

---

[4] Rural development forestry entails incremental additions in capacity and benefit to rural human welfare (through human-forest environment interaction), which itself is inextricably linked to environmental welfare. It can be used as a direct tool by the state for the development of forest citizens or as a paradigm that works as meeting point for the local people and the state (Warren 1995).

[5] This viewpoint is well accepted. Nygren (2000) and Saberwal (1997), for example, have shown agreement with this argument.

ecology, has pointed to the attention that is now commanded by the interaction between environmental and political forces. The stereotypes, such as population pressure (Ehrlich 1968), carrying capacity (Hardin 1968), measures of productivity, and poor indigenous management that had marked the studies of environmental degradation (as the standard reasons for environmental degradation) were sidelined by concepts of indigenous practices (Gadgil and Guha 1995; Peluso 1992; Sen 1992), policy, prioritisation of needs of the rural population (Jodha 1986; Agarwal 1986; Ghai and Vivian 1995), and the need to harness community interdependence to build sustainable institutions (Baland and Platteau 1996; Wade 1994). These approaches combined concerns of gender (Agarwal 1994; Sarin 1995, 1996; Shiva 1989), heterogeneity of interests in rural societies (Byres 1994), and even economic opportunities for the rural population in natural resources (Naik 1997). This trend has also informed the research practices that would, for example, follow participatory rural appraisal (PRA) methods using the 'farmers first' model (Chambers et al. 1989).

Again, as the boundaries of political ecology were being defined, the study itself did not remain limited to the academic community. Practitioners, environmentalists, conservationists, and journalists have all joined the environmental bandwagon and brought the attention of the world community to the environmental politics of developing countries in a significant and consistent manner. The 1972 UN Conference on Human Environment, followed by the Brundtland Commission Report in 1989, were key events in the internationalization of what earlier had been within the realm of local and national concerns. The positions taken by international forums, pressure groups, and voluntary organizations affected the very heart of environmental policies in developing countries. Environmental concerns crossed sovereign boundaries and caught the imagination of people worldwide with slogans that were designed and perfected by academics and quasi-political ecologists alike. The resultant rhetoric, backed by academic discourse, has been decidedly an important influence in making nation-states address global environmental issues (Agrawal 2001). The practitioners of political ecology stressed the global effects of local environmental disasters (Disilva et al. 1994). The natural ecosystems, such as tropical forests, for example, were to be treated as the 'heritage of world community' (Nygren 2000). These concerns have obliged international donors and lenders to stress policies that are conservation-oriented. More recently, funded environmental projects must demonstrate that they are responsive to the needs of local communities. NGOs routinely emphasize the need for greater public participation and community involvement when seeking solutions to environmental problems: 'management at the local level is necessary for achieving the global goal of sustainable development' (Ghai and Vivian 1995). The 1992 UN Conference added an important impetus by endorsing local participation, equity, and grassroots democracy in environmental agendas. These elements came to be at the very heart of ecological movements around the world (Castells 1997).

The political ecology discourse on forestry is no exception. Two important characters that have emerged as essential to understanding contemporary forestry are the multiple numbers of actors and institutions that are involved in forest dialogue and the standard 'language pack' that is used to address forestry issues. In India, although pressure groups, researchers, and environmentalists form a strong force in negotiating with the state on behalf of rural communities (Guha 1994), others such as NGOs, *panchayats*, and community-based forest protection groups are increasingly involved with the actual forest management. On the other hand, the vocabulary that is used by these numerous actors has common key themes, such as fulfillment of subsistence needs, use of indigenous knowledge, decentralization, participation, involvement of women and tribals – elements that are guided by the principles of moral economy.

The term moral economy was brought to popular attention by E.P.Thompson, who had supported the idea of a 'history from below' (Thompson 2001) advocating the importance of grassroots data to illuminate the politics that lie within marginal social groups. A number of studies since have highlighted the locally understood concepts of property rights, community membership, and the social good (Munro 1998). In a state-citizen perspective, the moral economy 'theories' (ibid.) are often used to explore the negotiations between rural citizens and state agents over the state incursions in social life. Scott, for example, has maintained that local knowledge is as important as formal and epistemic knowledge (Scott 1976) and has criticized the large-scale state inventions that are centrally administered and fail to appreciate the values, desires, and objections of their subjects (Scott 1998). The discourses have tended to attribute agrarian institutions with typical characteristics, such as equality, community values, and, 'above all, the right to subsistence' (Farmer and Bates 1996). They also link the breakdown of peasant institutions and conflicts in agrarian societies to the spread of markets and private interests (ibid.). The arguments have usefully contributed to how peasants are perceived and brought sensitivity to rural norms in mainstream discourses. Jeffery and Sundar (1999), on the other hand, note that the normative values that are proclaimed of rural community systems are not always exclusive to state and markets. Both market and the state, for example, have functioned with some normative support and, on the other hand, peasant economies are not completely independent of market exchanges (ibid.). Similarly, in India's forests, the rhetoric that makes up the 'new moral economy of Indian forests' (Jeffery and Sundar 1999, 18), terminologies, such as 'participation', 'community', and 'gender divisions' (discussed later in this chapter) remain contested. Jeffery and Sundar (1999) point out that the rural value systems are based on selected, even invented traditions, all of which are not necessarily inherent to the peasants and where the forest citizens can just draw 'unthinkably upon shared norms and values' (ibid., 18).

To be sure, the interests in community customary knowledge and practices were also helped by the increased worldwide concern with the increasing democratic control people had over their lives and political, social, and economic environment (Mathur 1997). Also, the period since the 1970s has seen dissatisfaction with mainstream development notions, and notions of development that are led by NGOs and community forums (as against the state) have gained acceptance (Pieterse 1998). Moreover, as the state has been blamed for failures to bring development and equity and carry out sustainable use of resources (ibid.), these new actors have challenged the state from a standpoint of 'peasant popular culture' (Munro 1998) and become the focus of attention to take up tasks that were earlier under the authority of the state. Indeed, in the context of forest, the interrelatedness of poverty, environmental degradation, and failures of state agencies (Jodha 1986; Guha 1994; Wilde and Vainio-Mattilla 1995) have not gone amiss.[6] The earlier development narratives that 'equated forest with idealized nature' (Jeffery and Sundar 1999) or explained deforestation in 'Malthusian terms' (ibid.) are on the decline. Instead, 'different calls on the forest' (Westoby 1987) are being made in which they are obliged to provide a flow of physical and social benefits to the peasants and balance the needs for timber production only when the community's needs are met on a 'priority basis' (GOI 1988).

### 1.2.1 Discussion

This section discussed the course that political ecology studies has taken since its inception more than three decades ago. The attention that political ecology has received owes a great deal to the collaboration of environmental activists and academics. These associations have been successful in bringing a variety of concerns from several fields to a relatively coherent body of work. Two significant elements mark the current approach to studying forestry: involvement of a multitude of institutions and use of a vocabulary that is guided by principles of 'moral economy'. A keen coupling of 'subsistence'-orientated ideologies with failures of the state to deliver better and equitable results in development and sustainable environment has shifted the attention to management where the foci are located at the community level. In investigating Joint Forest Management systems in India, this monograph finds several of the moral economy concepts, and ecological actors, such as the Forest Departments, village-based forest committees, village councils, and NGOs, and the concepts of development, participation, and forest use under scrutiny.

The next section examines key debates that underlie forestry studies in India. A similar combination of academic scholarship and activism is in evidence there. The prominent feature in the recent Indian forestry studies is the struggle that has existed between the modern Indian state and the rural community over control, use and management of the forest resources.

---

[6] Such concerns are apparent also at the international level. The Stockholm conference of 1972 linked the environment and development debates, and later, in 1989, the Brundtland Commision report made its famous, albeit contested (see Adams 1990) call for 'sustainable development' (Gupta 1998).

## 1.3 Indian Forestry Debates: The State-Citizen Dichotomy

A rigid state-citizen dichotomy dominates the forest discourse in which the dialogue about institutions and concepts that are used to address them has suffered from fetishization. Throughout history the state control over forest land has seldom been without ambivalence, and there have been continuous negotiations, latent or active, with the forest dependent citizens. On the other hand, villagers who depend on forests for fulfilling various needs do not necessarily conform to the stereotypes that are informed by such 'virtues' as sustainable indigenous management to fulfill the subsistence needs.

Although colonial foresters have chronicled the events as the processes of survey, settlement, and various other facets of scientific forestry in India (Ribbentrop 1900; Stebbing 1921, for example), the analysis of ecological history and the polity of India's forests is a comparatively new phenomenon. Indian political ecologists starting in the early 1970s took specific tasks onto themselves. Ramachandra Guha laid an important foundation for this genre of political ecology by trying 'to bring an ecological dimension to the study of agrarian history and peasant resistance' (Guha 1989, preface). The debate as to which regime of forest management, the British or indigenous, was more pertinent has brought available records under close scrutiny. The genre itself was galvanized into dizzy spells by the Chipko movement with celebrated writing by Ramachandra Guha and his colleague Madhav Gadgil. Another writer, Vandana Shiva, on the other hand, addressed issues such as gender, monoculture, and globalization, although in a vein not very different from Guha and Gadgil.

Guha has maintained that the state represents territorial and commercial interests that were counter to those of village communities where the interests of the forest citizens had been marginalized by the state. This 'theory' has informed the works of many researchers and indeed, dominates the political ecology discourse about Indian forests. The discourse about the struggle for access to India's forests consistently yielded two chief protagonists: the 'virtuous peasants and a vicious state' (Nygren 2000). In arguing the case of a state-citizen dichotomy, Ramachandra Guha, for example, challenged the central premises of the imperial historians – that the colonizers had saved the forests of South Asia from certain destruction by indigenous forest users (Guha 1983). Guha proposed that during the mid-nineteenth century, three schools of thought had developed with regard to the future treatment of the forests and forest land,

> ... the first, that of annexationists held out for nothing less than total state control over the forest areas. The second, that of the pragmatics, argued in favour of state management of ecologically sensitive and strategically valuable forests, allowing other areas to remain under communal systems of management. The third position, the populists completely rejected state intervention, holding that tribals and peasants must exercise sovereign rights over woodland. (However), of the three, the annexationists triumphed (Guha 1989).

Indeed, a corollary to Guha's annexationist theory is that such forest-land acquisitions and alienating land-tenure arrangements give forest-dependent communities a moral right to reclaim their 'share' in natural resources (Pathak 1994). Guha and Gadgil's idea of a predatory state finds support in select statements of colonial foresters. Ribbentrop, the chief-forester in colonial India, for example, argued that scientific forestry under imperial aegis marked the end of a 'war on the forests' (Ribbentrop 1900). Stebbing contended that rapacious private interests were brought under scientific supervision and control in the colonial period (Stebbing 1921). Arguing for sustainable indigenous practices, Guha reasoned that customary restraints on the use of trees had earlier ensured a renewal, but colonial land control and commercialization led to deforestation (Guha 1989, 29) and erosion of indigenous practices (Guha 1983, 1989; also Sen 1992). Gadgil views the period up to 1800 A.D., as a time of 'equilibrium' between people and nature (Gadgil 1985). In professing sustainable ecosystem practices, Gadgil and Guha, in their collaborated work, argue in favour of indigenous practices of *ecosystem people* as opposed to the reckless urban *omnivores* (Gadgil and Guha 1995).[7]

This approach rarely recognized different goals and methods that have been used to access forest usufruct at various levels in different regions and at different times. Guha and Gadgil overlooked the influence of the individual historical events that had marked the struggle between the state and the peasant for control and acquisition of forest lands. It was, for example, not until 1865 when, through a raft of legislation (see Appendix I), the Government of India reserved many forests to itself for production purposes that previously would have been managed as common property resources by forest-dependent groups. In many areas, such territorialization and state control was never accomplished (including in the Chotanagpur plateau containing Jharkhand and parts of southwest Bengal) (Sivaramakrishnan 1996). It is this latter phase of the colonial regime (1865-1947) that is particularly targeted by the likes of Guha and Gadgil who see the colonial forestry practices as an ecological watershed that disrupted the relationship of forest-based communities with the land (Guha 1983). Rangan agrees that in the period between 1918 and 1947, the emphasis of forest management had an industrial focus. She suggests, however, that it could achieve only limited success because of famines, world wars, and nationalist movements (Rangan 1997).

Rangan also differs significantly on the Chipko movement that is otherwise used by environmentalists to portray a notion of rural rebellion to protect their fragile forest environments that were being destroyed because of wrongful state policies and forestry methods. Chipko has been celebrated for the resistance that the peasant put up against the cutting down of trees by private contractors acting on

---

[7] This argument was extended by the authors in the context of independent India to explain the 'omnivorous' urban population who unethically exploit natural resources, making 'ecological refugees' out of the rural poor (Gadgil and Guha 1995).

behalf of the state. Rangan, instead, argues that the movement was orchestrated by village elites; the incentive that poor people had in their involvement with the movement was, in fact, principally to protest against the meagre amount of entrepreneurial activity they could secure from forestry. Rangan notes the doublespeak and the populist rhetoric of the Chipko leader, Sundarlal Bahuguna. She argues that he used the centralizing attitude of the central government to oust private enterprises and marginalize the power of the State's forest officials (Rangan 1993, 256). Orchestrated mainly by elites, Chipko failed to express the interests of the poor peasant society seeking employment opportunities and development (represented somewhat by the other Chipko leader, Chandi Prasad Bhatt). Rangan notes that,

> popular environment protests in India and arguably in other parts of the world all have a common concern, in pressuring states to intervene on their behalf to ensure equitable access to the potential benefits of economic development (Rangan 1996, 206).[8]

Rangan contests the idea of the state being routinely demonized by environmental scholars and activists (Rangan 1997). She argues that,

> representing the State as monolithic, eternally predatory, and always in opposition to civil society, is not only ahistorical, factually incorrect, and analytically flawed, but also precludes any possibility of exploring alternative ways of linking state institutions and civil society in shared projects in an attempt to translate ideas of regional economic and ecological sustainability through material and institutional practices (ibid., 2139).

The school led by Ramachandra Guha helps little to understand the contemporary phase of the state's weakened claims on pure forest regimes and its resultant paradigmatic shifts to seek participation from rural communities. The state-citizen dichotomy not only alienates the state from forest citizens but also perceives forestry in isolation. The influences of other facets of rural life, such as agriculture (Agrawal and Sivaramakrishnan 2000) and markets (Balachander 1995) that to villagers are not separated from their everyday life are seldom appreciated. Such discourses ignore the importance and potential of actors in civil societies, such as the NGOs (Raustalia 1997) and village forums, such as *panchayats* (village councils)[9] as well as community forest protection groups. The role played by environmental lobbyists, pressure groups, and international donors (Chatterjee and Finger 1994) are also played down.

---

[8] Haeuber, a few years earlier, had expressed a similar sentiment, 'What passes for environmental movements are, in fact, peasant movements draped in cloth of environmentalism' (Haeuber 1991, 181).

[9] *Panchayats* are statutory bodies established by the state. They are nonetheless meant for autonomous and decentralized governance of people at the village-level.

The detractors of Guha and Gadgil have tried to produce evidence from ancient Indian literature, however incomplete, that forest practices could have been as harmful and imperialist in approach as in British India. Nesmith (1991), for example, challenged those who espoused sustainable indigenous forest management in precolonial India. She sketched out the countenance of ancient and medieval forestry to emphasize that forest practices in ancient and medieval India could have been as harmful and imperialist in approach as they might have been in British-ruled India.[10] She argued that once the state found a forest resource of value, it has, through time, tried to exercise control over it.[11]

Sivaramakrishnan's (1996) thesis on the ecological history of colonial Bengal points to several instances of ambivalence that the state had demonstrated while laying claims to forest land.[12] The government, in face of contests from local

---

[10] Records on control and management systems of forestry in ancient and medieval India are far from complete. Information about forests during this period is available from dotted sources, such as Kautilya's *Arthashashtra* (321 B.C.), *Indika* by Megasthenes (305 B.C.), the inscriptions of Ashoka (273 B.C. to 236 B.C.), *Akbar-nama* (1650 A.D.) and so on. A commonly accepted notion accounting for forestry practices in the ancient Indian period follows: Aryans who migrated into India in the second millennium B.C. (Olivelle 1993) fought with the indigenous population (proto-Austroloids, who are represented, now, by the tribals or the *adivasis*) and pushed them into remote areas (Nesmith 1991, 47) and dense forests (Singh 1997, 84). The Aryans established political institutions not only of the king but also of chieftains and large landowners (Singh 1997, 64), soverign territory, and the authority to maintain law and order (Singh 1997). They started organized agriculture and forestry practices. During the reign of Chandra Gupta *Maurya* (320 B.C., see appendix), there was a regular Forest Department administered by the *kupyadhyaksha*, or superintendent of Forest products, assisted by a number of *vanpals*, or forest guards (Rawat 1991). Forests in the *Mauryan* Empire came under direct control of the sovereign, and both ownership and control of use were highly differentiated (Agrawal 1985). Forests remained a major source of revenue in the Gupta period (320-550 A.D.), and the state had strong control over them. Records from this period indicate that there was a collection of revenue for forest use from the citizenry (Nesmith 1991). Also see Appendix I.

[11] Nesmith also draws on the wider picture of how 'nature' was understood. Nature, which was regarded as *mother* in a pre-1500 A.D. phase had taken the notion of a *resource* by 1700 A.D. (Nesmith 1991). She calls the shift a 'male, mathematical, and mercantile approach' (ibid., 8).

[12] Sivaramakrishnan's thesis deals with the ecological history of the *Jungle Mahal*, the forested regions of southwest Bengal. His arguments rest on the ground that this region is one of the 'zones of anomaly' in Indian forestry history and had unique characteristics when its forest frontiers were charted out, its territories marked, and rights settled. The British, he contends, in early phases of colonization were apprehensive about the ways of 'extraordinary primitive' inhabitants and resorted to unique forms of 'territorialization' while trying to bring various forested regions under control (ibid., 105).

He states that Jharkhand and *Jungle Mahal* share the history of the Chotanagpur plateau along with ecological history. The Kol uprising in the early 1830s (p 144) and the Santhal

residents and an abiding need for legitimacy, constantly overrode its own revenue (ibid., 684) or territorializaton goals. Rangarajan (1996), on the other hand, pointed out that there has been an existence of subsidiary control by forest citizens using the forest for different purposes, arguably, in manners that may not necessarily be in opposition to those of the state. Singh strengthens the argument by stating that how forest land is accessed and used provides a possibility of the existence of '*de jure* and *de facto*' forest tenurial arrangement (Singh 1997, 3).[13] Vasan (2000), examining the perspective from the state side, points at the heterogeneity in the Forest Department and argues that its operational methods vary at different levels and are often considerably removed from the stated policies. The lower-level foresters, for example, in many instances act as active or passive allies of villagers (Vasan 2000).

In another important set of contributions, scholars have challenged the vocabulary used to bolster the state-citizen dichotomy. Nesmith (1991, 1994) took up the monoculture debate (the protest against the plantation of the fast-growing eucalyptus trees as part of the state-sponsored Social Forestry plantation programmes [see Shiva 1992, Guha and Martinez-Alier 1997, for example]) and argued that eucalyptus was in fact viewed positively by villagers and often used in a complementary fashion to homestead tree planting, and was seldom, as was alleged, found harmful to agriculture. Jewitt's (1996) research challenged the ecofeminist theory of Vandana Shiva that women are a 'repository of ecological knowledge' (Shiva 1989). Among men and women in Chotanagpur, Jewitt found little that demonstrated any essential difference in the sets of agro-ecological knowledge systems between the two sexes. Brodt's research in Central India, on the other hand, showed that there has been both a persistence and a demise of knowledge systems among rural populations: those that are useful have survived (Brodt 1998). In effect, these authors have argued that the romanticization of gender, indigenous knowledge, and practices is not only less helpful but is often untrue.

Although several environmental scholars have appreciated the ambiguity that is embedded in India's forest studies, many continue, partially or totally, to claim 'deeper unities' (Rangarajan, 1996, 92) in the working methods of the state in general and in forest management in particular. To draw a lesson for contemporary forestry, Sivaramakrishnan, for example, extrapolates on contest characteristics that had existed between the state and the citizens during the colonial period. He criticizes a Corbridge article (1993) for not maintaining the distinction between

---

uprising of 1855 (p 147) brought unique protectionist legislations for the tribes. The *Khuntkatti* system of taxation by tribal leaders was left in place.

[13] He complains that, although the state upheld the 'existing' rights in practice, there has been no survey of practices by individuals nor were classifications done for the different conservation measures in different types of forest (Singh 1997, 138).

reserved and protected category forests 'as they emerged in the aftermath of forest conservancy' (Sivaramakrishnan 1996, 249). He asks for appreciation of the uniqueness of the processes of acquisition (of forest land) when the state had used 'divergent and partial strategies' and resulted in 'contentious emergence of Protected Forest' (ibid., 257). However, he overreaches his arguments in seeking to draw lines of solid continuity from colonial forestry to the present that can be used for prescriptions for the current state of forest management. The transposition of his analysis that cuts through time and institutions is problematic. Joint Forest Management, he states, is a field of argument about these very elements of scientific forestry and colonial discourses  (Sivaramakrishnan 1996, 412).[14] He stops short of stating (as Guha does) that undoing the processes of territorialization and assertions by the state hold the keys to the success of forestry in India. Similarly, other authors have recommended a further 'retreat' or a complete reorientation of the state if it were sincere in seeking participation from the rural community in the management of forests. For example, it has been suggested that the *panchayats* be given substantially more control and say in forest management (Burman 1996), private investors be kept out of forest lands (Saxena 1994), the community management groups be given statutory status (Pattnaik and Dutta 1997), rural communities (particularly tribal[15] and women) be involved at each stage of managerial decision, that silvicultural decisions should be made by the rural community (Poffenberger 1996), and the Forest Department be completely reorientated if a meaningful participation were sought (Khator 1991).[16] Although these arguments hold certain positive lessons for participatory forest management, it is clear that there continues to be suspicion and even contempt for the Forest Department. On the one hand, such thinking robs the state of opportunities in which it can use its infrastructure to participate with the people in managing the forest while pursuing a number of goals,  including extending the benefits from the forest land for the purpose of rural development, and, on the other hand, it gives

---

[14] In chapters 4 and 5, I discuss how perceptions and practices at village-level do not follow bureaucratic and historical categorization, and why this alternative position needs to be appreciated if participation from forest citizens is to be taken seriously.

[15] The Indian Constitution relinquished in 1950 the Gandhian goal of tribal integration (Chadha 1997) in favour of affirmative action for a traditionally exploited population, the *harijans*, or the untouchables among the Hindus, and the *adivasis* (Warren 1995, 4). Jawahalal Nehru, the country's first prime minister, instead strived for the preservation of *adivasi* integrity through various forms of state intervention (through reservations of places in government offices, for example), protection (in matters of labour and land transfer), and assistance (development projects) (Khilnani 1997). The sixth schedule established district and regional councils for arbitration over *adivasi* land. In article 19 of the constitution, tribals were granted freedom of movement and settlement anywhere in the country. Article 244 restricts transfer of rights from *adivasi* to a non*adivasi*, and Article 244 A restricts exploitation by moneylenders in tribal areas.

[16] Khator (1991), for example, states that in India, unlike in the west, the bureaucracy has seldom responded to public awareness.

the state only limited choice to pursue a conservationist or commercial interest on select patches of forest lands if even a marginal interest from the community can be demonstrated there.

I do not see JFM as a course of 'deterritorialization' of the processes that were started during colonial rule or as the victory of local people who have challenged the 'state-industry' nexus (Pathak 1995).[17] Access to forest land and its management have instead been in continuous phases of bargaining (Kant 1996) between the state and people. The Forest Department is seen by the rural community as a legitimate institution that can play a crucial role in arranging amicable access to forests, providing solutions to intervillage conflict, and even bringing development into the villages. JFM holds potential for a synthesis of several claims from a number of institutions (including the state) to fulfill a number of goals. The JFM framework not only allows the enlargement of the forest constituency to include several institutions, but it also combines the roles and expertise of these institutions to bring a fresh approach to integrated rural development. The research engages with two 'external' institutions – *panchayats* and NGOs. It remains conscious of heterogeneous rural societies and tests the difference in methods that are employed by different sections within the communities for forest access and use, and those (both actors and institutions) who do not engage in an active manner with forest management and, indeed, compromise forest interest in exchange for other incentives.[18] Methods that are inherent to the communities are compared with those that are subscribed to by the state in the JFM framework.

### 1.3.1 Discussion

Recent studies have begun to illustrate shifts in perception (incentives, reasons) and management (methods, approach) of forest resources both at the state level and at the level of forest-dependent populations. However, the theme of 'vicious state and virtuous peasants' remains dominant in contemporary research and informs the studies and policy recommendations of key researchers. This approach is of limited advantage in addressing the goals of the multiple actors who are involved in participatory forestry today. The work of Guha's school of Indian political ecologists provides important starting points for investigating forestry management

---

[17] A different type of territorialization is discussed in chapters 4 and 5, in which villagers mark boundaries in their local forests to secure usufruct. Again, a different type of deterritorialization is recommended in chapter 6, where the forest department is envisaged with a role to address agrarian issues and rural development apart from their normal silvicultural management, thus ending, in principle, the strict separation of 'fields from forests'.

[18] My book is concerned mainly with the protected category of forests (PFs) where JFM is allowed (certain concessions have been extended in reserved forests in West Bengal). The duality that the state exhibits in allotting PFs for JFM is noted in chapter 3.

in the subcontinent. Corbridge and Jewitt (1997) mention their debt to the work of Ramachandra Guha in pointing to limitations of studies of a similar nature,

> Forest intellectuals such as Guha have done sterling work in the service of more transparent and ecologically sustainable systems of forest management in India. However, while highlighting the virtues of an assumed moral economy was critical to the struggles waged in India in the 1980s to reclaim the country's unquiet woods from a hostile Forest Department,[19] highlighting those same *assumed* virtues as a guide to practical forest management strategies post-1988 is more problematic. New tasks lie ahead for India's forest intellectuals (Corbridge and Jewitt 1997, 2162).

More recently, Agrawal and Sivaramakrishnan (2000), albeit recognizing the 'activist' trait in Guha and Gadgil's research, too have paid rich tributes,

> Indeed without their [Guha and Gadgil] contribution, it would be that much harder to call for studying agrarian environments, or to argue for dismantling the easy separations between nature and culture, indigenous and scientific, community and state, that are erected and enacted in the defense of disciplinary boundaries' (Agrawal and Sivaramakrishnan 2000, 11).

The Guha school of thought, however, provides an insufficient explanation about the nature of contemporary forest institutions, particularly when the state has shifted the management paradigm to accommodate institutions that were traditionally not involved with forestry and now add their own influences to the management of forest land.

## 1.4 The Evolution of Forest Tenure and Institutions

This section continues the argument that a number of factors over several decades played a role in determining the colonial and postcolonial policy framework and the nature of the state's involvement in forest lands. It was not until the later phase of the colonial period that a consolidated forest policy and practices emerged. Some continue to guide the management of forest land after Independence.

If the Mughals had shown little interest in forest management,[20] the British pursued a highly interventionist forest management. However, throughout colonial forestry, both the control of the forest resources ('processes of territorialization' [Sivaramakrishnan 1996], for example) and the actual management (fixing priority

---

[19] However, Rangan reasons that environmental protests in independent India were due to uneven regional development (Rangan 1997, 2139).

[20] The medieval period (1400 A.D. - ) inscriptions such as *Baburnama, Ain-i-Akabari* and *Tuzuk-i-Jahangiri* record extensive hunting for sport along with the sovereigns' *love* for flora and fauna. Rulers, particularly Akbar and Jehangir, though fond of roadside trees and gardens, had shown little interest in forest conservation (Agrawal 1985). Extensive damage occurred in the wars with other ruling states during the medieval period (Grove 1995, 417).

of interest and categorization of forest land, for example) were shaped by a variety of forces, both local and those situated at the national and international levels. British forestry combined concerns about the timber supply, revenue, agriculture, indigenous management, and even wider forces of global economic networks. The newly established British administration in India was initially not alive to the need for careful husbandry of forest resources and was under the impression that the forest wealth of India was inexhaustible (Grove 1995). The British themselves were new to the ideas of systematic forestry and had no developed forest organization in Britain (Agrawal 1985). The forces that shaped the control and management philosophy ranged from a scientific, conservationist approach to 'notions stimulated by literary evocations and romantic images' (Grove 1995, 483). Although the earlier colonizers were attracted to keeping commercially viable species in perpetual production (Rangarajan 1996), another school championed the notion of fulfilling the forest needs of peasants and other ideas that are connected to moral economy. Grove (1995) argues that, until the 1830s, indigenous control had remained somewhat intact despite several attempts to reserve both timber and forest land. The history of acquisition of forests by the state is made more complex by the fact that the government faced unique confrontations from forest citizens and regional elites in different regions of the country, frequently resulting in the grant of exclusive concessions to the rural population of that region (Sivaramakrishnan 1996). Clearly, the period from 1800 to1858, as Rangan has noted, was a period of 'reflection on the different purposes of forest conservation and management' (Rangan 1997, 2139).

The Forest Act in 1878 provided for the constitution of reserved and protected forests. During this period (1880 to 1900), forest settlement, demarcation, and survey were actively in progress in the various provinces. In 1893, in another twist to the conservation-orientated scientific management focus, came Voelcker's report prompting the Government of India to declare in its forest policy that permanent cultivation should come before forestry (Singh 1997), that the satisfaction of the needs of the local population at non-competitive rates, if not free, should override all considerations of revenue, and that after the fulfillment of the above conditions, the realization of *maximum* revenue should be the guiding factor.[21] The Forest Policy of 1894 established that expansion of agricultural cultivation was of greater importance than forest preservation (in Vira 1995).

> Wherever an effective demand for cultivable land exists and can only be supplied from forest areas, the land should ordinarily be relinquished without hesitation, even though that land may have been declared reserved forest under the Forest Act.

By the mid-nineteenth century, the process of territorialization of forests by the state had begun to take a more certain and uniform outlook. Although the

---

[21] For the same period, Gadgil and Guha have argued that the 'state was concerned above all with removing the existing ambiguity about the absolute proprietary right of the state' (Gadgil and Guha 1993).

government continued to dabble in assigning priority of interest on forest resources, on the whole, scientific forestry with strong commercial interests had been put into practice. The progress in organized forestry in the years between 1925 and 1947 ensured that the working plans[22] and forest research had had a history of more than eighty years of 'scientific' management of Indian forests by the time the country gained independence in 1947.

After Independence, the forest continued to be managed by the legislation and policies that had been established during the later phase of the colonial period (Haeuber 1991).[23] Upon abolition of *zamindari*, or the landlord system in the 1950s, large tracts of private forest land were vested with the state, making the Forest Department, as Gadgil and Guha (1995) say, the 'biggest landlord in the country'. The National Forest Policy of 1952 that hinged strongly on scientific forest management also drew from existing forestry practices in the United Soviet Socialists Republic and the United States of America (Nesmith 1991). The principle was to encourage the maximization of forest revenues and give priority to agriculture and industry. The second five-year plan (1952-1957), which had followed the National Forest Policy, directed the provinces to aim to put 33% of their land under forest cover. The five-year plans, however, progressed from consolidating the tenurial policies and management infrastructure that had been inherited from the colonial period to one that addressed issues of rural equity and sustainable use of forests and was in 'harmony with the nature' (Haeuber 1991).

An important shift in the management paradigm resulted when the Agricultural Commissions recommended in 1976 (during the national Emergency period), that forests that had remained under the control of individual provinces were to be made a *concurrent* subject between the States and the centre. The government in New Delhi was to play the core role in formulating policy guidelines and coordinating forestry programmes. The private contractors who had worked as intermediaries in forest work such as harvesting and sale of timber were not permitted to enter forest land, and, instead, the Forest Development Corporation (FDC) was established to carry out forestry work on behalf of the government. It was reasoned that because the interests of the centre and the States did not coincide, the government in New Delhi could arguably take a long-term view (Vira

---

[22] Forest working plans are documents usually printed for each forest division, describing in detail the resource facts, based on which prescriptions are made for future management of forest lands. The recommendations are for a given period of time, usually ten to twenty years.

[23] The Indian Forest Act of 1927, which is modelled on an even earlier act of 1878, continues to define the legal framework for forest management in the country. The Act covers vast ground, including rules on claims on forest land, settlement operations, categorization of forests, rights and concessions, and forest offences. In a slender booklet, the Act defines each of the forestry regulations quite broadly with a wide margin for interpretation (GOI 1927). However, it unambiguously leaves all executive and managerial powers, particularly regarding policing, land tenure, and exclusion with the state.

1995). This arrangement, Guha argued, allowed conservationists, international agencies, and voluntary groups, despite their low numerical strength, to have a considerable influence on the direction of policy at the level of the centre (Guha 1994).[24] State governments were subject to regional and local pressures, which might not be a factor for decision making at the centre, it was argued (Vira 1995). However, the centralization of control of forest resources left the forest departments with less power to deal with regional realities and bargain with pressure groups from the community and other institutions from civil society (Rangan 1993).

## 1.4.1 Discussion

The colonial period had settled on a mix of scientific and revenue-oriented forest management schemes while allowing limited access to the forest land by the local population. Several factors, however, influenced the evolution of colonial forest policies, which were influenced by regional realities and wider influences nationally and internationally. Forest land under direct state management increased more than three-fold after Independence (on abolition of *zamindari*) and were governed fundamentally by legislations and policies that had taken shape during the colonial period. In the last three decades, the state began to address sustainability of forests, fulfillment of subsistence needs and, more recently, to seek participation from the local people in the management of state-owned forest lands. However, several of the old legislations and top-down management attitude combined with concern for local realities have produced promising if contradictory results.[25]

## 1.5 Participatory Phase

This section explores the origin and meanings of participatory programmes that have been taken up by the Indian government. In face of forest contests between the state (the Forest Department) and forest-dependent communities, there has been growing support for the idea of placing 'power' back in the hands of the rural

---

[24] Guha argued that conservationists have an influence on forest policy which is completely out of proportion with their numbers and suggests that this is because they share a similar social and educational background with important decision makers at the centre (Guha 1994, 2192 in Vira 1995).

[25] In contradiction to participatory JFM policies, the central government had tabled in the parliament in 1994 a draft forest bill called 'The Conservation of Forests and Natural Ecosystems Act' to replace the current forest management legislations. The draft took a strong conservationist stand and hardly mentioned the JFM concepts (Hiremath et al. 1995). It was strongly criticised for trying to increase its bureaucratic hold over forest management, contain commercial interests, and permit only a small role for people in the management of forests (Hiremath et al. 1995; Rego 1995). The bill was, however, not passed by the parliament.

poor. In addition, there was the realization that the Forest Department had failed to 'arrest forest vandalism and destruction' (Bannerjee 1996). Starting in the late 1970s, a number of Social Forestry[26] programmes were developed, and the stated emphasis of the state forest policies shifted from commercial forestry to that of meeting the needs of the forest-dependent population on a priority basis. The most recent of these programmes has embraced a philosophy of Joint Forest Management (JFM).[27]

The involvement of village communities is a result of several factors including failures of state protectionist mechanisms, the continued dependence of villagers on forest resources, and recognition of their claims over access to forests. Agrawal (1999, 100) notes that,

> the failure of other alternatives, the demise of grand teleological theories of social change, the importance of community in writings on development and democratization, the simultaneous valorization of such related concepts as the local context, indigeneity, common property, participation, and decentralization, have all fed into the streams nourishing the growth of community-in-conservation.

However, meanings and uses of the terminologies, such as 'participation' and 'community', remain far from clear. The *participatory* forestry programmes in India, for example, are, for all formal purposes, designed and managed by the Forest Department. At best, they are a 'participatory top-down' approach (Inoue undated) where, despite several concessions, the departments continue to pursue the older goals instead of principally becoming a facilitator to the aspirations of the villagers. On the other hand, the paradigmatic shift of involvement of villagers on state-owned forest land provides villagers with the opportunity to lay claims to their rights and negotiate better terms of reference (Roy 2001) with the state, and even engage in several activities that are not formally recognized in the framework that the state draws for *participation*.

To best address village-level participation, the villagers are often treated as a singular unit, as a community that is defined in simple homogeneous terms where relationships are based on common territory, shared norms, and values (Jeffery and Sundar 1999). However, the concept of a community as an ossified unit (Roy 2001) masks the several differences, such as in caste, wealth, status, group cohesion, incentive to participate in forest management, etc. Also, community-level property rights do not address the equity aspect or that individual households

---

[26] The adjective 'social' is used both in a descriptive way – indicating public involvement, and a normative way – involvement in fulfilling human needs (Warren 1995).

[27] Ajit Bannerjee has opined that in the 1950s, the government-sponsored *van mahotsava*, or the 'festival of trees' was a form of community forestry where the FD encouraged tree plantation on non-forest lands (Bannerjee 1996). The results, he admits, were dismal.

have divergent interests (Reddy 1999).[28] The optimism based on these assumed commonalities of place, values, and needs may not actually inform the actual practice by villagers or groups of villagers who are taken as a community.

A particularly important set of concerns relates to gender division in forestry practices. The gender-specific discourses have highlighted the niche that women villagers occupy in use and management of forests. A prominent voice in highlighting these concerns is that of Vandana Shiva (her opposition to Social Forestry schemes is noted in the next section). Acknowledged as an ecological activist, feminist, scientist, ecofeminist, and cultural-religious commentator, Shiva's strategy in highlighting women's special place in ecology management is not surprisingly multidirectional. She has consistently criticized the Western notions of development that eroded those practices that were harmonious with nature. Her ecofeminist approach that conceptualizes the relationship between gender and environment sees women as the 'natural custodians' of the environment. Shiva states, for example, 'All religions and cultures of the South Indian region have been rooted in the forests, not through fear and ignorance but through ecological insight.' (Shiva 1989, 57). Shiva's (1989) argument about women being 'repositories' of ecological knowledge discusses how women in India have struggled to keep this knowledge alive in the face of modern development schemes, such as the Green Revolution, commercial forestry, and major water projects.[29] Similar accounts (see Sontheimer 1991) describe women in developing countries carrying unique gender-based struggles to sustain the ecological activities and overcome shortages caused by short-sighted decision making on the utilization of these resources.

These ecofeminism arguments have been criticized as playing on the essentialist (Locke 1999b) women/nature connection (Dodson Gray 1979). Biehl (1991) has argued that ecofeminism is regressive in associating women with 'nonhuman nature'. Agarwal (1992) is critical of ecofeminism but instead suggests a 'feminist environmentalism' approach that attempts to connect women's and men's relationship to nature with their material reality. The wide-ranging concerns have ensured that gender-based forest studies and policies that are attentive to

---

[28] Jeffery and Sundar (1999) note the ambiguity in the national JFM resolution over defining the village management unit for the purpose of JFM. The resolution leaves it open to the Forest Departments and the villagers on how exactly a 'village community' be organized into an institution for forest regeneration and protection. The dual membership for forest committee members with the *panchayats* and the contradictions that arise from the situation are noted in chapter 6.

[29] The popularity of Shiva's arguments is, arguably, partly to do with the apologetic stand that academics take in face of her critiques of Western value systems and the ill effects of colonial history.

gender equity and sensitive to women's role in forestry are common.[30] The JFM policy design, for example, has incorporated several women-promoting measures. This research has addressed gender issues mainly in considering forest work-patterns of men and women in the research villages.

### 1.5.1 Social Forestry

The Social Forestry programme emerged as part of a larger national rhetoric on equity and poverty eradication. This section addresses the achievements and failures the programme faced and the lessons that were learned from the Social Forestry projects. The major criticism Social Forestry faced was the disjunction between its intended goals and actual products. Villagers, for example, found the income generation a prime incentive for participation. To secure fuelwood from the programmes was often relegated to a secondary priority. There were also criticisms of the promotion of monoculture, the low participation of women and tribals, and the benefits awarded richer sections of society.

Social Forestry, taken up during the sixth five-year plan, had followed the social justice call of the prime minister, Indira Gandhi (made during the fifth five year plan, see appendix). As a leader in Social Forestry (Warren 1995, 54), India took a series of participatory interventions: village woodlots, strip plantation (roadsides and along railways), farm forestry, agroforestry, home gardens, urban forestry, fuelwood plantations, festival of trees (*van mahotsava*), education camps, nurseries, research and training, and so on. The Forest Department's inability to conserve forests and the ever increasing pressure on forests had visibly challenged the state's control over forest resources. Social Forestry was in some ways the state's effort to keep the pressure off the natural forest resources by creating pools of fodder and timber that would cover the needs of people and also arrest the deterioration of natural forests. Every Indian State took up Social Forestry and engaged in distribution, raising, plantation of seeds and saplings either free of cost or at highly subsidized prices. Large afforestation programmes were conceived with trees with rapid growing bio-mass.

A clear disjunction between the programmes' intended goals and actual products emerged. Although the targets of farm forestry in many States, for example, were considerably over-achieved, those from community forestry were less successful (Bannerjee 1996). Larger farmers primarily took up farm forestry, adopting commercially viable species such as eucalyptus. The participants invariably had an incentive in income generation. The project was alleged to have encouraged little participation from the tribal population (Nesmith 1991, 242), and villagers were reluctant to make long-term investments (Shepherd 1985, 1990). Vandana Shiva was vociferous against the programmes, which she thought promoted monoculture (Shiva 1992, 1993), did not encourage involvement from

---

[30] Indeed today, 'women' as a unit of analysis is as common as other methods that are used to address rural societies.

women (Shiva 1989) and from which particularly poor seasonal migrant labourers lost employment because tree planting is not a labour-intensive occupation. Afforestation of wasteland, to her, was 'privatization' of the commons (Shiva 1989, 84). Warren (1995, 32) noted failures in 'distributional characteristics' of usufruct that were generated from Social Forestry schemes. The Social Forestry programmes found willing funding bodies in the World Bank, the United States Agency for International Development (USAID), the Danish Agency for Development Assistance (DANIDA), the Department for International Development (DFID), the Swedish International Development Agency (SIDA), and Overseas Economic Cooperation Fund (OECF).[31] These donors were, however, accused of attempting to influence the direction of policy especially for regeneration of degraded forest areas and wildlife conservation (Vira 1995). The international agencies came under increasing attack for promoting a 'top-down' approach, which the participatory programme, in theory at least, was to eliminate. They also were alleged to have a vested interest in the country's corridors of power (Nesmith 1991; Shiva 1989).

Notwithstanding the criticisms and failures that Social Forestry faced, the various programmes had, nonetheless, initiated the process of involvement of communities with the Forest Department in addressing forestry. Although participation in Social Forestry remained limited largely to private and village lands, it was still unprecedented for the forest department to arrange devolution of forestry decisions (Baumann 1997), recognize villagers' subsistence needs (Poffenberger and McGean 1996), and invite choices and debates on species selection (Warren 1995; Chatterjee 1995) in the management of forested lands. In several ways, the Social Forestry projects prepared the Forest Department to execute similar projects of community involvement on state-owned forest land, thus paving the way for the transition to a more radical programme such as JFM. The National Forest Policy in 1988 concurred with lessons from Social Forestry in recognizing the need to fulfill the requirements of fuelwood, fodder, minor forest produce, and small timber for rural and tribal people (Naik 1997). In 1990, the Ministry of Forestry and Environment in New Delhi advised the State governments to take up Joint Forest Management (JFM).[32]

### 1.5.2 Joint Forest Management

The June 1990 letter from the Secretary of the Environment and Forests, Government of India, was worded simply (GOI 1990),

---

[31] Projects worth Rs. 9,940.44 million were initiated with external assistance in the period between 1981 and 1986 in fourteen states (Vira 1995).

[32] It should be noted that the announcement of JFM did not necessarily mean that Social Forestry had ceased to exist. Many States carried on with several components of Social Forestry, such as farm forestry and plantations (Bannerjee 1996).

> ... for giving to the village communities living close to the forest land usufructory benefits to ensure their participation in the afforestation programme. ...if they successfully protect the forests, they may be given a portion of the proceeds from the sale of trees when they mature.

The JFM announcement was to build on the tone set by the National Forest Policy of 1988 that had called for creating a 'massive peoples movement' to minimize the pressure on forests. The letter, however, left it to the various State governments to work out the modalities of the actual implementation of the JFM programme. The States were swift in response, and by 1992, nearly half of the Indian provinces had put JFM into place in one manner or another (Khare 1992); others soon followed suit. The FDs in each State interpreted the resolution with some variances including how to name village forest committees,[33] the structure and size of the management unit, the percentage of the share from forests and the modes of distribution of forest usufruct. As was the case in Jharkhand, the new resolution had to accommodate concessions that had been sanctioned by the State during earlier arrangements (see chapter 2).

Joint Forest Management is unprecedented not only in inviting legitimized forestry activities on state-owned forest land, but also in promising a managerial and cash incentive for forest citizens to participate in the management. The crop-sharing arrangement in JFM is seen as a bargain between the state and rural communities (Kant and Nautiyal 1994). Not surprisingly, the Joint Forest Management system grabbed the attention of writers such as Guha and Gadgil (see Hiremath et al. 1995) who wish to see in JFM the chance for restoration of a moral economy through increased tenurial and usufruct rights for rural communities and the exercise of indigenous practices, and those such as Rangan, who, on the other hand, are keen to find solutions within existing institutions by way of 'pressuring states to intervene on behalf of marginalized communities, to ensure equitable access to the potential benefits of economic development' (Rangan 1996, 206).

The reports on JFM that started to pour in were encouraging (Hobley 1996). JFM was reported to be instilling new attitudes and behaviour in the forest bureaucracy towards the villagers (Poffenberger 1995; Kurian and Bhatia 1997). Many forest beat officers reported that their primary incentive to encourage JFM

---

[33] Forest Protection Committees are known by various names in different States: Forest Protection Committees (FPCs) in West Bengal, Village Forest Management and Protection Committees (VFMPCs) in Jharkhand, for example. (A recent policy guideline has suggested that these committees are uniformly called as Joint Forest Management committees [JFMC] [GOI 2000].) In this book, the term FPC has also been used to represent those forest management groups that have been registered by the FD under the JFM agreement. Voluntary forest protection groups, however, refer to the committees in Jharkhand that were constituted through the initiatives of the villagers (some of whom have been registered by the FD). The term community (village-based) forest protection groups, on the other hand, refers to both the registered and voluntary forest committees.

was the vastly improved relations they came to cultivate in the community (Poffenberger and McGean 1996). NGOs too found themselves accommodated in the new regime as agents of change and promotion (McGean 1991). Through group exercises, discussions, meetings, and monitoring, the NGOs were to promote participatory practices in members of Forest Protection Committees and the Forest Department officials.

A number of studies have deconstructed the tenets of JFM. Researchers who had experienced the older forest regimes or the Social Forestry programme were, however, most helpful with their opinions of Joint Forest Management. Nesmith (1991) concludes her thesis on Social Forestry in West Bengal with the opinion that many lessons from Social Forestry are usefully addressed in the principles of JFM. Warren (1995) mentions the transformations that are apparent at the 'managerial' level and how NGOs working on rural development can now engage in the forestry realm. Baumann (1997) writing about *van panchayats* (village councils) in Uttarakhand, and Jewitt (1996) and Balachander (1995), examining practices in two different forest types in north and south India were equally optimistic about JFM. Foresters employed with the Indian Forest Service reported issues that needed to be addressed. They advocated improved skills in communication between foresters and forest citizens (Luthra 1994) to raise the political clout of villagers with the Forest Department where they could participate at policy and decision making at the State level (Khan 1995) (also see chapter 3). If further support were required, one needs only to look beyond India to see that similar systems of joint or co-forest management are being initiated in countries as diverse as Australia (Brown 1997), Canada (Hall 1997), Kenya (Blomley 1996), the Philippines (Gauld 2000), Indonesia (Nanang and Inoue 2000), Bangladesh (Khan 1998), Nepal (Chakraborty et al. 1997; Campbell 1997) Sri Lanka (Carter et al., 1994), Thailand, and parts of west Africa (Corbridge and Jewitt 1997).[34]

However, many others shared apprehensions about Joint Forest Management. JFM is a 'novel experiment to protect forest from anthropogenic forces' wrote Mukherjee (1995) in her introductory notes, only to conclude her article by asking 'what is so great about receiving 25% of the harvest revenue?' She asks if the programme is acceptable to participating communities and if the compensations are good enough (ibid., 3132). Burman (1996) brought out a series of questions to 'ponder upon' concerning JFM. He too is concerned whether the opportunity costs that farmers put in will be recovered and if there will be occasions for support activities, such as bee keeping, fisheries, etc. within JFM. He compares Bengal with other States (e.g. Orissa) where, for example, he argues there is a more democratic involvement of people with the *panchayat* (unlike in Bengal, where the beat officer, a petty FD official, heads the committee). Burman finds even the incentives in Maharashtra better than those in West Bengal (25% of standing crop,

---

[34] Corbridge and Jewitt (1997) note that assumptions about the merits of moral economies and forest citizens are being made in these places as well.

mainly Sal trees, and 50% of plantations, mainly eucalyptus trees, as against 25% in each case in Bengal) (ibid.). In another article, he questions the nature of participation, which, to him, remains top-down (Burman 1997). Kolavalli (1995), cynical about the programme, reasons that JFM is mostly a reflection of the FD's inability to enforce its own property rights any longer, and the department's primary motive is to reduce the cost of protection and management of state forests (Kolavalli 1995, 1933).[35] Based on their research in West Bengal, Beck and Ghosh (2000) reason that the newer form of community management of CPRs may only add to the exclusion of the poor and women possibly because it does not tackle what lies at the heart of forest destruction: agricultural intensification, population growth, and the commoditization of CPRs. Arora (1994) on the other hand, suggests a number of criteria that need to be met for successful implementation of JFM, including principles of empowerment, autonomy, self-realization, and effectiveness. Naik (1997) finds labour the major investment in JFM, and draws on theoretical situations in which, depending on available labour versus return, the success of FPC would be determined. He remains cynical about the Forest Department's attitude toward the actual process of participation (ibid.). Correa (1996) points out the dismal attitude of field-level staff who would neither register women on their rosters nor encourage them to join male members during FPC meetings.

### 1.5.3 The Design of JFM

JFM has departed from conventional and Social Forestry programmes through inclusion of 'outsiders' on state-owned forest land.[36] In exchange for forest management responsibility, the state has agreed to share cash from timber profits with forest citizens. Villagers have the opportunity to form committees and, in return for forest protection duties, are allowed to secure their subsistence needs from local forests and share profits with the FD. There are, however, a number of limitations to how Joint Forest Management is designed. The agreement, for example, allows management only in protected forests. Villagers living next to reserved category forests (and these make up 50.8% of the total forest area in India,

---

[35] Kolavalli (1995) has criticized, for example, Bihar's (and Jharkhand's) policy, where people are not able to decide what to do with their harvest share. He also quotes a Haryana government's letter that explicitly states that JFM would aid in reducing costs of protection and rehabilitation of forests and, in the long run, increase the revenue, despite sharing from the timber sale.

[36] However, the forest-based industries and private contractors who were sidelined on the Agriculture Commission's recommendation remain outside the JFM framework, as far as having direct access to forests and their management is concerned. Various tribal developments and the FD subsidiary undertakings that are involved in forestry work have had little instruction about the specific nature of their involvement.

see Appendix II)[37] may have similar sociocultural dependence on the forest, but they continue to have much more limited concessions in forests. JFM is subject to legislations, agreements, and goals that are present at State and national levels. The States, for example, still aim to put 33% of land under forest cover (envisaged in the second five-year plan, and further emphasized in the National Forest Policy 1988) and are restricted by the 1980 Forest Conservation Act to divert forest area for any purpose other than forestry without prior concurrence of the Government of India. The Act also prohibits creation of village forests from reserved forests, essentially disallowing the Forest Department from changing classification based on current realities. Such conditions not only bind the Forest Department to meeting targets (both in quantity and in principle), they greatly curtail the flexibility the FD may need to articulate local demands and provide incentives, such as rural development works, for participation. The arrangement in JFM usufruct share varies from one State to another, providing dissimilar incentives for forest works around the country. The programme has placed most of the managerial power in the hands of the Forest Department without, however, clarifying how the monitoring and enforcement of the JFM agreement would take place, particularly in situations where the level of utilities by the villagers is different (Ligon and Narain 1999). The JFM resolution announces little to recognize the heterogeneity of the rural population (for example, the difference in dependence on the forest by different sections of the population), the importance of leadership, or the degree of contribution of labour by individual households in the management of forests. The JFM programme instead provides for universal membership and an equal share in forest usufruct and other benefits.

In another key breakaway from earlier policies, village *panchayats* and NGOs have been included in the management scheme, principally to promote forest participation. In both cases, however, the exact nature of involvement is unclear. *Panchayats* are a traditional village institution that have a statutory status, several financial and administrative powers, and have been asked to play a supervisory role for the Forest Protection Committees (FPCs). The FPCs, on the other hand, do not share a similar complementary relationship with the *panchayats* – they cannot, for example, use *panchayat's* executive and judiciary powers for forestry or development purposes. Similarly, the NGOs, although recommended to play a supportive role to JFM, are excluded from any direct involvement in the forest land, and the exact nature of their responsibility has not been made clear.

### 1.5.4 Discussion

Joint Forest Management is removed from past management practices particularly in that several institutions are involved in forest land and usufruct management that was primarily reserved for the state. Although Social Forestry tried to redress

---

[37] Guha compares this provision to the recently amended Nepal Forest Act of 1993 where section 25 allows all national forests to be handed over to user groups in the form of a community forest (Guha 1994).

fuelwood need, JFM takes up a larger agenda and seeks to address the subsistence need and conservation by providing forest usufruct and cash incentives to villagers in exchange for participation in forest management. The new members of the JFM constituency – forest citizens (FPCs), *panchayats*, NGOs – are all invited to join JFM, although how they are to interpret their roles in day-to-day forest management is less clear.

## 1.6 Book Plan

The introductory chapter of the monograph discusses the nature of studies that have dealt with contextual sources of environmental change in general and forestry in particular. It argues that dominant opinions in political ecology studies are guided by principles of moral economy. In the context of studies on Indian forestry, the approach poses several problems. The chapter also discusses scholars who in recent research have made important departures. It noted key phases in Indian forest management and the debates that surround them. The final sections review participatory programmes taken up in the subcontinent and discuss the design of Joint Forest Management.

Chapter 2 scrutinizes the dominant politico-institutional setup in each of the two States of Jharkhand and West Bengal. It notes various achievements of West Bengal's Forest Department in fostering participatory forestry. It is stated that some of the failures in the celebrated Arabari Project remain entrenched in the JFM framework. The chapter also explains the methods used during fieldwork and while writing the monograph.

Chapter 3 starts with a discussion of the structural changes in the Forest Department in the two States that has happened in response to JFM. It then provides baseline data on each of the eight villages that were surveyed along with local forest histories. The chapter primarily examines the various ways in which the Forest Department interacts with the community in the JFM setup. The field realities are compared to the functions that were recommended to the foresters. The chapter demonstrates that the roles of lower-level officers have changed in the post-JFM scenario. Although strict adherence to the sets of responsibilities prescribed in JFM is seldom practised, lower-level forest officials influence forest activities in several informal manners.

Chapter 4 and 5 are devoted to examining the dynamics within village communities. Chapter 4 examines the forestry activities within the formal framework of JFM. It teases out the various elements such as meetings, forest patrols, conflict resolution, that are part of the JFM package. The chapter discusses the ways JFM requirements have been interpreted at the community level. It is argued that there is often a disjunction between village polity and forest politics, which, at times, jeopardizes forest management. Also, it is found that the forest interest is best served in cases where there is a high degree of dependence, good leadership, and homogeneity of interest.

Chapter 5, on the other hand, discusses the notion and beliefs that inform the autogenous and inherent characters of community forestry practices. It discusses the self-initiated forest protection groups of Jharkhand and compares them with the registered Forest Protection Committees in West Bengal. The chapter brings Jharkhand and Bengal on to a similar footing. It is argued that, given similar community characteristics, villagers demonstrate analogous forestry practices. The chapter, however, argues for an inherent instability that remains in such specialized systems. Autogenous initiatives cannot exist in a political vacuum and in the absence of support activities by other institutions. Communication, feedback, and directions that may emerge from these bodies would be essential to give sustenance and legitimacy to autogenous forestry efforts.

Chapter 6 compares forest forums such as FPCs and self-initiated committees to the traditional village body, the *panchayats*. The findings draw more from the Bengal experience. It is argued that, despite the marginal nature of FPCs as compared to the established *panchayats*, the committees create a power base and legitimacy of their own. This, however, depends on a number of factors including a dependency on forests, leadership patterns, and relationships with other villages in the *panchayat*.

Chapter 7 discusses two NGOs, the Indian Institute of Bio-Social Research and Development (IBRAD) and Ram Krishna Mission (RKM) working on rural development forestry in Bengal and Jharkhand respectively. This chapter argues that although IBRAD has been useful with some of its experimental models, RKM has proved more useful with conventional goals and methods. The chapter also states that villagers when involved with institutions from outside, strongly demonstrate expectations for multisectoral and integrated rural development agendas to be included in the NGOs' work plan.

The concluding chapter draws from the entire research exercise. It combines various findings of the research and comments on the institutional arrangement that is working in the JFM atmosphere. More specifically the chapter summarizes the findings in relation to the research questions and issues that were put forward. While testing the institutional structures and sturdiness of Joint Forest Management, the chapter makes several recommendations that can render JFM more meaningful. Finally, it extrapolates on the future directions forest management should take in India, and highlights areas that need further research.

## 1.7 Conclusion

I compare two States, Jharkhand and West Bengal, while identifying historical and contemporary debates about forest management in India. The introductory chapter presented characteristics that have marked political ecology studies in general and Indian forestry studies in particular. It argued that approaches that treat state and citizen in opposition to each other pose problems. The chapter discussed contributions from scholars who in recent studies have appreciated the heterogeneity and ambivalence that are shown by these two forest actors at several levels and through time. Others still remain informed by the state-citizen dichotomy discourse. It was argued that contemporary forest management must acknowledge the potential of new actors and institutions. At the same time, forest management must engage the state in managing forests to address a number of goals including an equitable distribution of usufruct and rural development. The fetishization of romanticized community characteristics that are often guided by principles of moral economy are misleading, it is stated.

The final section of this chapter discussed participatory programmes that have been taken up in forestry in India. It was argued that Social Forestry programmes, despite many failures, paved the way for Joint Forest Management, which, despite certain constraints, shows good potential for addressing forest management and rural development forestry. It is unclear, however, how local institutions, such as the villages' Forest Protection Committees, *panchayats*, and NGOs operate to render various goals, such as fulfillment of subsistence needs, rural equity, sustainable forestry practices, forest cover conservation, that are assumed in JFM to last on any long-term basis. Albeit radical in inviting villagers to partake in forest management, JFM reflects a conservatism on how it is designed. The Forest Department is conscious of its historical legacy, wary of outsiders and unclear on who should participate and how they should be involved.

The next chapter discusses the politico-institutional set-up in Jharkhand and West Bengal. The State of West Bengal is commonly seen as a pioneer in official Indian attempts to promote Joint Forest Management systems. Jharkhand, in contrast, has only promulgated JFM since 1990. The chapter discusses the forestry institutions and JFM framework in each of the two States. It notes the achievements of West Bengal's Forest Department, including the celebrated Arabari Project, in fostering participatory forestry.

Chapter 2

# Participatory Forest Management: The Context of Jharkhand and West Bengal

## 2.1 Introduction

This chapter sets the tone for the rest of the monograph. Principally, it provides the setting for the research, the southwestern region of West Bengal and southern Bihar, now a new province, Jharkhand.[1] The first part of the chapter locates both the States in their sociopolitical setup. The next section situates the forestry infrastructure in the contemporary polity and bureaucratic structure of Jharkhand and West Bengal. The chapter also analyzes the nature of participation in the Arabari Socio-Economic Project (ASEP), arguably, the progenitor of JFM. It is suggested that Bengal's acclaimed success in participatory forestry, although noteworthy, is state-driven. The goals of the Forest Department have remained in variance with those of the rural community from which it seeks participation, and the bureaucracy does not challenge the divisions that lie at the heart of the variegated and heterogeneous societies. All these factors were evident within the ASEP and continue in the JFM setup. The final section compares the institutional arrangement (FPC, FD *panchayat*, and NGOs) in both States. It describes the responsibilities that have been 'prescribed' to FPCs in the Joint Forest Management system and the roles that have been taken by other ecological institutions.

---

[1] The southern districts of Bihar (including Ranchi where the research in Bihar was conducted) were separated from Bihar on 15 November 2000, to form a new province, Jharkhand (see Map 2.1). However, the newly formed Jharkhand has the same institutions and legislations in place that it had when it was part of Bihar.

The new province of Jharkhand is made up of the following 22 districts: Ranchi, Gumla, Lohardanga, East Singbhum, West Singbhum, Hazaribagh, Giridih, Kodarma, Chatra, Dhanbad, Bokaro, Palamu, Garhwa, Dumka, Devghar, Godda, Pakaur, Sahibganj, Latehar, Simdega, Saraikela and Jamtara. Southwest Bengal, on the other hand, is understood to comprise the districts of Midnapore, Bankura, Purulia, Burdwan, and parts of Birbhum (Khare et al. 1995).

## 2.2 Jharkhand and Bengal: A Political Profile

The Indian States of Jharkhand and West Bengal have provided the backdrop to the study. The areas that were chosen for research are the more forested regions with high community dependence on forests and areas, which contain the greatest amount of protected category of forests (PFs) where Joint Forest Management arrangement is sought to be instituted. The following section discusses the physiography and polity of each of the States. The main purposes of this section are to introduce the differences that mark the post-Independence polity of Bihar, Jharkhand and Bengal and draw on similarities, such as a comparable ecology and history of forest and management infrastructure. It leads to my larger contention that both provinces are similar in how the communities secure forest resources for subsistence use and how they seek to interact with other institutions.

During most of the British rule, Bihar remained a part of the Bengal presidency and, until the partition of Bengal in 1911, was governed from Calcutta. In 1911, Bihar and Orissa together formed a separate governor's province. In 1936, as a result of the State Re-organization Act, the five British districts of Orissa were to form still another province. In 1947, after Independence, Bengal was further partitioned into east and west, the former becoming a part of the newly formed Pakistan.[2] Tribal-dominated Chotanagpur, however, remained, to the 'discomfiture of tribals' (Blair 1969, 30), a part of Bihar until the recent split of Jharkhand from Bihar. Chotanagpur plateau, which comprises most of Jharkhand and much of southwest Bengal, is a hot subhumid ecoregion with red and lateritic soils (Gangopadhyay 1991) and a growing period of 150 to 180 days. Both Jharkhand and southwest Bengal share a generally hot and dry climate with a rainy season (average rainfall is around 1300 mm) extending from June to September (GOB 1994; GOWB 1966). The dominant natural forest in the region is the tropical dry deciduous type, and Sal (Shorea *robusta*) of coppice origin is the predominant species.[3] The forest area that has been reforested under the Forest Departments' *plantation*-schemes, however, comprises mainly of eucalyptus trees (Nesmith 1991). The population structure in both regions is a mix of caste-Hindu as well as

---

[2] On the merger of princely states with the Indian Union, Seraikela (400 sq. miles) and Kharsawan (153 sq. miles) were made a part of Singhbhum district in south Bihar. In 1956, as part of linguistic reorganization of Indian States (States Reorganisation Act, 1956), some 733 sq. miles of the Purnea district and 2,407 sq. miles of Manbhum district were transferred to West Bengal. In the process, a small part of Manbhum was attached to Singhbhum district, and the rest of the nontransformed portion was made into a new Dhanbad district (Blair 1969, 26). From 1956 until November 2000, there had been no change in the territorial jurisdiction in these two States.

[3] The major *associates* of Sal are Pterocarpus *marsupium* (*pea sal*), Madhuca *latifolia* (*mahua*), Diospyros *melanoxylon* (*kendu*), Schleichera *oleosa* (*kusum*), Terminalia *tomentosa* (*asan*), Holoptelia *integrifolia* (*challa*), Aegle *marmelos* (*bel*), Bombax *ceiba* (*semul*) and Cleistanthus *collinus* (*parashi*). See Nesmith (1991) and Jewitt (1996) for an exhaustive list of flora in southwest Bengal and Jharkhand respectively.

pockets of Muslim population. On the other hand, despite shared features such as a contiguous boundary and ecological history, Bihar (and Jharkhand) and south west Bengal present a number of contrasting features, particularly in the nature of state polity, bureaucratic initiatives, and entrenchment of rural institutions, such as the *panchayat*.

### 2.2.1 Bihar: Failed Measures?

Bihar has performed abysmally on several counts. The State is marked by land-reform inefficiency, land-liberation struggles, populist politics, and, more recently, corruption scandals and political instability. It has been caught up in corruption and inefficient bureaucracy (Chaitanya 1996), opportunist political alliances (Prasad 1997), agrarian violence (Hauser 1997), and a general 'lawlessness' (Das 1989). The initial period of enthusiasm from the Central government to develop the State (with the sumptuous mineral resources in southern Bihar, now Jharkhand) with 'temples of modern India' (Khilnani 1997) soon dissipated. A few private enterprises that started in Jharkhand area in the pre-Independence period have continued to operate in the State. In recent years, however, the region has been plagued by the closures of several smaller industry units, and the industrial output has been in decline. Caste affiliations remain a prominent feature in the allegiance and defection in politics and other spheres of public life.[4]

The Bihar Land Reforms Act, amidst strong opposition from the landed gentry, was passed in the Bihar Legislative Assembly in 1950 (Das 1992) to abolish the *zamindari*, or the landlord system in the State. (*Zamindari* had been in place since the Permanent Settlement Act of 1793). Earlier, in 1949, the *panchayati raj* system had been introduced in the State. Notwithstanding the intentions of these policies, their potential was never realized. The agricultural lands that came to be vested with the State could not effectively be redistributed to the landless and marginal farmers (Bharti 1992). The *panchayats*, on the other hand, remained dominated by prominent people from the caste-Hindu population. In 1997, the *panchayats* were declared non-functioning by the State High Court on grounds of overdue elections. Urbanization in Bihar had remained low at 8.4% limited to 8% of cultivated land, and literacy rate and landholding at about 0.9 ha is among the lowest in India (Kumar 1996, 18).

---

[4] V.S. Naipaul describes the *zamindars*, or the landlords of Bihar living in plain brick houses in similar wretchedness as the rest of population (Naipaul 1964). Nirad Chaudhuri, on the other hand, does not stop short from espousing a near renaissance for Bengal in the late nineteenth and early twentieth century (Chaudhuri 1965). A series of articles in *Economic and Political Weekly*, notably by Bharti (1989, 1990, 1992), Bhatia (1998), Das (1986, 1989, 1992) and Gupta (1981) chronicle the dismal record of social and economic performance in Bihar in recent years.

Blair's thesis on the 1967 national elections in north Bihar finds caste loyalties to be the most significant factor in Bihar's electoral politics.[5] Although his hopes for the replacement of 'caste in favour of multi-party system' (Blair 1969, 358) might elude the State for longer, his thesis was prophetic. Reading into early cases of the execution of solidarity by lower caste members in the wake of fragmentation of the higher caste *Bhumihar* population, Blair anticipated a possible future where the lower castes would come to power capitalizing on similar caste fractures and defaults in Bihar's electoral politics. He had hoped that the mechanics of caste politics would work in *their* favour too (ibid., 19).

This indeed came true when Janata Dal (JD) became the ruling party at the centre, on an anti-Congress wave in the early 1990s, and Bihar received a new government under a low-caste Yadav leader, Laloo Prasad (Gupta 1992). Whereas Janata Dal subsequently disintegrated in the rest of India, Yadav has remained the chief executive in the State, (with his party rechristened Rashtriya Janta Dal [RJD]). This has occurred despite some important electoral setbacks to the RJD resulting mainly from an alliance between BJP and Samata–JD (U) political parties (Sengupta 1999). Despite some novel beginnings and proposals on justice and equity for marginalized communities, Yadav did little to pull the State out of misery (Hausser 1997; Thakur 2000). His period has marked the State with corrupt and inefficient government practices and a particularly sluggish economy.[6]

---

[5] This continues to be the case. See Verma (1991) and Prasad (1997) for a discussion on the subject. Prasad (1997) reporting on the elections of 1996, for example, argued that caste and social factions continue to play important roles in elections in Bihar, contributing to the violent and corrupt nature of elections in the State.

[6] The sympathizers of Bihar reminisce about a golden past of the State (Das 1992). A confluence of Indian religions (Buddhism, Jainism, Sikhism), Bihar is said to have been a place of pride in an era that goes as far back as the seventh and eighth centuries B.C., when the kingdoms of Magadh (Chanakya, the author of Arthashastra, had served as the sovereign of the empire) and Licchavi had used relatively advanced political systems of governance and linked statecraft with economics. This phase of Bihar was in decline by the seventh or eighth century A.D., when the ruling Gupta dynasty fell victim to the conquest of almost all of northern India by invaders from the Middle East. In medieval times, the Mughal and successive Afghan and Persian rulers governed Bihar from Delhi like the rest of northern India, as part of a provincial administration. The only remarkable person of these times in Bihar was the Afghan ruler, Sher Khan Sur, a ferocious warrior who was also known for welfare activities and land reforms.

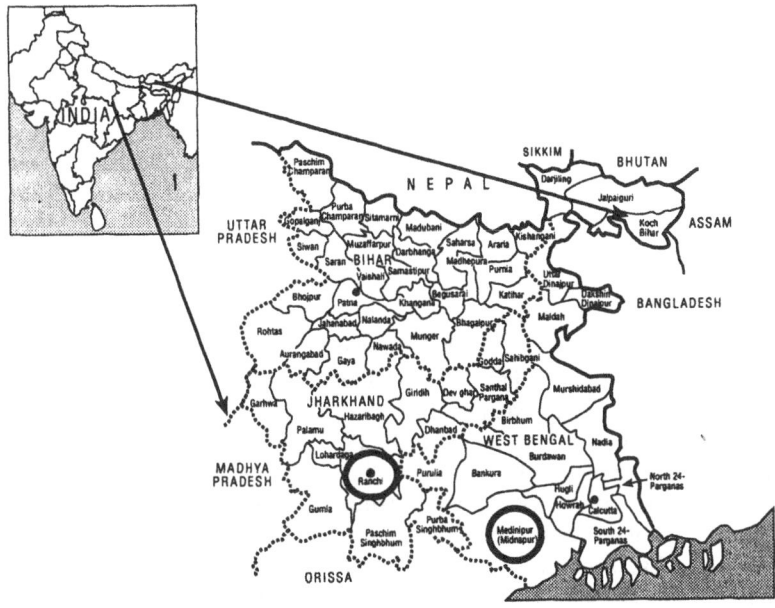

**Map 2.1 Location of Research Sites**

## 2.2.1.1 Jharkhand

Academics from both social and physical disciplines have been quick to point out the artificiality in Bihar's boundaries. Blair cites the pre-Independence Simon commission report that labelled Bihar 'the most artificial unit of all Indian provinces' (Blair 1969, 29). Although differences, particularly in physical features, are present in other States including West Bengal, the inconsonant politics between north and south Bihar has kept the disparity rife in post-Independence Bihar. The Congress Party that had ruled Bihar during most of the years after Independence (until 1992) was dominated, both in party and polity, by caste-Hindus from north Bihar. In 1949, Jaipal Singh, a Munda tribal from the south, recognizing nonrepresentation of tribals, formed a political party called the Jharkhand Party (Das 1992b),[7] with the proposal to carve out a separate Jharkhand State from the States of Bihar, Madhya Pradesh, Orissa, and West Bengal. The party returned over twenty Members of the Legislative Assembly (MLAs) in State elections held just after Independence in 1952 (Blair 1969, 53). In 1963, Singh, however, agreed to merge the party with the Congress, and Jharkhand's cause got smothered in the calls of (Nehruvian) nation-building. Following Jaipal Singh's departure from the Jharkhand scene, several other contenders for a new State revived Jharkhand parties and various sociocultural forums. Despite many promises from the centre, the realization of separate Statehood (increasingly limited now to south Bihar) remained a furtive dream for its pursuers (Corbridge 1986). In the last decade, Jharkhand politicians were back in the political limelight for one scandal or another, and sporadic protests and demonstrations have continued despite Bihar's ruling party, Rashtriya Janta Dal's (RJD) staunch opposition (and amelioration of *Jharkhandis* with several key posts at the centre and in the State) to the demand. This scenario changed when the Bharatiya Janata Party (BJP) came to power at the centre. BJP had promised in their election manifesto the creation of Jharkhand,[8] a separate province from Bihar. After several delays (Das 1998), the Bihar State Reorganization Bill was finally cleared by the BJP in the Indian Parliament in the summer of 2000. The creation of the Jharkhand province is a victory of sorts for its champions and a challenge for a region, which, despite its mineral wealth, several land-right privileges, and autonomous administrative councils (for development and tribal welfare), has remained one of the poorest regions in the country. Jharkhand, in any case, in essence inherits the bureaucracy and, to a certain degree, the polity of north Bihar. How it will articulate its goals in the coming years is something to look forward to.

---

[7] Jaipal Singh had earlier headed an organization called the *Chotanapur Adviasi Mahasabha,* which had come up in the 1930s mainly to protest the exploitation of tribals by the *dikus*, or outsiders. In 1949, the older body was, however, consolidated under a new name, Jharkhand Party (Das 1992b) and with a larger political canvas.

[8] BJP also endorsed similar non-secessionist demands for the creation of separate provinces (Mawdsley 1997) in Uttar Pradesh and Madhya Pradesh.

### 2.2.2 West Bengal: Grassroots Success?

West Bengal above all reflects the results of governance provided by Left coalition parties for more than two decades. One of the most prominent aspects of the rule has been their assertive actions in grassroots politics, commitment to land reforms,[9] and other social programmes to empower poor rural communities (Dréze and Sen 1997, Lieten 1992). Starting in 1977, sharecroppers and landless persons were given a 99-year lease (*pattas*) on lands that had been vested with the State after the Land Ceiling Act. Since 1979, the State government implemented 'Operation *Barga*'.[10] The programmes resulted in the provision of land to the landless and tenurial security to sharecroppers and small landholders. Also, *panchayati raj* (governance through village councils) was strengthened and restructured during the period (Williams 1997). Members of *panchayat* were made integral to decision making and the overall management of rural development.

However, this is not to imply that West Bengal has done considerably better than Bihar (and Jharkhand) in overall development. The statistics show that West Bengal and Bihar (along with Orissa) have the highest concentration of people living below the poverty line (Sengupta and Gazdar 1997). Although the population living in urban areas in Bengal is on a par with the rest of India, its industrial output has gone down from 23% of India's total in 1961 to under 7% by the end of the 1980s (ibid., 130).[11] The political equations in West Bengal have changed since the successful alliance of Mamta Bannerjee's Trinamaool Mamta Congress (TMC) with the Bharatiya Janta Party (BJP) in the 1998 general elections (Gillan 1998).[12] In the 1998 election, the BJP made its first substantial inroads in Bengal's electoral politics. Although the TMC took 24.3% of the votes, and the Left Front garnered 46.83% (while Communist Party of India (Marxist) [CPI (M)], on its own, could get only 35.41%), the TMC-BJP alliance received 51.07% of the

---

[9] The legal requisites for land reforms, such as abolition of *zamindari*, a ceiling on the size of land holding, were, however, in place before the Left parties came to power.

[10] Under this programme, the *bargadars* (sharecroppers) had their names recorded in revenue records in meetings organized at the village level by officials of the Revenue Department. By March 1989, 1.255 million acres of land had been declared surplus under the Land Ceiling Act, of which 0.835 million acres had been redistributed to about 1.7 million beneficiaries at an average rate of 0.49 acre per beneficiary (*Source*: the district land and land reforms office [DLLRO], Midnapore).

[11] Also, see Dasgupta (1998) and Raychaudhuri and Chatterjee (1998) for a discussion of the slow down of industrialization in West Bengal, and Bagchi (1998) for the overall development in West Bengal since Independence. Banerjee (1998) blames the decline of West Bengal manufacturing business from its prime position at the time of Independence on the regional bias the big business houses came to have against the State.

[12] The alliance between the BJP and TMC has remained unsteady as both parties attempt to remain at the forefront of opposition politics (Gillan 1998).

total votes (Acharya 1999), demonstrating a slim but sure non-Left majority (Chakrabarty 1998). The Left Front, however, is still in power and organizationally superior to the TMC-BJP alliance. Until now, the party has been led by a power-loving but seasoned leadership capable of maintaining a *bhadralok* (literally, gentleman's club) appearance (Acharya 1999). Although the TMC's high rhetoric has challenged the left's entrenchment in rural politics, it has often resulted in severe conflicts between supporters of each party. During the research period in Midnapore, several TMC-led demonstrations were witnessed, and there was frequent news on clashes and even deaths.[13] Mamta Bannerjee has emerged as a champion of suffering people and, although she has positioned her party well in the rural polity of West Bengal, she provides little assurance for genuine governance. With the frustrating little that CPI (M) achieved in its long, unbroken rule of more than two decades and the recent exit of the long-reigning chief minister, Jyoti Basu, CPI (M) seems destined to be put into an even weaker position by non-Left parties, who are not necessarily any more efficient.

### 2.2.3 Discussion

Despite the current political impasse and economic stagnation, it is commonly agreed that the Left-coalition parties have been able to bring important changes to West Bengal. The land reforms have reduced wealth differentiation in rural Bengal (Lieten 1992, Sanyal et al. 1998), and village institutions are competent to deal with bureaucracy and various state initiatives. Improved agricultural and labour productivity has helped to reduce rural poverty in the State (Ghosh 1998). The rural forums in Bengal, such as *panchayats*, continue to assert their agenda clearly and are, as pressure groups, widely noticed by the public and the State's press. On the other hand, pressure or interests groups (Blair 1969, 82) have remained nearly nonexistent in Bihar.[14] However, I will argue that in similar circumstances of dependence on forestry with management designs resting within the community, villagers, particularly those who represent a uniform, cohesive, and homogenous set of interests, articulate their interests in similar fashions.[15]

---

[13] Roy (1994) reports cases of police brutality in curbing protest demonstrations by non-Left political groups.

[14] Blair (1969), however, recognized Jaipal Singh's Jharkhand party as a pressure group (which, nevertheless, got liquidated in 1967). He assigned caste politics as the main reason for underdevelopment, where *Biharis*, in exchange for psychic income from caste loyalties, are prepared to forego actual material development.

[15] Expression of such interests, however, may remain invisible to an indifferent bureaucracy, as is the case in Bihar, which is crippled with several structural and constitutional constraints.

## 2.3 Forestry Infrastructure in Jharkhand and West Bengal

The forest cover of Bihar (including Jharkhand districts), as assessed by Forest Survey of India (FSI 1993), is 26,587 sq. km (15.29% of its geographical area; of this 13,172 sq. km are under dense forest and 13,145 sq. km are open forest). The forest cover in West Bengal (FSI 1993), on the other hand, is 8,186 sq. km (9.22% of its geographical area, of which 3,362 sq. km are dense forest, 2,119 sq. km are open forest, and 2,705 sq. km are mangrove forest).[16] Both Jharkhand and *Jungle Mahal* (the forested region in southwest Bengal) share similar ecology, and both States inherited a vast amount of forest lands (that were vested in the state upon abolition of *zamindari*) and the edifice of colonial bureaucracy to manage their forests. Both Bihar and Bengal had an all-India bureaucratic cadre overseeing forestry with the help of lower-level staff selected within the State. Working plans (Nautiyal and Chowdhary 1982) have remained essential to the planning and execution of forestry works in both States, with the primary aim to obtain the largest possible flow of forest produce on a sustained basis (ibid., 22).[17] In recent years, conventional forestry practices have been unable to protect and regenerate forests. Lacking the resources to enforce restrictions (Palit 1993), vast tracts of forests have suffered serious depletion in Jharkhand and southwestern Bengal. Although recent innovations and successes in West Bengal mark distinctive departures in the FD's approach towards community involvement, the history of dependence, conflict, and deforestation have not been too different in the two States. The Forest Departments in both provinces have incurred a progressive loss of revenue from protected forests (GOB 1994; Kurup 1996). With a number of common characteristics, community forestry practices compare well between the States.

### 2.3.1 Jharkhand: Custodial Forestry

Much of the forest that was vested in the Bihar State after the abolition of *zamindari* was degraded (Jewitt 1995), and a long contest over forest resources, despite a complex arrangement of rights to the villagers (Kumar 1996), had left a desperation and alienation between forest citizens and the forest bureaucracy (Corbridge and Jewitt 1997).[18] Responding to participatory and equity rhetoric in

---

[16] As against this, the recorded forest area of Bihar is 29,226 sq. km. (GOB 1988), whereas West Bengal has 11,879 sq. km of forest land on record (GOWB 1996). (It was noted in chapter 1 that a land registered with the government as forest land may not necessarily have sufficient or any forest cover).

[17] The forest productivity in Bihar has generally been higher (an average of 20.47 million cubic meters/year) compared with Bengal (9.83 million cubic meters/year) (Nautiyal and Chowdhary 1982).

[18] Kumar (1996), however, argues that the Forest Department of Bihar (and Jharkhand) has continuously pursued, at least in principle, a policy of managing Protected Forests (PFs) with the sole aim of satiating the needs of the local right-holding tenants of the village in

the nation, Bihar embarked on Social Forestry projects that were 'in operation' until 1990. The programme, funded largely by the Swedish International Development Agency (SIDA), however, produced unconvincing results. The survival rate of the farm forestry plantations, for example, was as low as 20% (Kumar 1996, 8), leaving the donors with little interest in investing in Bihar's forestry in the future.

Joint Forest Management was officially announced in 1990. However, initiatives from the Forest Department have, at best, been moderate. Forest bureaucracy, for example, has been unable to shake off the power structure that is conditioned to emphasize policing and protection. The FD is lacking not only ideology but also the institutional infrastructure necessary to back up the participatory rhetoric of JFM policy. The department is plagued by structural constraints, such as an insufficient number of staff, lack of funds, and a constitutional bottleneck (for example, the working plans that enable the harvest of forests have not been sanctioned by the State for the past several years). The department has not been exempt from corruption, lack of funds, general inefficiency, or work strikes by lower-level staff – the features that also characterize other public domains in Jharkhand.

On the other hand, the forest citizens in several pockets in Jharkhand have turned to self-initiated forest management strategies to secure forest usufructs (Krishnaswamy 1995).[19] The Joint Forest Management (JFM) has, arguably, supported the belief among resident villagers that protection of forests would yield legitimate shares in the forest usufruct. Armed only with limited knowledge of the new tenurial arrangement, the villagers have consolidated various autogenous activities in forest management. They have, when possible, also used their formal status as Village Forest Management and Protection Committees (VFMPC) (the Forest Department, in an initial bout of enthusiasm, registered a few hundred committees) to regulate access to forest usufruct.

---

which the PF is situated. He asserts that such joint action concepts were the outcome of recurring rebellions in the tribal hinterlands, which forced the British to show more concern about safeguarding the (customary) rights of *raiyats* (the cultivating inhabitant of the village) as well as those of the tribals (ibid., 11). The Bihar (Jharkhand) Forest Department, Kumar states, had tried cooperative measures, when, in the years from 1956 to 1958, it handed 50 PFs to *panchayats* for management and revenue control (ibid., 11); the experiment failed. A more ambitious arrangement was later carried out when the *mukhiya* (headman) of the *Gram Panchayat* was to receive the villagers' share after the annual harvesting coupe (timber, pole, small wood). These programmes proved ineffective, and the forests handed over to villagers soon disappeared.

[19] Voluntary forest protection groups are also found in the neighbouring province of Orissa. Saxena (1996) lists high dependence on forest usufruct, remote location of village hamlets, and the ambiguous tenurial status of the forests as key factors responsible for sustaining self-initiated forest protection groups in Orissa.

## 2.3.2 West Bengal: Innovative Strategies towards PFM

In 1945, Bengal enacted the Private Forest Act to provide guidelines to owners of private forest lands for management of forests (Pattnaik and Dutta 1997). It was not, however, until the abolition of *zamindari* in 1955[20] that these forests, upon the enactment of the West Bengal Estates Acquisition Act, were vested in the State. There was forest destruction, as in Bihar, in areas where forests changed hands from *zamindars* to the State. The north Bengal forests, already under control of the State, on the other hand, suffered little damage. West Bengal's forest management has continued with (and not unlike Jharkhand), dual commercial and conservation interests in forests. During Social Forestry, West Bengal proved more efficient than Jharkhand,[21] although other states, such as Gujarat, Maharashtra and Madhya Pradesh achieved greater targets in plantation and farm forestry.

The government of West Bengal, building on Social Forestry and Arabari experience, ratified a series of participatory forestry schemes. In 1980, the West Bengal government's '*New* Directives on Forest Management' enlarged privileges and concessions to the tribal population that was living in the vicinity of forests. The encouraging results prompted the government to form a statutory body called *Bhumi Sanskar Sthayee Samiti*, or the Land Society in 1985, which involved the Forest Department and members of the *panchayat*. One of the duties of this body was to identify beneficiaries among the members of scheduled castes and scheduled tribes who could benefit from plantations created under the Social Forestry project and the Integrated Tribal Development Programme (ITDP). Later, in 1986, the *Bhumi Sanskar Sthayee Samiti* was renamed as *Ban-O-Bhumi Sanskar Sthayee Samiti*, or the Forest and Land Society, and was to address various forest concerns. In 1986, in another development, the Forest Department agreed to share 50% of the usufruct from the plantations raised on wastelands and other public lands under the Rural Landless Employment Guarantee Programme (RLEGP) scheme. The *panchayat samiti* was made responsible for the protection of these plantations (FD memo no. 1925, dated 24.4.86). In another order, it was specified that 25% of the usufruct from plantations that were raised under the 'rehabilitation of degraded forests' programme of the Social Forestry project would be distributed to local residents selected by *Ban-O-Bhumi Sanskar Sthayee Samiti* (FD memo no. 2379, dated 11.6.86). The strip plantations created by the Forest Department under Social Forestry projects were handed over to *panchayats* for maintenance and protection. The *panchayats* were given authority to identify poor people who would receive usufructory benefits from these plantations (FD memo no. 2914, dated 22.7.86). A new scheme called 'Economic Rehabilitation of Fringe

---

[20] Between 1865 and 1878, the government of India had recognized forests held under *zamindars* as privately held (Sivaramakrishnan 1996, 431), which, in essence, dissolved the distinction between forests and agricultural land in these estates (ibid., 442).

[21] In Bengal, the Social Forestry Project, funded largely by the World Bank, was extended for three more years, up to 1993 (Nesmith 1991).

Population' was drawn up through which various development schemes would be used by forest citizens to generate income through forest-based activities. Other socially beneficial measures, such as the drinking water supply, the construction of earthen dams, and minor irrigation projects, were planned by the Forest Department as part of larger efforts of PFM.

The State of West Bengal and the Forest Department took several innovative steps to foster a participatory environment. Their efforts to share forest revenue and combine rural development with forest regeneration and rehabilitation projects are particularly noteworthy. The string of achievements that Bengal had attained not only instilled confidence in the bureaucratic setup in general but complemented grassroots-level institutions that were already in place and could deal effectively with initiatives being provided by the forest bureaucracy.

The next section discusses the Arabari Socio-Economic Project. It is argued that there are conflicts between interest groups within a community, which the FD fails to recognize. This is not, however, to take any credit away from Bengal's progressive and transparent bureaucracy, but chiefly to illustrate that Bengal also faces challenges similar to those faced by the States that have been slow, even reluctant, to signal the onset of participatory forest management.

## 2.4 The Arabari Socio-Economic Project (ASEP) (1971–1998)

In 1971, a radical attempt at participatory forest management was made on the initiative of a Division Forest Officer (DFO), Ajit Bannerjee, in Arabari villages in the Midnapore Forest Division of southwest Bengal. This unprecedented undertaking was named 'Arabari Socio-Economic Project (ASEP)'. An area of 1256 hectares of forest land was obtained from the Forest Directorate with the objective of improving the degraded condition of natural vegetation (mostly, self-regenerating Sal), while giving economic incentives to villagers in exchange for cooperation in forest management. Eleven villages, which shared their boundaries with forest, were incorporated into the project (see Table 2.1). The project proposed to enhance overall economic activity in the area through planting and protection activities. Additionally, a groundbreaking promise was made to share 25% of income from the sale of timber in the case of harvests. Sal trees were to be harvested on a ten-year coppice rotation practice; however, no formal protection committee was formed, and, instead, voluntary community protection was sought.

The ASEP covered 601 households (1981 census) in eleven villages, two of which were uninhabited. The cash income level in the community on average was low (approximately Rs. 3000/year/household); the majority were marginal farmers with a few cultivators and service holders in tow (GOWB 1993c). A member from each of the households was made a member-beneficiary to the usufruct share and received an equal portion of the 25% of timber harvest returns. Since 1987, the villagers received 25% of the net revenue from the sale of poles and firewood.

Apart from the share in timber-harvest, villagers earned money from the collection and sale of non-timber forest products (mostly, Sal leaves, Sal seeds, mushroom, fallen firewood and cashew-nuts). The ASEP beneficiaries, for example, earned Rs. 1,391 per household in the year 1988 (GOWB 1993c).[22]

**Table 2.1 Arabari Villages**

| Villages (*mouza*) in Arabari Socio-Economic Project | Number of Beneficiary Households |
|---|---|
| 1. Guchisole | 58 |
| 2. Satsole | 151 |
| 3. Sakhisole | 48 |
| 4. Jorekeudi | 27 |
| 5. Majhigarh | 51 |
| 6. Mohisdubi | Uninhabited |
| 7. Chandmura | 30 |
| 8. Gutiamara | Uninhabited |
| 9. Sankrui | 103 |
| 10. Sapadiha | 34 |
| 11. Urami | 99 |

Of the three villages that I surveyed during the first phase of my field work, it was evident that the forest cover in the ASEP area was remarkably better, both in diversity and density, than in the neighbouring villages of Sokhisole and Buaramara (where Forest Protection Committees have now formed under the JFM agreement, although only in 1993 and 1996 respectively). In twenty-five years, ASEP came to include 700 ha of Sal forests, 300 ha of eucalyptus and *akashmoni*, 60 ha of cashew plantation, 190 ha of scrub forest and 2 ha for research nurseries. The ASEP was successful in two key respects: regenerating forests in wastelands and providing growth to the local economy through legitimate forest activities. The plantation selected and raised as part of the project has met the fodder, fuelwood, small timber, and minor forest produce needs of village communities. Additionally, the project aided the local community in increasing its income and with various village development works.[23] In that sense, some of the important goals and rhetoric set out by the FD were served through the project.

---

[22] The figure contrasts favourably with the JFM harvest return of Rs. 1,248 to FPC members in Bhagwati Chowk village, the highest in the Gopegarh Beat in West Bengal (see chapter 4).

[23] Villagers were initially even allowed to grow paddy, maize, groundnut, and fodder grasses on the deforested State lands (Khare et al. 1995).

### 2.4.1 The Duality Embedded in ASEP

A dichotomy existed between the government's incentives in seeking participation and those of the forest citizens. However, despite a divergent set of primary incentives, the JFM, as the ASEP had done, touches several common grounds. The first section argues that JFM, which is informed by ASEP's framework, faces similar difficulties that were inherent in the ASEP.

Subramaniam Palit, a contemporary of Ajit Bannerjee who implemented the ASEP, summarized his feeling towards participation in State forests (in Khare et al. 1995).

> In the early 1970s, I was Divisional Forest Officer (DFO) of Purulia Division. As a young DFO I too organized raids with great zeal to recover stolen forest produce from all over the district. During one such raid in June 1973, we encountered stiff opposition from the people bringing in the produce, which led to the police opening fire. Two people were killed and three injured. A number of forest and police personnel were also injured by missiles hurled by the miscreants. This incident resulted in my telegraphic transfer from the district, a judicial inquiry into the firing incident and a Government order discontinuing the *haat* (village market) raids. The staff was totally demoralized and the illegal trade continued to flourish. This was in fact a turning point in my career as I became convinced that there was no alternative to Joint Forest Management (JFM) if forests were to survive.

The author in the passage above recognizes that the policing practices had reached a head and the state could not overlook incidents of mass-scale violence against what, albeit, remained 'illegal' forestry activities by 'miscreants'. As the Forest Department takes up JFM, the variance of goals remains; whereas the collection, use, and sale of forest usufruct appears as a key incentive for forest citizens, the FD strives for conservation and territorialization (assertion of an absolute tenurial right on the forest land). It is, nonetheless, commendable that the Forest Directorate in Kolkata had cleared a project that was unprecedented and based on the conviction of one individual rather than one that came as a result of standard procedures, either through working plans or from departmental meetings.[24]

However, many of the successes of the ASEP remained on the surface. First, the location of Arabari itself was significant for its success. A pocket in southwest Bengal, Arabari villages had degraded forest land (in PF category) as well as agents (elites, *panchayat*) who could interpret the FD's initiatives to the rest of the community. The special status of Arabari cannot be denied; the FD had taken special interest to bring about a showcase example of its breakthrough participatory intervention. The project had attempted to fulfill a large agenda (drafted by the FD), which included the communities' access to local forests and a

---

[24] Similar individualistic initiative would, for example, find little encouragement in Jharkhand.

share of timber revenues, raising revenue for the FD, and regenerating forests through community-FD collaboration. Although all the sections have benefited in some respect, the project remained primarily an FD- and Arabari's elite- controlled venture (Chatterji 1996). The communities did not enjoy ownership nor were they responsible for charting the course of the project. The design of the project did not specify responsibilities and duties to an extent that management would not depend on arbitrary protection methods. Participation from the community on any sustained basis was seldom there, and the prime benefits were typically captured by the elites. Angana Chatterji, who has researched Arabari more intensively, concludes that the FD did not endeavour to create a distinction between caste and *adivasis* (tribal) groups, and instead included all households as *equal* shareholders to usufruct benefits (Chatterji 1996). Forest Departments dealt with the project through these elites, whereas marginalized groups were involved in protection and guarding forests.

This form of state-run 'participation' demonstrated its implications in several ways. Whenever support from the Forest Department waned (e.g. on transfer of the DFO in-charge to another station), community involvement in ASEP faced serious threats. Similarly, the sociopolitical divisions within the community, which went unnoticed by the FD, had a detrimental impact on forest management. The differences in the community could often be traced to the allegiances the villagers shared with two main political parties: the Communist Party of India (Marxist) and the Congress (Indira). In 1971, when ASEP was conceived, Congress was the ruling political party in the State. However, since 1977, CPI (M) has been in power. This change significantly reversed the role of groups that influenced decision-making processes in the ASEP. Consequently, members of CPI (M) could operate both informally and formally (through the local governance of *panchayat*) to influence various aspects of rural development forestry, not to mention the immediate ASEP activities.

The Forest Department failed to foster sustained and uniform participation. It did little to appreciate the heterogeneity in terms of class and social status. Hence, the variance in needs and goals in participation of different groups were never addressed. This was also true in terms of gender, ethnicity, and age.[25] No attempt was made to put forest resources under the control of smaller or cohesive committees. The share of labour in the protection of forests did not reflect a universal and equal dividend for the entire community. In the last few years, there was also an increase in discontent within the community over the stagnation of

---

[25] A limited amount of specialized approach, however, was made in terms of access to usufruct in the ASEP. There were two categories of entitlements, fixed after consultation with Arabari's elitist executive committee and the Forest Department: those that were available to all households (such as the collection of dry leaves, resin, and gum), and those that were exclusive to select (poorer) households (collection of dead trees, paid labour in cashew plantation activities) (Chatterji 1996).

benefits received from the ASEP. The ASEP beneficiaries, for example, demanded a share as high as 75% from the rotational fellings of Sal (Chatterji 1996, 92). Communities also demanded the inclusion of development projects (irrigation, roads, education, electricity, etc.) in the ASEP (ibid.); however, little microplanning entrepreneurship was carried out in the area.

Since the coming of JFM, there has been a constant debate to formalize the ASEP under JFM and place it back in the Midnapore East Forest Division. The officer in charge of ASEP in 1998 asserted that 'a project' by definition must have 'a start and a finish date', and that a period of more than 25 years must surely be a long enough time. In 1998, the project status of Arabari was finally removed, and Arabari was put under the standard JFM system. Now comes one of the key tests for Arabari forestry. The deprivation of the special status would imply splitting the project area into a number of smaller FPCs. Although this might arguably improve certain community management practices (e.g. the recognition of resources and fixing of responsibility), the removal of current special status, apart from the removal of generous support from the FD, would mean putting up smaller areas for harvest (as is the practice in the rest of the Midnapore Forest Division). This could threaten a key goal (i.e. income) that sustained villagers' enthusiasm, and, in turn, further impair the participatory activities on the very breeding grounds of JFM.

### 2.4.2 Discussion

Joint Forest Management, mandatory now all over India in state-owned protected forests, is arguably an effort by the government of India to universalize what had started as an experiment in Arabari.[26] The characteristics that mark the ASEP illuminate the complexities that enshroud the replication of a unique project such as the ASEP. I argued that although Arabari established the need for participation in state-owned resources, particularly those that are keenly contested, it failed to produce a synthesis of various goals that are pursued by different user groups and stakeholders. Such duality is constantly present between stakeholders and is followed through out the monograph.

In this sense, ASEP did not challenge the power dynamics of a heterogeneous rural society and failed to reflect the forest management needs and priorities of different and often contending groups of villagers. Limited in approach, it did not address the development needs and opportunity costs of the community. As the objectives of the state and people were joined, Arabari became a showcase for the

---

[26] Sukhomajri in Haryana, India provides another example of a participatory experiment through 'social fencing' (Sarin 1998; also Gupta 1995). Here, the villagers formed autonomous bodies to manage both forest and non-forest lands and improve living conditions. Sarin (1998), however, agrees that Bengal's framework has served as a model for JFM in most of the Indian States.

inevitability of the participatory approach. Nevertheless, the rules are still made and managed by the Forest Departments according to their own goals.

## 2.5 Institutional Arrangement in Joint Forest Management in Jharkhand and Bengal

The earlier section examined the Arabari Socio-Economic Project and showed that the symmetrical relationship (Pattnaik and Dutta 1997) professed between the FD and the local institutions in ASEP was, despite many successes, not the case. This section introduces the institutional setup of JFM in Jharkhand and West Bengal. It does so by examining the nature of the roles that are assigned to various institutions in Jharkhand and Bengal and outlining the different directions the FDs have taken in these States. In Bengal, the activism of the FD presents a certain agenda; in Jharkhand, on the other hand, the FD's work-style is markedly threatened by a series of constraints. The section discusses the composition of registered Forest Protection Committees and the benefits that are promised in the JFM. It also notes the presence of intermediary institutions in JFM, the *panchayats* and NGOs.

### 2.5.1 The Village Forest Management Committees

Joint Forest Management in Bengal was declared an official practice in 1989 (GOWB 1989). Bihar was prompted by the Central government to devise its own resolution and came up with an elaborate framework outlining the structure of Village Forest Management and Protection Committees (VFMPCs) and distribution methods in JFM in 1990. VFMPCs in Bihar are made up of one member from each household. An executive body, made up of fifteen to eighteen people including leaders of *panchayat*,[27] the village religious leader, a local school teacher, four members from the schedule caste/tribe, and three to five women, is established to head the committee. The forester holds the position of member-secretary to the executive body and acts as a coordinator between the villagers and the Forest Department. The forest guard is an invited member and is expected to attend the committees' monthly meetings. The structure of the Forest Protection Committees (FPCs) in Bengal is similar to, albeit simpler than, that in Jharkhand. FPCs are made up of one member from each household where the spouse is a joint-holder in the membership.[28] The executive committee is made up of six people with two members who are representatives of the village *panchayat*.

---

[27] The FD recommends the inclusion of elected and defeated *mukhiya* (council leader) and *sarpanch* (judicial officer) in the executive body.

[28] The collection of forest product, such as firewood, is, however, not limited to this membership. As has been the practice, both adult members of a household and children (mostly females) forage forest floors for firewood and other usufructs.

Foresters hold the position of member-secretary with duties similar to those in Jharkhand.

### 2.5.1.1 The Distribution Mechanics of Harvest under JFM

The forest departments have proposed elaborate distribution mechanisms to share profits from the timber harvest with members of forest committees. In Jharkhand, the members are to receive, in addition to timber output from the periodic thinning of forest, a share of the final harvest in accordance with rights set out in village records known as the *Khatiyan* registers. The committee can then sell any surplus timber, either to local villagers or on open markets. The members of the Village Forest Management and Protection Committee (VFMPC) are responsible for carrying out harvesting for which they are to receive wages. Of the harvest produce, 20% belongs to the Forest Department as its royalty. Of the remaining 80%, 30% goes to meet the 'bonafide' domestic needs of the village,[29] whereas the other 50% is to be put up for sale. The revenue from the sale, after paying for the managerial expenses of the VFMPC, is to be divided into three equal parts.[30] Two parts go toward village development and forest development respectively, whereas the third part is to be paid in cash to each member of VFMPC.

A typical harvest operation in West Bengal is as follows: once an FPC completes its mandatory five years of shareholding (or time since formal registration), an area is identified by the FD and notified to the Forest Development Corporation (FDC) for harvesting. The FDC then sanctions a loan to the FD, which pays wages to the FPC members (who alone are entitled to be employed for the purpose) for carrying out the felling, logging, and transport to Sal-depots. Once the sale is done, (through auction, tender, negotiations, or pre-destined institutions like Coal India Limited), the cost of harvesting is subtracted from the gross sale value. Of this, 25% is paid to the Forest Protection Committee concerned. Of the balance, 10% is deducted by the FDC as a service charge. Of the remaining amount, a further 10% is deducted by the FDC as interest on working capital and establishment charge. The balance is then paid to the Divisional Forest Officer as a royalty to the forest department. In the year 1996-1997, the FDC (south) paid (for the sale in 1995-1996) an amount of Rs. 8,881,229 as FPCs'

---

[29] The 'bonafide' domestic need is the quantity of forest produce as ascertained by the FD officials for an individual village under the requirement of the forest settlement order and is maintained in the village file called *Khatiyan* II. However, the rights recorded in *Khatiyan* II are subject to the prescriptions that are made by the Forest Directorate in the Working Plans. This provision leaves the routine exercise of rights by villagers at the mercy of the efficiency with which each of the plans is prepared and executed.

[30] It is noteworthy that members of the FPC not only receive a share from the sale of timber, but also have been promised secure wages for forest work during harvest operations.

shares.[31] The gross value collected in the division was approximately Rs. 70 million for that year (FDC [south] office records).[32]

### 2.5.2 *Panchayat*

Joint Forest Management juxtaposes a traditional village institution, the *panchayat*, with the newly-instituted Forest Protection Committees. In West Bengal, the FD started to involve the *panchayat* quite early in forest management, such as through the *Ban-O-Bhumi Samskar Sthyayee Samiti*. *Panchayat* records were used to identify economically backward rural populations, and their cooperation was sought in exchange for forest usufruct. However, with the coming of JFM, the equations have changed. A much larger population, nearly anyone in a village living next to a forest, is invited to join the JFM programme. Vis-à-vis territorial configurations, the arrangement presents a myriad of complex situations. Although the jurisdiction of *panchayats,* for example, is decided using various population characteristics and is territorially demarcated within revenue villages, the forest committees are formed from villagers living next to state-owned forests. It is easy to see that there would seldom ever be a 'one FPC-one *Panchayat'* situation. Nonetheless, in several instances, the FPCs have fitted well within the tight space that the bureaucracy and the *panchayats* relinquish; however, in others, they have remained marginal and have been used for vested interests. Chapter 6 addresses many practical situations with which FPCs members must deal while sharing dual membership with the *panchayat*. These conflicts are explored in the West Bengal case, which has an elaborate three-tier *panchayat* system. In Jharkhand, the *panchayat* was not functional during the research period. The

---

[31] Harvesting of timber remains under the jurisdiction of Forest Development Corporation (FDC). However, unlike in north Bengal where the FDC enjoys a monopoly on harvesting because of its well-established infrastructure, lack of a similar infrastructure in southwest Bengal has led the FDC to request the Forest Department to carry out harvesting in its respective territorial division. The FDC, however, remains the sole institution to market harvested forest timber and poles. The marketing of timber products is done either through auctions, tender, or sale to institutions (coal fields, the army, mills, Bharat Coking Coal Limited, North Frontier Coal Fields, etc.). Earlier, marketing was done solely through auction, which resulted in select merchants controlling the price of forest products. Now, however, due to a high demand from big institutions, the FDC has been able to get a better price and a speedy disposal of timber (*Source*: FDC [south] office).

[32] The figures are for the FDC (south) Division, which is comprised of West Midnapore, South Bankura, North Bankura, Panchet Soil Conservation Division, and parts of East Midnapore. It may be noted that there is a negligible role played by the Bihar (now, Jharkhand) Forest Development Corporation Limited (FDC) in the harvest and sale of forest timber. Unlike Bengal, where the FDC plays an important role in timber extraction and sale, in Jharkhand, timber, firewood, and bamboo are sold through the State trading wing of the Forest Department. However, the non-timber forest products fall largely under the jurisdiction of Tribal Cooperative Development Federation of India (TRIFED), Large Area Multi-Purpose Society (LAMPS), and Jharkhand State Forest Development Corporation Limited.

chapter instead addresses the continued importance of the former leaders of the *panchayat*.

### 2.5.3 NGOs in Jharkhand and Bengal

Unlike other parts of India, West Bengal has a surprisingly small number of NGOs working on rural development forestry. The forest directorate, for example, identified only two NGOs to participate in JFM efforts. The NGOs were invited to the 'apex body' committee meetings at the department headquarters in Kolkata to discuss ways to promote JFM in the State.[33] Chapter 7 discusses one of the two NGOs, the Indian Institute of Bio-Social Research and Development (IBRAD). S.B. Roy, the founder and director of IBRAD, has given an individual shape to the organization that he conceived in 1985. After working in diverse fields, such as health and agriculture, the NGO is now engaged mostly with JFM activities and related support and research. The Ford Foundation is the major funding body of IBRAD's JFM activities.

NGOs in Jharkhand, on the other hand, have cropped up in large numbers. A rickshaw-ride in Ranchi alone shows dozens of billboards advertising *registered* NGOs pursuing development or environmental causes. During the first phase of field work, offices of the Society for Rural Industrialization (SRI), Agrarian Assistance Association Trust, and *Divyayan*, a branch of a large NGO, Ram Krishna Mission, were visited. SRI was established in 1985 in Ranchi, and initially functioned as a 'technology resource centre'. In 1995, however, it inaugurated a 'technology demonstration centre' in Chamghatti in Annagarha Block, Ranchi. The Agrarian Assistance Association Trust, on the other hand, is an example of a low-key organization which is doomed to work when funds are available and only in areas for which it can get funds. It is run by Aspand Khan, a local resident of Maheshpur in Annagarha. For the past few years, the NGO has organized festivals on Environment Day (5 June) where, amid cultural activities and festivities, group discussions are held to promote awareness about use and protection of local forests. However, I mainly discuss the work of *Divyayan* and the nature of the participation and factions it has created (see chapter 7).

### 2.6 Notes on Methodology

The research compares the States of Jharkhand and West Bengal that share a contiguous boundary and similar forest ecology. It examines characteristics that mark forest activities (extraction, consumption, protection) among forest citizens in Jharkhand and Bengal in the participatory forest management (PFM) atmosphere. I examine decentralized forest management while testing rhetoric

---

[33] The 'apex body' committee meetings were organized by the Forest Department at its head office in Kolkata. Representatives from key NGOs were invited to discuss their JFM-promotion plans with the senior bureaucrats (also see chapter 7).

against the ground truths in two provinces of eastern India. One way to investigate this is, obviously, to see the forces that have led to JFM and opportunities that have been created in its wake. The nature of evolution of both polices and institutions (through creation, marginalization, inclusion, adjustments) is important to locate the incentives and goals that each of the stakeholders has in participating in JFM. It is also imperative to deconstruct the rhetoric that has surfaced in the wake of new discourses on participation. And then there is a need to examine the actual functions of institutions that work at several levels to contribute to and derive from the pool of resources in PFM. The interinstitutional relationship and modes of operation of each of the JFM institutions are studied. Also, those community characters that make up the tenets of moral economy vocabulary are examined. The following research issues form a backbone to the examination and were investigated during the course of research:

1. The Forest Protection Committee, a key stake-holder in JFM, will be motivated enough to invest time and other household resources, over a number of years, to meet the mandatory demands of JFM (protection of forests, monitoring, attendance in meetings and forest works) in anticipation of sharing the usufruct gains (including share in cash from timber harvest) associated with afforestation and other forest management schemes. The management roles that are prescribed for in the JFM are in consonance with indigenous forestry practices of the rural communities.

2. Forest Departments are competent, well-equipped, and sensitive enough to participate in tandem with local communities in Joint Forest Management. The earlier participatory arrangements have given them the required experience and lessons to be able to obtain participation from rural communities in regeneration, protection, development, and management of forest lands and in sharing the usufruct benefits with the rural communities.

3. The 'equity' rhetoric would be served. JFM would aid the local community in various village development works, and in increasing its income. Women and the tribal population will find adequate representation in forest management and share in the benefits.

4. Joint Forest Management would help in reconverting wasteland into forest land and possibly assist in putting unforested areas under forest cover as well. Also, it would go to meet fodder, fuelwood, small timber, and minor forest produce needs of village communities. The number of forest-related offences would decrease.

5. Institutions (*panchayats*, NGOs) that are traditionally involved with rural development, and earlier had a limited role in forest activities, will find useful roles in the present forest management structure. *Panchayats*, as hoped in the JFM agreement, will play an efficient supervisory role towards participatory forest management. NGOs in their supporting roles will sustain and improve the dialogue between the state and the forest citizens. The resultant institutional arrangement would properly and fairly reflect forest management needs and priorities of different, and possibly contending, groups of villagers.

6.   JFM effectively reflects the major concerns of sustainable use of natural
     resources. In its current shape, Joint Forest Management holds the answer to a
     stable and agreeable (forest-) land tenurial and usufruct arrangement between
     the state and its people.   ·

### 2.6.1 Research Focus: Community Forestry Groups

This section discusses the focus of the monograph and the approach that has been
used in the research. The point of entry for the research is examination of JFM
institutions and sociopolitical positions that are taken by them. The institutions
include the chief stakeholders in JFM – the Forest Department and community
forest protection groups – and the peripheral institutions, *panchayats* and NGOs,
who are to work as promoters. The examination is, however, primarily at the level
of community-forest interface. In other words, the institutions have been examined
for their operational practices within village communities.

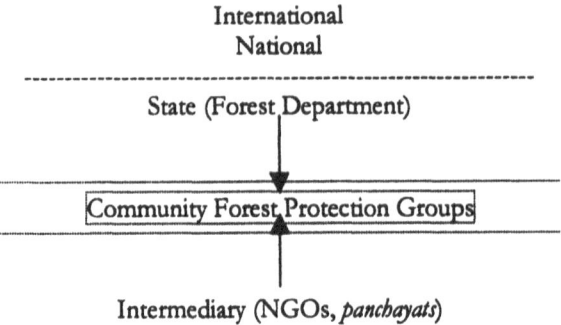

**Figure 2.1 Research Focus: Involvement of Institutions at the Community-
Forest Interface** (modified from Warren 1995)

Warren (1995) identifies seven levels at which institutional involvement can be
analyzed: individual, household, community, intermediary, state, nation, and
international. This research sets out to investigate the theoretical and functional
robustness of JFM at the village community level. It examines the manners in
which FPCs or voluntary forest committees interact with the Forest Department,
*panchayat*, and NGOs (see Figure 2.1). The research revolves primarily around the
village community. Institutions that work at the community-forest interface are not
only examined for modes of operation, but also for how they are perceived by
various groups in the community.[34] A considerable amount of attention is given to

---

[34] The interaction between rural people and forests is through networks of relationships
(Agrawal 1995), both private and at the level of institutions. Factors such as gender, class,
caste, seasonal cycles, and a priority ranking of forest usufruct may influence this

community leaders, those key individuals who give a unique shape to individual FPCs. A limited attempt has also been made to engender the study; my observations are, for example, reflected against findings by other researchers.

After setting boundaries for the research, a set of explicit questions was devised to investigate the research issues and form the basis of interviews, questionnaires, and discussions with members of the stakeholding institutions. The questions that would lead the inquiry mechanism were grouped into three clusters: ecological history, forestry functions, and forest usufruct; for each cluster, I investigated the interaction of village-based forest committees with other institutions (also see Figure 2.2). While grounded and practical in expression and containing both conceptual and thematic dimensions, the clusters had the potential to unravel perceptions and opinions held by each of four institutions: community forest committees, FD, *panchayats*, and NGOs (see Appendix III for questionnaire and interview formats).

- **Question set 1. Ecological history:** What have been the roles of policies, institutions, and the nature of dependence on forest resources in establishing the current practices, environmental values, and incentives for involvement in Joint Forest Management? How have institutions and policies evolved? How have various dimensions of participation or contradiction in the interinstitutional set-up evolved? How have people responded to these changes? What have been the perceptions regarding various participatory paradigms and the factors at play within them?
- **Question set 2. Forestry functions:** What are the roles played by various members of Forest Protection Committees or self-initiated forest protection groups? How do other institutions aid them, and what is the nature of interinstitutional dependence? What are the incentives for each institution to participate, defect, or maintain an ambiguous status? How do established critical practices in specific social and official set-ups affect the functions of institutions? Do individuals (charismatic leaders, NGO leaders) shape institutions at the grassroots level? What is the nature of devolution of decisions and responsibilities? How are responsibilities (meetings, protection, plantation, etc.) decided and enforced? What are the constraints for cooperation?
- **Question set 3. Forest usufruct:** What is the nature of access and rights to forest resources provided for in Joint Forest Management? How are they different from indigenous practices and needs? What are the implications for rural development forestry and for an increment in the community's and Forest Departments' income? What are institutional incentives to be party to JFM? What are the assumptions about the benefits? Who benefits? Who loses? Do benefits fulfill the promises (equity, access, development), and expectations they started out with?

---

interaction. This monograph tests both the complementary relationship between institutions and the differences that mark the community forestry.

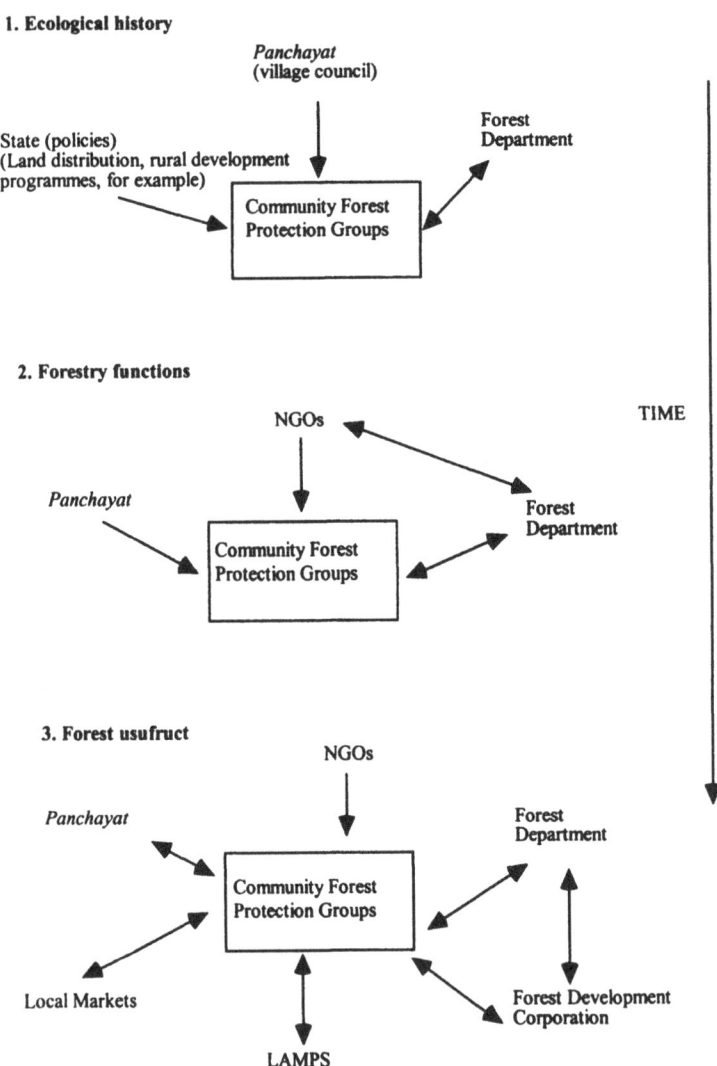

**Figure 2.2 Interaction between Ecological Institutions at Different Stages of Participatory Forest Management**

Two intensive field works were conducted. The forest villages that were surveyed during the first phase of field work indicated the representative features of JFM activities, helping to narrow down the study to a select number of villages for the intensive research. The intensive research was carried out in two forest beats, Annagarha in Jharkhand and Gopegarh in West Bengal. The first phase was to become familiar with a number of villages in the area; then four villages in each of these two beats were selected for intensive study. Although executive members of FPCs (and leaders in the case of self-initiated protection groups) were key informants for the research, approximately 120 households in each of the provinces were interviewed to represent a wide cross-section of the society.

*Forest Protection Committees*

The initial phase of survey and baseline data helped to determine the villages to be used for intensive research. An effort was made to choose villages that had the involvement of other JFM institutions. I remained aware of how each would compare in multicase analyses and with villages across the border. During this time detailed forest management inventories were conducted using participatory research techniques (discussions, interviews, participatory observation, meetings) for different groups of forest-dependent populations. Standard demographic data (age, gender, class, ethnic group) were collected for each respondent. The questionnaire and interviews were geared to investigate both historical and contemporary aspects of local forests.

I depended on oral histories from elderly villagers to get impressions of forestry operations as early as Independence. All respondents were asked to give their opinion of contemporary operational methods in forestry, rural development works, and involvement of neighbouring villagers, the FD, *panchayats*, and the NGOs. These would provide information about modes, attributes, and efficiency of intra- and inter- institutional communications. Defection within the village community and contest from outside the community over management of forests were also examined. Of particular importance for an overview of the entire set-up were the leaders, both in JFM and *panchayat*.

To get an account of gender division, both men and women were interviewed about work distribution, representation, and usufruct access in forestry practices. It became apparent that the spatial identification with forests played an important role for villagers in the use and management of local forests. These territories, would, however, often be in variance to that demarcated for management and protection by the FD under the JFM agreement. Resource maps were drawn to locate the hamlets vis-à-vis forests. The research also gained from minutes from village meetings (the records are often held by community leaders) and records of occasional Forest Department microplans for rural development forestry (with beat offices).

*Forest Department*

The Forest Department's records provided the baseline data on FPCs. Also, maps of forests vis-à-vis the location of villages under study were seen. The FD records also helped to understand changes in organizational structure in the wake of JFM. Attempts were made to view records of revenue and expenses for each forest beat. This was frequently granted in Bengal, whereas in Jharkhand it was not made available. Also, data on recorded forest offences for both the regions were accessed. Interviews and discussions with the Forest Department officials were helpful in clarifying several aspects of regional forestry and in getting to know the attitudes of the department officials in light of JFM. Discussions about the department's long-term view of the tenurial arrangement of forest land, usufruct rights, species selection, and infrastructural lapses were taken up with senior officials. Discussions and observational study with beat officers and forest guards provided insights into the relationship between the foresters and local people.

*Peripheral Institutions: Panchayats and NGOs*

An approach similar to the one taken with the Forest Department was used while contacting *panchayats* and NGOs. The records available with these institutions were consulted. Evidence there was further bolstered with discussions and interviews with office holders in each of the institutions. Participatory-observation methods were followed when members of these institutions were working in villages.

### 2.6.2 Opportunities and Constraints

The field work in Jharkhand involved working in villages that are predominantly tribal. As a north Bihari, I was conscious of the *diku-*, or outsider-, label I might carry in Jharkhand villages. I had known several *adivasi* students and employees in my boarding school in Hazaribagh, in Jharkhand. Despite the familiarity with the region and its people, I had wondered if I would face the problem of resistance that Annagarha tribal residents might typically employ for outsiders. This was, however, seldom the case. I took care to establish that I did not represent any organization or government office, including the Forest Department.[35] Apart from several rounds of introductions (particularly in the non-tribal Mahespur *khas*), I was left alone 'to look and ask around'.     However, it took some time before the villagers 'opened up'. Indeed, some key interviews and discussions (such as the ones with the Maheshpur tribal leader, Saubhagya Munda, see chapter 4) happened

---

[35] I had also frequently clarified that my report was not a part of any survey that would bring 'development projects' into the region. One evening I was returning from Lemha *toli* to my room on the Annagarha highway. I was on a motor scooter when I saw an old woman carrying a thin pile of Sal twigs and leaves on her head. She must have been returning to her house in Lemha. She was alone and walked slowly. When I got nearer, she stopped walking and bowed in a deep *namaste*. She did not turn towards me, nor did she meet my eyes – ritual she must be used to, to acknowledge the authority of forest staff who might still be on a patrol-duty. I instinctively returned the *namaste* with a nod. Only when the scooter had rolled ahead, did I realize the association that the old woman had made.

during the later part of my field stay. The usual shyness prevented women, particularly the younger members, from speaking out to a male outsider. Thus, the percentage of women is less among the respondents. I was also conscious that I had joined the league of anthropologists against whom villagers guard their privacy; I respected this in each case, even if the *data* were unyielding. My ability to speak Hindi, on the other hand, helped me to cover a large number of *tolis* and villages and talk to the residents. Also, my language facility made it easy to go through *panchayat* records, minutes from village meetings, and the Forest Department records at the beat level. In West Bengal, however, with limited grasp of Bengali, I depended on villagers who understood Hindi, or someone who could translate (often a fellow villager and occasionally student translators from Midnapore town). I found the West Bengal's Forest Department (both at higher and beat levels) at ease in assisting someone for 'pure research' purpose. (Access to records from offices of the Forest Department in Jharkhand, on the other hand, despite several instances of assistance, was tricky.)[36]

It has been an ambitious project to compare participatory forestry in two States. The strict selection of methods that became obligatory for the research design has meant foregoing certain examinations and also focusing only at certain levels. The institutions have been examined mainly in relation to community forestry practices (whereas secondary data were collected to inform several other facets for each of the institutions). For example, the revenue returns of the Forest Department in the pre- and post- JFM scenarios or the weight of influence of donor bodies such as the World Bank in facilitating changes in the FD's organization in West Bengal were not analyzed and only referred to. Also, it was beyond the scope of this work to examine in any depth the sociological reasons for cohesion and conflict within village communities.

Rural populations were classified into three groups: those who participate in forest management, those who do not (and have conflicting interests with the managing bodies), and those who are indifferent to participatory forest management (PFM). This method of classification could have marginalized results if, for example, other population characteristics such as age structure, gender, income, land holding were taken as primary perspectives of examination. Standard demographic data were, nonetheless, collected for each of the respondents.

---

[36] Harry Blair, in his thesis on Bihar's electoral politics of the late 1960s, mentions the paucity of data on Bihar, particularly those at the community level (Blair 1969, 13). He found information on Bihar 'unquestionably' miniscule as compared to what is available for other Indian States (ibid., 17). This continues to be the case. (The journal *Economic and Political Weekly* [India], however, occasionally contains reports and anaylyses of incidental events, such as elections, scams, and violence in the State).

### 2.6.3 Analysis of Data and Composition of Case Study Report

The dominant modes of analysis include pattern-matching, rival explanations, and explanation building, which ·may, in turn, use either convergent (where each evidence is directed to test a single hypothesis) or divergent (where evidence from interviews, surveys, document analysis, etc. yield separate bodies of conclusions) methods to arrive at results (Yin 1989). A general strategy that was used to analyze the evidence from the case studies included laying out the theoretical propositions that led to the case study. Then case descriptions based on field interviews, discussions, and empirical evidence (both quantitative and qualitative) were prepared for comparisons. The next stage was to develop a cross-case analysis (across States and institutions) and write the case report.

### 2.7 Conclusion

Chapter 2 has intended to highlight the forestry infrastructure that is in place in the unique settings of the Jharkhand and *Jungle Mahal* forests. The initial sections outlined the sociopolitical profiles of Jharkhand and West Bengal. Low overall development indicators mar the polity of both the States. Bengal, however, contains stronger grassroots organizations, which, in turn, have had a close and working relationship with the state bureaucracy. More significantly, the Forest Department in West Bengal has been progressive and transparent. Jharkhand's Forest Department, on the other hand, has done little to advance JFM causes in forests that are already heavily right-burdened. Although the chapter commends the participatory initiatives of the Forest Department in Bengal, it reiterates that the variance in goals between the community and the FD continue to pose a difficulty in achieving the high rhetoric of JFM. This was demonstrated in the Arabari Socio-Economic Project (ASEP) and is key to understanding the assumed goals of Joint Forest Management. The final section of the chapter introduced various institutions that are working at the village-forest interface in each of the States. It also discussed the research design and outlined the methodologies taken up during the initial phase of research and subsequent intensive field work. It lists the key research issues and sets of questions that have been used to investigate each one of them.

# Chapter 3

# Forest Departments: Changed Roles, Conventional Goals

## 3.1 Introduction

This chapter analyzes how the Forest Departments in Jharkhand and West Bengal have worked with village communities to achieve participation in forest management. It discusses the policy framework that the departments have adopted towards forest management and introduces the settings in the villages where the research was carried out. Baseline dataset for each of the villages is provided and is referred to in the following chapters. The chapter begins with a discussion of the scale and quality of JFM efforts in West Bengal. It is argued that the concentration of a number of JFM committees in southwest Bengal betrays a target-oriented approach by the department to raise the percentage of forest cover in deforested parts of the State. The Forest Department in Jharkhand, on the other hand, despite a prompt declaration of the JFM resolution, has shown meagre bureaucratic initiatives to encourage villagers to protect forests under the JFM agreement. The section nevertheless extrapolates on a project proposal the FD submitted to the World Bank to gain insights into the State's long-term plans for forest management.

The later sections of the chapter analyze how the Forest Departments have performed in each State vis-à-vis three key parameters of JFM: registration of villages under the JFM agreement, sharing responsibility for the protection of forests, and distribution of usufruct and benefits. It is argued that the lower-level officials are key actors in shaping the attitude and providing legitimacy to the protection mechanisms in villages. The nature of interaction between the officials and the villagers, however, depends on a number of factors, such as the relationship of the beat officials to the village leader, the history of the local forest, and the status of the village in the larger set-up. The beat officials, in the absence of explicit instructions from the higher offices, often combine older practices with those that are sensitive to participatory forestry. This includes permitting members of FPCs to extract usufruct on a regular basis, as well as allowing them to handle forest offences on their own. However, a considerable amount of insularity continues to exist between FPCs and the Forest Department. The latter interacts mainly through leaders with whom it is comfortable. The women and even the larger community remain conspicuous by their absence both in FPC meetings and routine interaction with the forest department's officials. Last, among the usufructory return from the JFM, the meagre share from the harvest of timber appears to be an unsteady and often insufficient source of incentive for participation. The share depends on the ratio of household to forest area that is harvested, and is, more often than not, a paltry sum of money. In Jharkhand, harvest of timber under the JFM agreement has not occurred. However, the previous harvest operations have left village communities with bitter memories. Villagers, on the other hand, demonstrate the expectation that the Forest Department will involve itself with rural development. The chapter ends with the suggestion that the FD enlarge its constituency to areas of rural development.

## 3.2 Joint Forest Management: A Shift in Paradigm

Although a greater part of the chapter is geared to an analysis of the gaps that remain in the implementation (and interpretation) of JFM rhetoric, this section discusses the overall direction each of the States has taken vis-à-vis implementation of participatory forestry. Joint Forest Management has marked a clear departure from management systems of the past. There are two ways in which JFM has had impacts on forest management in Jharkhand and West Bengal. First, the States have decided to subdue their revenue interests in forest land and instead focus to meet the dual goals of equity for forest citizens and conservation of forest cover. Second, the forest department that had once keenly guarded its hold over forests has invited rural communities (through Forest Protection Committees) and other institutions such as *panchayats* and voluntary agencies to assist in JFM efforts.

In West Bengal, the shift in paradigm is visible in how the department has modified its organizational structure and operations and in its effort to include outside institutions, particularly the *panchayats*. In Jharkhand, despite a change in rhetoric, this transformation is less apparent in actual practice. The following sections discuss how Bengal has, with greater articulation than Jharkhand, adjusted its management paradigm to suit the overall design of Joint Forest Management.

### 3.2.1 Bengal's Directions in JFM

West Bengal's Forest Department has shown innovation, promptness, and transparency in the implementation of JFM. In July 1990, on receiving the Government of India's (GOI's) order on JFM, the Forest Department of West Bengal improvised on its previous format (GOWB 1989) with a new resolution (GOWB 1990). The only major change in the new resolution, however, was that the State government agreed to provide 'any family' who would be interested in 'work of protection' of forests the option to become a member of a Forest Protection Committee (the earlier provision allowed only 'economically backward people living in the vicinity of forest' to become beneficiaries). In another progressive step, the government, in November 1991, extended the JFM pledge, which, until then, had remained restricted to southwest Bengal, to *degraded* (my emphasis) forests of the northern Bengal plains. A similar resolution followed for Darjeeling's Gorkha Hill areas and for Sunderbans where beneficiaries were entitled to 25% from the sale of firewood and poles (from thinning operations) (GOWB 1991). The widening of JFM in West Bengal establishes that the FD was convinced that a share in revenue and forest usufruct would encourage protection in degraded forests. Also, the enlargement of the JFM constituency from southwest Bengal to the northern plains and Sunderbans indicates that the endorsement of JFM has become a unique tool for managing forests in the State.

Indeed, as was frequently pointed out in early feedback on JFM in the State, through inclusion of newer categories of households and regions from other parts of the State, the Forest Department reflected a willingness to put equity goals ahead of generating revenue from forest resources (GOWB 1995b, 1997; also Kurup 1996). One of the assessments of 'success' of JFM in the State is, for example, summed up in a report published by the Forest Department. It reports a survey (carried out in southwest Bengal) where members of FPCs were asked why they chose JFM membership,

> while 56% of FPCs felt it was due to betterment of life, 23% due to conservation of nature and in 9% FPCs it was for aesthetic value (GOWB 1997b ).

The report concludes,

> this shows high awareness level of the villagers on their own as only 13 FPCs have said that it was mainly due to publicity by FD (GOWB 1997b).

The survey further weighed the reasons villagers do not participate and based them on the following criteria: lethargy 22%, conflict based on class 14%, lack of publicity 9%, not sure of benefit 5% (GOWB 1997b). The (quantitative) survey was, hence, keen to show that the JFM has taken root on its own and, where rural communities shared the vision of the FD, provided both better living conditions and conservation of forests through the programme. Similarly, Khare et al. (1995), for example, in commending the efforts of West Bengal's Forest Department to implement JFM, cited figures on the number of FPCs and households that have been drawn in by JFM to manage forests. He stated that between 1987 and 1991, JFM had spread from a near zero representation to its peak in the State. With a bar graph, he tried to establish the argument that the area of forest covered under JFM is proportional to the number of households that have been drawn into membership (Khare et al. 1995, 22).[1] Although not stated explicitly, the argument suggests that a great amount of symmetry and proportion existed between the FD's initiative and the response of the people.

---

[1] For example, villages that do not share contiguous boundaries with forest are not usually invited to JFM membership. Also, rural people living next to reserved-category forests are usually precluded from JFM benefits (as in Jharkhand, particularly).

Closer scrutiny, however, reveals that the programme was driven largely by the State apparatus and implemented chiefly in areas that have degraded Sal forest. In this sense, JFM appears foremost as a FD-sponsored tool to serve the primary motive of restoration of forest cover in southwest Bengal.[2] For example, the proportional distribution of FPCs in the State indicates that the Forest Department fostered JFM most vigorously in southwest Bengal. In 1994, when the southwestern districts of Midnapur, Bankura and Purulia accounted for 802, 809, and 591 FPCs respectively, the deltaic 24-Paraganas had 6 FPCs, Burdwan had 37 FPCs, and Birbhum accounted for only 58 registered FPCs (GOWB 1994). Notably, the northern districts of Darjeeling, Jalpaiguri, and Coochbehar combined accounted only for 160 FPCs (GOWB 1994). By 1997, West Bengal had nearly 3,300 officially registered FPCs within the State (GOWB 1996b). However, the distribution characteristics of the FPCs located in 13 Forest Divisions continued to have the earlier characteristics in that the FPCs remained concentrated in the southwestern districts of Bengal.[3] Similarly, the southern district of 24-Paraganas, with its expansive mangrove forests (which in turn accounts for 37% of the State-managed forest) has minimal representation within the FPC commune.[4]

Hence, apart from a constitutional conduciveness (the presence of protected-category forests), JFM in southwest Bengal made sense to the Forest Department because there are many degraded forests and wasteland (GOWB 1997) in the area. Indeed, southwest Bengal has only 37.91% of the recorded forest lands of West Bengal but accounts for 69.60% of total wastelands of the State (Bagchi and Phillip 1993). The region also contains the maximum amount of land that was vested in the State (acquired by the government through various land ceiling laws):

---

[2] In this sense, both the centre and the State government have been consistent in opening the participatory dialogue primarily for degraded forests.

[3] Assuming that rural populations that live next to forests in regions other than southwest Bengal have similar dependence on forest usufruct, it is unfair that they are not entitled to the same usufructory package in exchange for forest management. It is likely that the Forest Department is reluctant to share timber produce because it has traditionally had greater economic interest in the forests of northern Bengal (25% of State-managed forests) and may not be prepared to give away the revenue from the region or change the nature of silvicultural operations in the area. JFM has been proposed for the protected category of forests (PFs), and many regions of the northern Bengal and Sunderbans have reserved category forests (RFs), which present a constitutional problem for allotting shares in timber in those regions. Last, the lower JFM activity in northern Bengal could also be a reflection of a lack of political clout the population of the area enjoys in mainstream State politics. By its own admission, the Forest Department feels that the migrant labourers, landless farmers, and refugee population that form most of the forest fringe population in northern Bengal do not present a possibility for an effective 'user-group management' (GOWB 1993b, 5).

[4] The number of FPCs, however, had risen in other areas too, and often doubled. By 1996, for example, 24-Paragana had 15 FPCs, Birbhum 133 and Burdwan 62 (GOWB 1996b, 4).The number of FPCs in north Bengal, however, increased only marginally (ibid.).

the districts of Midnapore (803,000 acres), Bankura (425,000 acres), and Purulia (287,000 acres) (ibid.). It is also a territory where people, including *panchayats*, have had involvement with schemes, such as Social Forestry, and *Ban-o-bhumi* projects. (It was also the host for the Arabari Socio-economic Project.) Finally, a not so untimely impetus came from donors, such as the World Bank and the Ford Foundation.[5] The State government also supported the projects taken up by the FD.

### 3.2.2 Jharkhand's Forest Department: Constraints and Conservatism

The Forest Department in Jharkhand has innovated little. The bureaucracy uses an approach that is guided by principles of returning high non-tax revenue to the State, working through conventional forestry methods (policing, scientific forestry)[6] and maintaining rigid bureaucratic stratification. In instances where other States have moved to decentralize office responsibilities (horizontally, by divesting certain responsibilities to parallel institutions such as FDC or vertically by investing certain others to junior officials), Jharkhand's Forest Department has done little to loosen the grip of senior officials on the forest machinery. When, for example, many of the Indian States constituted the Forest Development Corporation (FDC) to replace private contractors for timber harvest, Jharkhand's FD retained the harvest operation for itself and instead allotted relatively minor responsibilities, such as collection and sale of minor forest products, to the newly founded FDC.[7]

Recent years have witnessed a further deterioration in forest management in Jharkhand. As identified in the State's own reports, the revenue returns from forests have dwindled.[8] A workshop recognized that more than 50% of forests are in a dilapidated state (Anonymous 1994), and, despite several plantation schemes, there has been little improvement in the quality of the State's forest cover. The

---

[5] Arguably, to be accountable to the funding bodies, the Forest Department has turned up a high number of registered villages and the forest area that are covered by 'participation'.

[6] Scientific forestry includes methods such as regeneration through coppice, crop improvement by favouring valuable species, removal of weeds, and management of forest cover. Such systematic forestry, however, is recent, and, for example, in Bengal was established in any real sense only after 1858, when the province came under direct British rule (Sivaramakrishnan 1996, 392). Working plans that support systematic forestry provide 'superior surveillance and estimation of growing stock or merchantable timber' (ibid., 404).

[7] The decision to harvest timber (such as marking the annual coupes in the field) is taken by the territorial DFOs from the FD. The actual felling operation (transportation and marketing) is carried out by the trading wing of the FD (GOB 1994).

[8] In 1989-1990, Bihar's FD revenue stood at Rs. 379 million; this has decreased to nothing in recent years. The FDC too, despite earlier profits, has shown losses in recent years (GOB 1994).

department achieved abysmal results in Social Forestry schemes (Kumar 1996). Moreover, since the Social Forestry project (started in 1985 and funded mostly by SIDA) ended, little external funding has been granted to the Forest Department. The department annual report·states that,

> It has been six years since the SIDA-sponsored Social Forestry programme ceased to exist. During this period, due to want of large and organized project proposals, investment in the forestry sector has nearly stopped (GOB 1999, 5; my translation).

The annual report of the Forest Department, *Pratiwedan,* lists funds that are targeted for State forestry-related projects. In recent years, paltry sums have trickled in through the World Food Programme (mainly in the form of wages to forestry workers) and through marginal projects, such as for tourism (funded by the government of Japan in places of Buddhist interest), tiger-projects (central government-/State-funded), tribal development, etc. (GOB 1996). The Forest Department in recent years, however, had counted on receiving substantial funding for what it termed the 'Bihar Forestry Project', a proposal to revamp the entire management system (see next section). Initially proposed to run from 1996 to 2005, the decade-long project was to cost Rs. 2932.3 million (GOB 1998, 5). Despite several delays, the FD had hoped to clinch the project. However, in 1999, it acknowledged that the project was unlikely to be accepted by the World Bank. The department's annual report said,

> ... according to the World Bank, the financial condition of the State is not well. Also, the projects that the Bank has invested in in other sectors of the State have shown slow progress. Therefore, the Bank is unwilling to start new projects in the State (GOB 1999, 6; my translation).[9]

Despite the fact that the performance of the FD had stalled in many areas, the FD announced its willingness for participatory forestry through JFM. Following the Government of India's letter in June 1990 (GOI 1990), the Bihar (now, Jharkhand) Forest Department came out with its own set of directives on JFM in November in the same year. The bureaucrats were willing to concede (in workshops, for example) that 'conventional' practices of policing only distanced the villagers from the department (Anonymous 1994). They also admitted that communities that were dependent on forest (despite their 'quota' of rights) had little alternative but to cut forest and even sell timber and fuelwood (ibid., 4).

The Forest Department in Jharkhand reported that 1,242 villages are registered as Village Forest Management and Protection Committees (VFMPCs) that cover a forest area of 654,269 hectares (nearly 27% of the State's protected category of forests) (GOB 1994, Annex 9, 5). The department, however, was not sure how

---

[9] In February 2004, the World Bank was in an advanced stage of discussion with the State government of Jharkhand to reconsider funding the 'Jharkhand Participatory Forest Management Project', with emphasis on a 'broad, multi-sectoral approach to poverty reduction in forest-fringe communities' (*Source*: www.worldbank.org).

many of these committees were registered during the Social Forestry period and how many registered as part of JFM. In other words, old committees have been rechristened as VFMPCs without the villagers being briefed on JFM. The FD further admits that most of the Social Forestry committees are, in all likelihood, non-functional (ibid. 1994). In the project proposal to the World Bank, the department, on the other hand, pointed to the many self-initiated committees in the State that show strong promise for managing local forests on a sustainable basis. The FD proposed to bolster these initiatives although, yet again, it conceded that it had scant record of the actual functional status of these committees.

Vis-à-vis JFM, the project proposal demonstrates an awareness of the shortcomings of how the JFM resolution is worded. For example, it proposes to remove the clause that limits the number of women in a VFMPC to a *maximum* of five and, instead, open membership to all adult men and women in a village (GOB 1994, Annex 9, 34). Also, it proposes that the committees be able to convene meetings in the absence of foresters, and that offenders be reported via VFMPC representatives and not directly by villagers who apprehend them (to minimize conflicts between fellow villagers). The department recognizes the mistrust that the villagers continue to have towards the FD staff and proposes a system of annual feedback from VFMPCs. Taking a lesson from Bengal, the FD recommends certain, albeit fewer (than Bengal) privileges in reserved-category forests. The department also recommends free collection and sale of non-timber forest products (the rights to which are currently held by Tribal Cooperative Development Federation of India [TRIFED] and the State Forest Development Corporation [FDC]).[10] More significantly, the project proposes that the members of VFMPCs be able to use their share of forest usufruct as they want (and not as prescribed in the JFM resolution) (GOB 1994, Annex 9). However, it qualifies the usufruct share by saying that the feedback the department has received shows that villagers do not wish to harvest timber because it would spoil the crop they have helped raise over a number of years (GOB 1994, Annex 9, 6). Villagers oppose clear felling, however, largely because of the mistrust they have for the felling operations carried out by the FD.

### 3.2.3 Discussion

West Bengal is a pioneer in the attempt to address the failures of Social Forestry and, later, improvise its own JFM rules. Jharkhand, on the other hand, remains tied to top-down forest management and is plagued by problems, such as lack of funds. It has proposed to address its failings through external funding. Certain senior

---

[10] The Forest Development Corporations (FDCs) have apparently not functioned to satisfaction. It was suggested that FDCs were unsuccessful in attracting institutional finance (such as from National Bank for Agriculture and Rural Development (NABARD) and carrying out the forestry tasks assigned to them (Haque 1996). Several FDCs were non-functional and survived only because of the government's contribution. Most were far from generating profits (ibid., 22).

officers from the Forest Department admitted to the history of mistrust between villagers and the FD and several lacunae in the way the State's JFM resolution is worded. The next section shows that, despite raising important issues, Jharkhand's Forest Department proposes few tangible changes in its structure to deal with the situation on any long-term basis. It also discusses how the FDs in both States have attempted (as in Bengal) or proposed (as in Jharkhand) to restructure their bureaucracies so that they are in consonance with the principles of participatory forest management.

### 3.3 The Forest Department's Structure, and Reorganization

The forest departments in Jharkhand and Bengal, as in the rest of India, are run by Indian Forest Service (IFS) officers selected on an all-India level (Warren 1995). A number of forest officers chosen at State level assist the IFS officers (see table below). The result is a strong hierarchy where lower FD officials only 'translate' orders that are issued from the top (Correa 1996). In Bengal in recent years, there have been internal debates (and pressure from funding bodies) for reorganization of the bureaucratic setup. The reorganization, essentially to better suit the mood and needs of participatory forest management, has shown mixed results in Bengal. Although the actual line of command is unchanged, the Forest Directorate, acting on suggestions by senior officers, has made notable changes in the bureaucratic arrangement and responsibilities at lower levels. The FD has also been asked to work in tandem with *panchayats* (even approximating the *panchayat* design with their own). In the case of Jharkhand, there has been no similar process of reorganization. Drawing on the Bihar's Forestry proposal to the World Bank, this section notes that the department seeks to improve its information bank and planning unit and improve forest cover (largely through scientific methods). The department proposes assistance to self-initiated village committees, although it states little that could be interpreted as a willingness to change the top-down structure of the department (see Table 3.1).

### Table 3.1 Organization of the Forest Department

1.   Minister of Environment and Forests (political appointment)
2.   Secretary of Environment and Forests
3.   Principal Chief Conservator of Forests
4.   Chief Conservator of Forests
5.   Conservator of Forest
6.   Divisional Forest Officer
7.   Assistant Divisional Forest Officer
8.   Range Forest Officer
9.   Beat Officer
10.  Forest Guard.

### 3.3.1 West Bengal

Responding to the managerial needs in forest management, West Bengal has attempted to reorganize the forest bureaucracy in the State.[11] A series of letters written by field-based officers to the directorate in Kolkata provides glimpses into the postures the senior officers took over reorganization of the Forest Department.[12] The officers consistently expressed their wish to continue with controls that the current hierarchy permitted. They feared that after reorganization, a leaner department would not be able to provide support for overall management or security to the members of staff who were positioned in forests. There were frequent suggestions to increase the number of staff at lower levels where the actual protection and management were centred. There was also a consensus among the senior bureaucrats that Divisional Forest Officers (DFOs) (mostly IFS officers) must continue to have overall command of forest management. A DFO, for example, emphasized the need to continue with the consolidation of 'power and control of *cadre*-officers' (GOWB 1993). An IFS officer from the Forest Development Corporation suggested that 'the line of command' should continue to flow down from the top to maintain the 'discipline of the organization' (ibid. 1993). Although most did not mind the creation of 'sub-divisions' that could better reflect decentralized goals, some resisted the idea of splitting up existing forest divisions into smaller divisions. The officers suggested upholding an optimum 'size and status' befitting a division (GOWB 1993). However, what seemed acceptable to the DFOs was regrouping or splitting forest territories at range and beat level.

The communication by the senior bureaucracy, in the best sense, can be interpreted as an understanding that it feels that the existing line of command (which to some degree can take credit for the very onset of participatory forestry) can alone channel information for decentralized forest management. On the other hand, it could also be read as a clearly expressed disapproval by the senior officers of any suggestion that might result in decreasing their power over control of forest land and say in forest management.

Not surprisingly, the actual reorganization of the FD in West Bengal followed a pattern that was acceptable to the majority of DFOs. Although several State-level employees were promoted to higher ranks (some even to the rank of DFOs) as part of the reorganization, the changes were mainly at the lower levels of bureaucracy (though mainly promotions and territorial reorganization). The files on reorganization in Midnapore East Forest Division show that the debates over

---

[11] The reorganization was apparently part of the set of conditions for funding by the World Bank that invested in the State's JFM project.

[12] The letters, written by DFOs, were generously made available by the FD office in Midnapore.

departmental reorganization  continued into 1995, the year when actual results from decisions that had been taken by the headquarters started to pour in. By the end of the year, nearly two dozen State-cadre forest rangers in Midnapore Forest Division were promoted to positions of Assistant Forest Officers (AFO) and Assistant Divisional Forest Officers (ADFO) and two hundred posts of rangers were filled by officers from lower levels (GOWB 1995). In a separate initiative, two non-territorial divisions (Kharagpur Social Forestry[13] and Rupnarain Soil Conservation Divisions), that had been until then 'project-based' functional divisions, were made territorial with responsibility for managing forest lands. Therefore, Midnapore East Division parted with some of its forest to the newly created territorial division of Rupnarain Soil Conservation.[14] The officers at Midnapore East, however, admitted that it was only a small dent in their own holding of forest land. By November 1995, the DFO at Midnapore East, in compliance with the government order number 2655–For/ FR/O/D/4E-2/95 dated 27 June 1995, issued an order to transfer specific forest ranges to Kharagpur Social Forestry and Rupnarain Soil Conservation Division. This included transfer of both property and personnel from Midnapore East to the new divisions (GOWB 1995). On 22 November.1995, the DFO at Midnapore East Division confirmed that the reorganization of Midnapore East Division has taken effect. Similar reorganization took place in the rest of the State and, in 1996, the Forest Directorate published the list of reconstituted territories, forest circles, and their respective territories down to beat level (GOWB 1996b).

In yet another initiative by the FD, there have been debates about how the department can work in tandem with *panchayats* (village councils). There were suggestions to match the territorial jurisdiction of the FD with that of *panchayat's* three-tier setup. This could mean that the forest beats should be reconstituted to align themselves with the territorial jurisdiction of the village *panchayats*. It was suggested that the beats should also have the freedom to reorganize in the future (GOWB 1993) where they could make constant adjustments with the *panchayats*. The letter also suggested that the forest range office be equated with the *panchayat samiti* (the next level of *panchayat)*, and the divisional office be equated with the *zilla parishad* (the highest *panchayat* office). The letter also proposed bringing

---

[13] Social Forestry schemes that were on the wane in West Bengal (due to policy changes) did not stop right away. The programme that had mainly involved *panchayat* land or land held under private ownership was active as late as 1996. Sale of seedlings, for example, had continued in 1998. The department officials reasoned that old schemes of distributing free or inexpensive saplings was less effective because people have become 'tree-minded', and there is little need to prompt with free saplings. Also, many private nurseries have come up to supply cheap saplings.

[14] Until then Midnapore had two territorial forest divisions, Midnapore East and Midnapore West. Since reorganization, two new divisions,  Kharagpur Social Forestry Division and Rupnarain Soil Conservation Division, which were earlier functional divisions, were added as territorial divisions.

together tribal and environment departments in the larger forestry framework.[15] However, the DFO at Bankura cautioned that such simplifications might result in 'chaos' as had happened 'during the reorganization in Purulia' (GOWB 1993). Although the physical alignment of the FD with the *panchayat* has not taken place in Midnapore, the principle of working with *panchayat* leaders is increasingly finding a sympathetic place in FD work mechanisms. The *panchayat* members, for example, are invited to meetings and consulted in large-scale forest offences or an intervillage conflict over use of forest usufruct.

### 3.3.2 Jharkhand

As mentioned in the earlier section, Jharkhand's Forest Department recognized several shortcomings in its current setup. The project proposal to the World Bank lists several corrective measures, yet it suggests little in the way of a willingness to change the core structure of the department to bring the management out of its current impasse. The project proposal, for example, suggests increasing the number of staff members and strengthening the working plan unit. It proposes the purchase of better data-gathering tools (including Geographic Information Systems [GIS] tools) and solicits funds to train officers in mapping and acquisition of forestry information.[16] The proposal, as an explanation, states that the data bank and working plans have not been updated because of the poor capacity of the planning unit of the department. It observes that, although preparation of working plans may take a number of years, the officers in charge of the operations tend to stay in the unit for less than two years. Admittedly, the planning and monitoring unit commands a low status within the FD setup. The postings to the working plan unit, the document states, are 'often regarded as a punishment' (GOB 1994, Annex 7, 4). Furthermore, the department has suffered budgetary irregularities and a lack of funding. As mentioned earlier the returns from forestry activities have diminished in recent years, and although the current philosophy of forest management focuses less on realization of revenue from the forests, the situation adversely affects even the basic functions of the department (irregularity in availability of funds, for example, could affect season-based projects such as plantation).

---

[15] The same letter remarks that only territorial (p4) officers should be made Divisional Forest Officers (DFOs).

[16] The department particularly lacks information about qualitative factors, such as the nature and state of its forests and status of village protection committees. Furthermore, the territorial maps that form the basis of forest activities have not been revised since the 1930s in Jharkhand. The working plans are supposed to cover a period of 20 years and be reviewed after a period of 10 years. However, for one third of Bihar's and Jharkhand's forest, there is no working plan, or the plans have expired 10 to 30 years ago (GOB 1994, Annex 7). Also, data on socio-economic factors have not been long revised, and the records on plantation and forest cover are insufficient to enable efficient planning.

The framework that the department proposes for forest management is a mix of scientific forestry and participation by the people. However, these goals appear as two separate agendas with little in common. Although the department recognizes the importance of voluntary protection groups, the proposal mentions very little about how the FD would engage itself with these committees, let alone with those who do not have voluntary systems of forest management. Moreover, other institutions such as *panchayats* and NGOs are not envisaged with fruitful roles in the set-up. On another level, the department is least ambivalent in its assertions to continue with scientific forestry (such as provisions of closure of forests, nurturing better grasses, and other silvicultural operations, such as afforestation and 'treatment'[GOB 1994, Annex 8, 16]). Unlike in West Bengal where Social Forestry is being phased out, the Forest Department in Jharkhand wants Social Forestry to remain a part of JFM in which farmers could be encouraged to plant trees on privately owned lands. It envisages that this would help create fodder banks to relieve forest land from the demand of fodder (ibid.).[17]

Despite a resolve to revive its data bank, the department proposes few tangible changes, particularly those that are in consonance with the principles of JFM. The proposal does not, for example, mention how the lack of interest in the planning unit might be lessened unless the departmental suprastructure is altered to provide needed prestige to the reviled unit. Despite admitting the existence of pressing issues, such as a lack of trust between the FD and villagers, a paucity of funds and failure in earlier forestry projects, the department makes only half-hearted attempts to deal with them. Most of all, it remains apathetic to aligning itself with village communities and rural institutions to become involved in participatory forest management.

### 3.3.3 Discussion

The debate about reorganization of the Forest Department in West Bengal is in keeping with the changes and reforms in which the department has indulged for the past three decades. It is, however, argued that the reorganization produced mixed results, such as several promotions for junior-level staff, some territorial adjustment, and a progressive dialogue with *panchayat*. However, the reorganization did not challenge the grip of senior bureaucrats on forest machinery nor did it provide autonomy to lower-level officials to work more independently while dealing with routine situations at the village level. In Jharkhand, although the FD seeks to strengthen its planning unit, it makes insufficient suggestions about how to make the unit attractive to foresters. It takes insufficient cognizance of how

---

[17] The Forestry Project wishes to create a fodder bank so that forest timber can be saved from grazing pressures. It proposes to import grass seeds from Australia in collaboration with the Animal Husbandry Department (the latter has been in the news for years because of corruption, kickbacks, and inefficiency in what came to be known as the Bihar Fodder Scam; see Joseph [1997] and Roy [1997] for discussions on the fodder scam).

it can combine participatory rhetoric with various other interests, such as scientific forestry, and it must overcome poor staffing, lack of interest, information, and funds.

## 3.4 The Setting of Research Sites and JFM Membership

The case study in West Bengal refers to the Gopegarh forest beat in Midnapore East Forest Division. Four villages are referred to in West Bengal: Bhagwati Chowk, Amratola, Phulpahari, and Khairulla Chowk. In Jharkhand, the research was carried out in Annagarha forest beat in Ranchi East Forest Division. Forestry practices in the villages of Mahespur, Nawagarh, Ober, and Vanadag are discussed (see Tables below).

The forest area in the Midnapore East Forest Division is 46,952.86 hectares of which Sal accounts for 26,739 hectares. There are nine territorial ranges and 26 forest beats (an average of 2.8 beats per forest range). 87.12% of forest in the division is under JFM (less than 7,000 hectares remain to be put under JFM in East Midnapore in 1996), and there are as many as 40,000 beneficiaries (GOWB undated). The forests of East Midnapore, unlike in Jharkhand, are spread out in disjointed patches of varying sizes and, in many instances, as islands among cultivated fields and habitations. The FD recognizes that lack of 'compactness' has contributed to the general degradation of forest (GOWB undated, 2). The forest area in Gopegarh forest beat, on the other hand, is 1,498.87 hectares. The FPCs that have been studied in the beat are part of the Konkabati *panchayat*. In the case study in Jharkhand, there are 28,328.76 acres of State forest land in Annagarha beat, of which 27,405.55 acres make up the protected-category forest whereas the rest are of reserved category. Annagarha has two *panchayat* centres, one each in Nawagarh and Maheshpur. The villages are laid out along the sides of the Annagarha-Hundru waterfall road. The forest distribution in Annagarha is more dense and compact that in Gopegarh.

### 3.4.1 JFM Membership in West Bengal

The Gopegarh forest beat accounts for five registered FPCs,[18] whereas three villages in the area, including Khairulla Chowk, are still unregistered. Amratola and Phulpahari were the first villages in Gopegarh beat to be registered as a Forest Protection Committee (FPC). Early the following year, Bhagwati Chowk was registered by the Forest Department. The document declaring the agreement is held in triplicate, one each in the forest beat office, range office, and FPC executive members. The document lists rights and duties under the JFM agreement followed by a list of JFM beneficiaries (a member of each household), and a *declaration of intent* signed by the Divisional Forest Officer and *panchayat* leader. Many of the

---

[18] One of the villages in Gopegarh, Delua, which had been registered under JFM, was struck off the list of FPCs because of poor forest management and a number of forest offences.

FPCs take membership from more than one village; this is true for other parts of West Bengal as well.

**Table 3.2 Forest Protection Committees in Gopegarh Forest Beat, Midnapore**

| FPC/ Date of Registration | Area of Forest (ha) | Popul- ation | FPC leader | Number of Beneficiaries | Functional Status |
|---|---|---|---|---|---|
| Bhagwati Chowk 6.1.92 | 150.8 | 190 | Poltu Singh | 37 | Successful FPC |
| Amratola and Phulpahari 18.11.91 | 226 | 900 | Ranjit Pandit Madhuri Chalak | 246 | Large-scale felling in village forest |
| Khairulla Chowk (unregistered) | N.A. | 1830 | Jeevan Pandit | N.A. | Accused of several offences |

As mentioned earlier, following the GOI's JFM letter, the FD in West Bengal modified its resolution to invite all rural families that might be interested in forest protection to become members in JFM:

> The beneficiaries ordinarily shall be economically backward people living in the vicinity of the forests concerned. Every family living in the vicinity of the forests shall, however, have the option of becoming a member of the Forest Protection Committee, if such family including the female members is interested in the work of protection (GOWB 1990, clause 1 [ii]).

In practice, each household of a village is registered, with the membership recorded against the name of the eldest male in the family. The order in which villages are registered does not, however, necessarily reflect the status of forestry management in a village. The registration is principally on invitation by the Forest Department.[19] The order could often result from impressions that beat officers have of each village and the nature of communication between villagers and the beat officer. Amratola-Phulpahari villages had had poor forests and poor management potential but were the first to be registered. This could be because Amratola is the centre for *panchayat* activities in the area, and leaders regularly interact (as equals) with the Forest Department. Bhagwati Chowk was registered soon after. This village also has a seasoned leader and has maintained a good relationship with lower officers in the FD. One of the residents is also employed in the Forest

---

[19] A GOI-sponsored workshop discussed methods for forming joint management committees (Anonymous 1990). The suggestion covered how to establish communication, prepare a microplan, and conduct beat-level meetings with villagers and forest officials.

Department. Khairulla Chowk, on the other hand, has remained outside the purview of JFM. The village arguably carries a stigma because the majority of its residents are political refugees from Bangladesh and on numerous occasions have been blamed by the villagers and the FD for being behind forest offences.[20] Despite the bias towards granting membership, it cannot be denied that the FD appears committed to placing all its protected forest under JFM. Indeed, this principle has guided the work pattern for lower-level officials for several years now. However, the beat officer, Amitabh Singh Deb, complained of the massive amount of chores that JFM has brought to his office. He stated that the registration mainly reflected the order in which formalities could be carried out and, with time, he would have all the forest under JFM.

Indeed the process of registration alone involves a number of formalities including delineation of forests,[21] village meetings, consent of the DFO, coordination with *panchayat* leaders, and so on. Nonetheless, the intense process of negotiation between Forest Department and villages has had some positive consequences. Most respondents, those who are now members of Forest Protection Committees and those who are not, for example, are aware of the basic tenets of JFM. They are alert to the incentives from the FD, and have sought JFM institutions – the FD, but also the NGOs and *panchayats* – in imaginative ways.

### 3.4.2 JFM Membership in Jharkhand

In Jharkhand, all the villages in Annagarha have some experience with voluntary forest protection. Three of them, Maheshpur, Nawagarh and Ober, were registered by the Forest Department as Village Forest Management and Protection Committees (VFMPCs) (see Table 3.3). Vanadag is yet to be formalized as a VFMPC. Maheshpur was registered as an all-woman VFMPC (in which all the primary members, including the executive committee, are women), the only all-woman VFMPC in Jharkhand. The committee was placed under a woman leader

---

[20] It has been alleged that the dates when villages are registered under JFM agreement do not reflect the period from which villagers actually started to protect their local forests (Burman 1996). (This is important because harvest of timber, in which FPCs are entitled to a 25% share, can be carried out only when the committee remains intact five years after registration [GOWB 1990].)

[21] In Gopegarh, one of the most sensitive tasks for the Forest Department has been to tackle disputes over allocation of forest areas to FPCs. Bhagwati Chowk has been given a large area of Sal and eucalyptus. This forest has traditionally been used by the neighbouring villages, and the demarcation has resulted in conflicts between the villages. The Forest Department has intervened in such cases either to consolidate the claim of control of the forest that was allotted to a FPC (as in Bhagwati Chowk) or to *redraw* the boundaries of the implicated resource (as proposed in Amratola-Phulpahari).

from Maheshpur *khas*, a *tola*[22] composed predominantly of a Muslim population. However, the well-meaning initiative produced few results in the long run.

**Table 3.3 Village Forest Management and Protection Committees (VFMPCs) in Annagarha Forest Beat**

| VFMPC/ Date of Registration | Forest Area (ha) | Population[23] | Forest leader | Functional Status |
|---|---|---|---|---|
| Maheshpur 16.11.91 | 172.59 | 1232 | Baratan Khatoon (woman-committee) | Defunct |
| Ober 28.9.93 | 226.68 | 1028 | Lahru Bediya Pahlu Bediya | Loyalty divided between two groups |
| Nawagarh 28.9.93 | 172.76 | 1226 | Kunwar Munda | Mixed results |
| Vanadag (unregistered) | N.A. | N.A. (50 households) | Mahadev Oraon (self-initiated) | Highly organized voluntary protection |

While registering VFMPCs, Jharkhand followed a path similar to West Bengal, albeit in a simpler fashion. The process was much less intense, and the department took little cognizance of circumstances at the village level. Although the lower-level officers are aware of the attitudes that villagers (and their leaders) have towards forests, the nature of the recommendation they might have made to the DFOs in Ranchi is unclear. The Forest Department, for example, registered one VFMPC per village. However, unlike in Bengal, the villagers in Annagarha identify more solidly with *tolas* than the entire village.[24] A village committee,

---

[22] *Tola* (also called *toli*) is a subunit of a village and is usually composed of a population of the same ethnicity.

[23] From *panchayat* records (1991 census).

[24] Maheshpur is made up of several *tolis*: Maheshpur *khas*, Lemha, Jinga, Salya Tongri, Mahli, and Khapcha. Similarly, the village of Ober is made up of two *tolis*: Ober *khas* and Harra Bera. Nawagarh has six *tolis*: Garh, Nawagarh *khas*, Marai, Maini Chapar, Khankhi, and Nawatu.

hence, would seldom represent the interests of all the groups living in the village.[25] Unlike Bengal, there was no discernible pattern in the order in which the VFMPCs were registered. Although aware of the dynamics that exist in voluntary forest protection groups, the lower officials did not take them into account when recommending villages for JFM. Vanadag, which has maintained an exceptional record of vigilance of its local forest, was, for example, not registered.

Once the villages in Annagarha were selected for registration, the process was swift. Village meetings were convened on various pretexts, including visit of senior forest officers, during which the key tenets of JFM were verbally explained to the villagers. A committee was recommended during the meeting, its executive body constituted, and a leader was chosen to head the committee. Following this, the villagers signed (or put thumb-prints) on the membership form. Due to the brief period in negotiation and interaction for JFM agreement, only a few villagers (mostly VFMPC leaders) were aware of the nature of the agreement in JFM. Most of the respondents remained unclear about the actual usufruct arrangement that JFM provides for. Although while Maheshpur has a copy of the agreement (which I could not see), the villagers in Ober and Nawagarh were provided with no record of the JFM agreement.

### 3.4.3 Discussion

It is noteworthy that although the larger policies of the Forest Department in West Bengal indicate a preference for degraded forest lands for JFM and a target-oriented approach towards registration, the process of registration at the village level (particularly in forest-degraded southwest Bengal) shows varying characteristics depending on the FD-village relationship and other factors, such as, the history of the local forest, nature of offences, etc. The case studies, not surprisingly, demonstrate that the selection order of registration hardly represents the way forests fare in the hands of FPCs. However, despite a certain partisanship (evidence of the varied relationship that the FD has at the level of villages), it is certain that the Forest Department wishes to put all its protected-category forests under JFM. In Jharkhand, except for a brief period of massive-scale registration, there has been a lack of interest in implementing JFM. The process of registration has not taken into account the unique nature of voluntary protection – *tola*-wise protection, rather than village-wise, for example. In both States, however, starting with the process of registration, lower-level officials, particularly the beat officers, assume enormous responsibility in participatory forestry. They are key agents in getting villages to formally agree to participate in JFM (even selecting the order in which they are registered) and translate the tenets of JFM for the benefit of

---

[25] The JFM resolution (GOB 1990) prescribes a committee for one village or a cluster of villages. It does not recognize a situation in which one village can have more than one VFMPC.

villagers. The next section elaborates the roles which the lower-level officials assume in routine forest management following registration of the villages.

## 3.5 Shares in JFM Responsibilities

The members of forest committees in both States are responsible for protection of forest cover, informing forest personnel of forest offences, and preventing trespass, encroachment, grazing, fire, theft, and damage to forests. The committees are also required to help provide assistance and labour for forestry work including those needed for timber harvest (GOB 1990; GOWB 1990). The power to terminate membership in JFM lies with DFOs (appeals against which can be made through the *panchayat*).[26] The FPCs in West Bengal must also hold a general body meeting every year to take stock of the various issues regarding JFM. They are responsible for keeping a roster with a list of beneficiaries and maintaining records of 'proceedings of the meetings of the executive committee that are to be held from time to time' (GOWB 1990). In Jharkhand, the resolution differs slightly in that it addresses the responsibilities through the executive body rather than the members of village forest committees. The committee is supposed to meet every six months, whereas the executive body is to meet every month to discuss protection and development of the forest in accordance with the directions from the forest directorate. The members are, however, asked to report not only forest offences but also the 'erring members' of the executive committee (GOB 1990).

### 3.5.1 The Forest Department - Village Interface

The foresters in Gopegarh, West Bengal, had established a relatively friendly rapport with the villagers even before the onset of JFM. In the Social Forestry set-up this was made possible both formally, through projects managed by *panchayats*, and informally, through the sociable attitude of the lower-level foresters, particularly the beat officer at that time. JFM, nonetheless, has brought notable changes in the forest management in Gopegarh. First, the relationship between the officers and villagers stands on a more solid and context-specific ground. The process of registration of FPCs that involved several rounds of briefing by the department officials about the new status of forest management and role of villagers (as members of FPCs), for example, created a formal space where the Forest Department and villagers could interact on issues related specifically to forest management. The department could now interact directly with villages during meetings or in other facets of JFM, such as in plantation, protection, and harvest.

---

[26] There is no provision for an individual defaulter's name being struck from the FPC list. Instead, the entire village stands to be penalized in instances of serious forest offences.

However, despite having gained important ground for participation with the villagers, the Forest Department in Gopegarh did not, in any active way, seek to enforce the 'duties and functions' onto the members of the FPC once the registration phase was over. The department has, however, invited NGOs to encourage villagers to participate in forest management as discussed in chapter 7. (This points to the earlier argument that the department invests a vast amount of time in bringing in the maximum number of villages [in southwest Bengal] under JFM agreement.) The JFM resolution itself provides little information about the role of the department in participatory forestry, and there are few expressed instructions from the senior official about facilitating joint management in the villages. The lower-level officers, as a result, combine the formalities that they used to in early days with the current realities of field situations.

Foremost among the transformation resulting from JFM is that the lower-level officials face a situation in which vast amounts of forest land, indeed the majority in Gopegarh in West Bengal, have been put under the management of village communities. To be sure, JFM finds substantial support among field-based forest officials. It not only promises to lighten their protection responsibilities (although many complained of increased work-loads, particularly during the registration and harvest period), but the foresters praise the amicable environment that JFM (or voluntary protection, as in Jharkhand) has ushered in. However, their response to community management varies from one village to another depending on many factors, such as the history of forest of a village, the relationship with the villagers, the interaction with the leaders, status of the village, and so on.

If the lower-level officers are instrumental in registration and formal invitation to the JFM, they are no less important in its actual implementation. Although they have restricted their patrolling of forests to more vulnerable areas, the officials remain vital as conduits of information to the villagers and feedback to the forest office. In addition, the officials are key to shaping the reputation of forest committees and providing legitimacy to the protection mechanisms adopted by a particular FPC in the larger beat set-up. If the beat officials were to rank the villages on participation in Gopegarh, West Bengal, the order could well be Bhagwati Chowk as the best FPC, followed by Amratola-Phulpahari in a transient stage, and Khairulla Chowk (unregistered) as the worst village with the most difficulties. On the other hand, in Jharkhand, the villages could well be in order with Vanadag as the best (although unregistered), followed by Nawagarh and Ober, and then Maheshpur (with a defunct, all-woman VFMPC). The evaluation somewhat reflects the actual forest protection (forest cover); it is also a pointer to the relationship the officials share with the villagers, particularly with their leaders. Bhagwati Chowk, for example, enjoys support from the foresters. In an instance when the villagers were involved in a fierce fight with the neighbouring Amratola villagers when they attempted to use the forest allotted to Chowk FPC, the beat office was instrumental in resolving the dispute (see chapter 4). On the other hand, the villagers in Khairulla Chowk, for example, did not receive similar support to establish an effective forest management scheme. This is not to suggest that the

Khairulla Chowk villagers were not at fault, but perhaps not any more than those in Amratola-Phulpahari who also have a number of forest offences against them.

In Jharkhand, the foresters are no less important. The forest leader of Ober, Lahru Bediya, for example, shows no less resolve than the leader at Vanadag. However, in the absence of support from the Forest Department, he has been unable to provide effective leadership or gain consensus for forest management in his village. (Chapter 5 discusses how the loyalty of villagers switched from Lahru to the leader supported by a local NGO. Also see chapter 7.) The rival faction that is supported by an external agency, an NGO, fares better than the forum headed by Lahru Bediya. The forest officials, for their part, have not provided support to either of the factions. They pointed out that different groups in Ober 'make too much noise'. In other words, forest offences to which Lahru might be pointing to get attention from the FD officials are commonplace, and the officials do not want to get involved in intravillage feuds and constant reports of petty offences.

The lower-level officials play a key role in endorsing forestry practices of the community at large, including activities that are not permitted in the JFM agreement.[27] They rarely judge the performance of FPCs based on how the members adhere to JFM rules. Most of the FPCs, for example, do not follow a regime strictly to protect forest (by patrolling, for example) or convene meetings on a regular basis to discuss forestry. The officials cited three different reasons for the lack of observance of formalities by members of the FPCs. First, this is the case, when FPCs are not functioning well, and hence there is no agreement within a community on forest patrol, meetings, and usufruct extraction. Second, FPCs have internalized the protection attitude, and, in these cases, forest offences seldom occur, and moderate patrol during routine forestry work is enough to take care of forest resources. Third, depending on the season, for example, during the peak cultivation period, it could be difficult for FPC members to attend meetings or care for forests. The lower-level officials are aware of and even sensitive to these informal practices and notions. They would, for example, seldom recommend that an FPC be removed from the JFM just because the rules were not followed by the book.

### 3.5.2 Points of Contact: FPC Meetings and the Leadership Cone

Forest forums in villages are typically represented by a single leader. The foresters find it more acceptable if they can deal with one leader who can effectively communicate with the villagers. Since the onset of JFM, several meetings have been held with executive bodies and the department officials of Gopegarh beat.[28]

---

[27] This may include activities such as extraction of timber poles from forest land for personal use.

[28] DFOs would often attend these meetings.

The meetings are usually held in a Forest Department building near the beat office. Minutes are kept during the meeting and, depending on the agenda, topics such as harvest plan or rural development plans are discussed, noted, and passed on to relevant authorities for further consideration. The FPC meetings have been successfully used to address issues such as harvesting, microplans, intervillage conflicts, and even elephant scares. These meetings have served to consolidate the participation between the department, *panchayats*, and the FPCs. In Annagarha in Jharkhand, on the other hand, meetings held at the behest of the forest department have been less common, and the beat office holds no record of such meetings (except those held for the purpose of registration). The foresters in Annagarha who are responsible for convening these meetings complain of being understaffed and tied up with other pressing problems such as patrolling the vulnerable areas.[29] Nonetheless, two features mark the forest committee meetings with the Forest Department. First, the presence of women in the meetings is negligible.[30] Second, it is usually the village leaders who are the most visible members in these meetings. Although the invitation is made to each of the executive leaders, the representation is typically through a unique leader who represents communities' interests in the forest (but can also be a leader on other issues as well, which usually is the case). Indeed both the characteristics – little direct representation of women and interaction of the Forest Department with specific individuals – extend to the routine interaction between the Forest Department and forest committees. The forest *beat* officials, for example, usually speak to male members of the community, usually the leader.[31] They reason that it is socially awkward to address women, apprehend them, or discuss issues about forest management. In Gopegarh or Annagarha, if the forest officials need to convey information or caution the FPC about a forest offence, they usually contact the leader. Similarly, the FPC leaders are understood by officials to represent the consolidated imagination and needs of the village community.

The nature of the interaction between the Forest Department and the villagers can be envisaged as two inverted cones (see Figure 3.1). Here, the instructions, information, and feedback percolate through a number of actors where the point of contact between the two institutions, in effect, is held rather delicately between beat officers (and forest guards) and the villager forest leader. This does not mean that a member of the community does not get to speak with higher officials (or

---

[29] Meetings within villages are not uncommon. However, meetings are seldom held within a village setting for forestry purposes alone. The discussion would usually combine concerns of other topics at hand, such as agriculture (see chapter 5).

[30] The case would be different in an all-women FPC such as Maheshpur where women were prominent in meetings.

[31] This is despite the fact that the involvement of women is distinctly higher in day-to-day forest activities (in employed labour, collection of firewood, and collection, process, and sale of non-timber forest products [NTFPs], etc.).

vice-versa) or that the beat officer does not interact with other members of the community, but that the interaction is located most commonly between these two agents.[32]

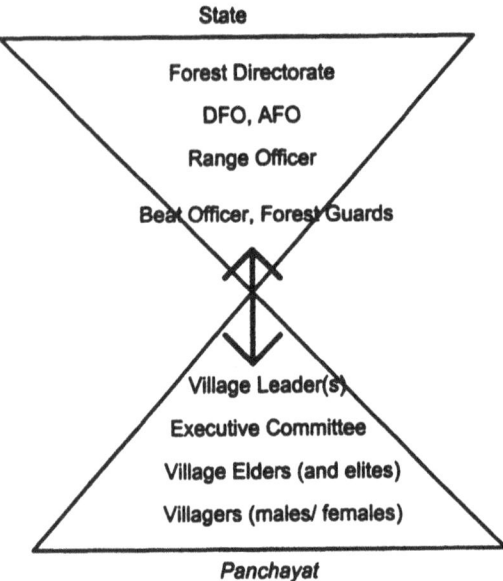

**Figure 3.1 FD-FPC Interaction Cone: Point of Contact**

### 3.5.3 Discussion

The nature of responsibilities asked of members of forest committees is similar in Jharkhand and in Bengal. They may be put into three broad categories: protection of forests, apprehension and reporting of offenders, and forestry works. The Forest Department makes almost all (formal) management decisions including formation and annulment of committees, invitation to meetings, harvest plans, and plantation. However, the role of the Forest Department, particularly of lower-level officials, remains unclear. The interaction of villagers and lower-level officials instead is shaped by such basic truths as forest cover, nature of forest history, relationship

---

[32] Dove (1994) identified a similar situation in social forestry practices in Pakistan where the foresters preferred to work with wealthy farmers, because the latter are 'easier to work with and are in a position to return favours' (Fortmann 1988 in Dove 1994). In my research, the foresters' bias, however, is towards (male) leaders in a community (some of them are marginally better off than the rest of the population). It must also be noted that the foresters' knowledge of peasants' needs (Dove 1992) or the 'official construction of reality' (ibid. 1994, 333) is not seen as a uniform entity here but is also varied at different official levels in practice and conception.

between beat officer and forest leaders, and status of the village. The interaction between the Forest Department and villagers revolves around beat officers and forest guards and the village forest leader(s).

### 3.6 Offences: Felling, Encroachment, Election Sell Out

The JFM resolution in both States is unambiguous about the protection role that the village communities are required to assume as part of the agreement. The forest offences are not only to be checked, but the members of committees are to 'assist and provide active support to the forest officers in arresting and prosecuting the offenders' (GOB 1990). Villagers, however, seldom report offences from their own community to department officials and rarely single out individual members in their community for punishment by the department. As discussed in the next two chapters, despite little provision to deal with forest offences, the villagers handle offences by using exclusion and fines. On the other hand, people from outside one's community are often blamed and occasionally reported to the Forest Department. Again, the resolution in neither Jharkhand nor West Bengal discusses the actual *modus operandi* that the Forest Department should have towards FPCs in routine forest protection. The Forest Department, due to poor staffing, nonetheless revolves around patrolling forests (also markets, pathways, etc.) that are more vulnerable. The lower-level officials, in the face of this attitude, frequently adopt a two-pronged approach vis-à-vis forest offences. They either caution villagers or even look the other way in the case of reported minor forest offences and, on the other hand, continue with formal procedures when they apprehend the offenders themselves.[33]

The records at Annagarha's forest beat office contain few reports filed by villagers about illegal felling in the area. There is one report on a massive felling in Amratola forests in 1998, although no one is named in the list. In another case, however, ten villagers from Khairulla Chowk are accused of responsibility for a large-scale felling in Amratola forests and, in another case, a fight taken up by Bhagwati Chowk with Amratola residents is on record. In such rare instances, the Forest Department goes into action. The information from these reports is passed by the beat officer to the DFO (usually through the range officer). In the case of Khairulla Chowk, the DFO wrote a letter to the *panchayat samiti* office and requested him to confidentially ascertain if the suspects were guilty and if the booty could be recovered. The *panchayat* found that a few trees had indeed been cut and some of the people still had them in their houses. Following the communication, raids were conducted. In practice, however, the beat officers seldom expect the minor offences to be reported by the villagers. They might insist that the offences be handled by the FPC leaders. These procedures are similar in

---

[33] Such offences are also occasions for certain officers to ask for bribes.

Jharkhand. However, offences that were reported in Annagarha were registered and sent to the court; no consultation with the village leaders was attempted.[34]

The foresters in Gopegarh and Annagarha have continued with their daily rounds of patrols. The routes they take for routine patrols, however, have been noticeably influenced by participatory forestry. The patrolling by the department officials is more intense in areas that are not covered by JFM or voluntary protection or in the forest land that reports regular offences. On the other hand, they enter village forests usually being reported on or in instances of outright felling of timber or encroachment of forest land. In the event, beat officers and forest guards enter villages to consult leaders and, in the case of a reported offence, even reprimand the suspect. Such entry and easy consultation between the foresters and villagers was difficult in earlier days. When asked why the officials did not visit committee members or the village forests more often, the foresters complained of the poor infrastructure that supports the patrolling, including the low number of staff and poor facilities for travel in the forest area. The complaint was more severe in Jharkhand. A forester in Annagarha, Jharkhand reasoned, '*Ab lakdi pakden, ki van mein jayen?*' (Should we get hold of timber that is being smuggled or keep visiting forests just to keep an eye?) The beat office of Annagarha is located on the highway, and a check-post regulates forestry goods that pass, particularly between Jharkhand and West Bengal through Purulia town (see Map 4.1). Monitoring vehicular traffic is the key function for the post keepers. They, however, are also on the look out for local head loaders and bicycle-*wallahs* carrying fuelwood and woodcoke to local markets.

The forest offence records in Jharkhand and Bengal illustrate that the number of offences that are recorded has not changed in any distinct way since the onset of JFM (see Tables and Graphs below) This, however, is not an indication that there has been no change in quantity or indeed, quality, of forest offences. One of the most plausible scenarios could be that, due to JFM, the kind of offences, such as minor and regular offences, that would in any case have gone unreported, has dropped, but is not reflected in offence records. It may be noted that the forest offence records indicate that Khairulla Chowk residents, although often accused of forest offences, have seldom actually been booked by the Forest Department for committing forest offences (see Table 3.5).

### 3.6.1 Encroachment of Forest Land

The FD has been blamed because its participation in forest management may entail forcing villagers to abandon the encroachment they have made on forest lands

---

[34] The lower-level officers in Anngarha patrol forests in uniforms. The priority for the patrolling officers in Annagarha is to protect the reserved forests, which is not only not under the protection of any community but also has the best timber crop. Also, they are careful that species in research plots, where the department has grown a variety of species for study purposes, are not harmed.

(Sivaramakrishnan 1998). The West Bengal FD has indeed suggested coordination with other state departments such as animal husbandry so that they could provide joint incentives to people for returning land to the department in exchange for a commitment by the FD that those lands could continue to be used exclusively by the villagers to meet needs, such as fodder grasses. The 'benefit package' (GOWB undated, 15) could also include plantation and support activities of sericulture, mushrooms, etc. with help from other departments and agencies. There are also proposals to use appeasement tactics such as plantation with species of plants of the individual's choice and over which these people could retain a measure of control.

In Midnapre range, a total of 80 hectares of forest land were evacuated between 1991 and 1996 and plantation was attempted on this land. The beat officer in Gopegarh, for example, stated that Bhagwati Chowk FPC is a '90% success'; the only irritant that remains is that some of the forest land remains encroached on by village leaders (all of whom, incidentally, have been part of the FPC executive body). The FD is nevertheless hopeful of getting the land back. One of the officers said, 'Come back in ten years' time, and you will find the land back with us'.[35] The process of eviction has remained formal in Jharkhand. Records at Annagarha forest beat demonstrate that villagers are routinely evicted, recorded, and fined (see Table 3.4).[36]

---

[35] During my research, a newly built mud house erected by a migrant family on forest land next to Gopegarh village was demolished. The forest guard had warned the occupants, a recently migrated family. After being served with informal notices, the house was destroyed. Following the incident, the range officer and other senior foresters were informed, and apparently, little paper work was carried out to record the incident. A senior forester explained that recording encroachment is generally avoided because the records might be used to regularize the illegal occupation.

[36] In Jharkhand, the compounding operation has ceased for several years. This means that if an offence is recorded, it has to be referred to the court within 24 hours. This is unlike Bengal, where beat officers often judge the nature of the offence and settle cases 'out of court'. The process is however quite formal – records are maintained, and the receipts for fines are handed out to the defendant.

**Table 3.4 Recorded Forest Offences (category-wise) in Annagarha Forest Beat, Jharkhand**

| Year | Felling | Stone Quarrying & Wood coal manufacture | Illegal Transport | Encroachment | Total offences | Total Fine Collected (in Rupees) |
|---|---|---|---|---|---|---|
| 1986 | 33 | 1 | 4 | - | 38 | 186, 293 |
| 1987 | unavailable | | | | | |
| 1988 | 8 | 1 | 1 | - | 10 | 27,400 |
| 1989 | 15 | - | 1 | - | 16 | 166,366 |
| 1990 | 22 | - | 10 | - | 32 | 150,890 |
| 1991 | unavailable | | | | | |
| 1992 | 4 | 6 | 2 | 3 | 15 | 59,630 |
| 1993 | 14 | 10 | 3 | 4 | 31 | 307,555 |
| 1994 | 86 | 17 | 1 | 5 | 109 | 175,462 |
| 1995 | 21 | 11 | - | 5 | 37 | 76,200 |
| 1996 | 44 | 7 | 1 | 7 | 59 | 120,147 |
| 1997 | 21 | 4 | 6 | - | 31 | 302,189 |
| 1998 | 12 | 5 | 6 | 1 | 24 | 164,657 |

*Source*: Annagarha Forest Beat Office (Offence Records)

**Graph 3.1 Recorded Forest Offences (1986-1998), Annagarha Forest Beat, Jharkhand**

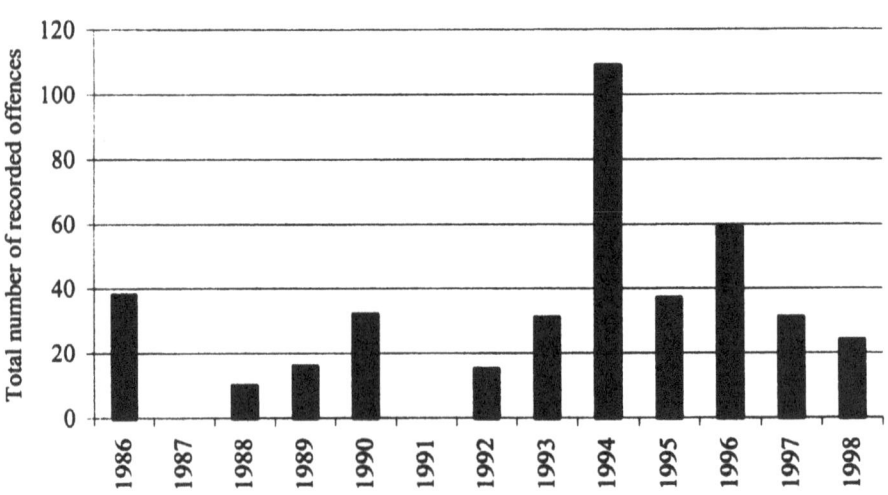

**Table 3.5 Recorded Forest Offences in Gopegarh Forest Beat, West Bengal**

| Year | Total Offences | Collection in fine[a] (in Rupees) | Type of case[b] POR | UDOR | Cases against Khairulla Chowk Residents |
|---|---|---|---|---|---|
| 1986 | 29 | 1,652 | 28 | 1 | 1 |
| 1987 | 32 | 2, 938 | 25 | 7 | 2 |
| 1988 | 21 | 1,055 | 21 | 0 | 1 |
| 1989 | 17 | 1, 050 | 15 | 2 | 1 |
| 1990 | 20 | 735 | 15 | 5 | 0 |
| 1991 | unavailable | | | | - |
| 1992 | 41 | 3,702 | 32 | 9 | 0 |
| 1993 | 54 | 5,523 | 40 | 14 | 0 |
| 1994 | 25 | 2,437 | 17 | 8 | 0 |
| 1995 | incomplete | | | | - |
| 1996 | 21 | 7,240 | 18 | 3 | 1 |
| 1997 | 24 | 12,993 | 10 | 2 | 0 |
| 1998[c] | 40 | 9,405 | 32 | 8 | 1 |

*Notes*: a. Figures have been rounded to the nearest whole number.
b. POR is Prosecution Offence Report; UDOR is Undetected Offence Report
c. Recorded until July 1998.

*Source*: Gopegarh Forest Beat Office (Offence Records)

**Graph 3.2 Recorded Forest Offences (1986-1998), Gopegarh Forest Beat, West Bengal**

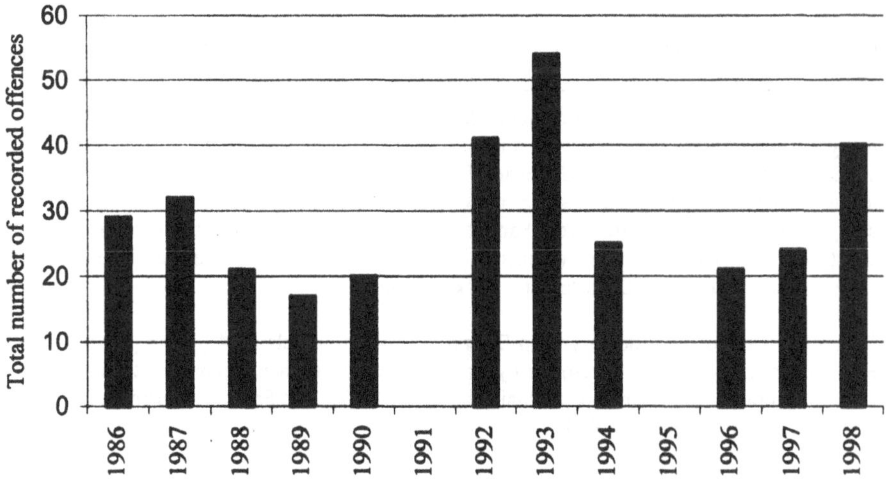

### 3.6.2 Discussion

In both States, the foresters have been given little guidance for their day-to-day activities on JFM. Their own interpretation and initiative are key to routine forest management. Bengal's supportive programme, however, has ensured effective communication with villagers, and is held mostly between the beat officials and village leaders. The officials continue to perform regular patrol duties. However, they are increasingly restricted to 'non-negotiated' territories, areas that are not put under a village's jurisdiction, such as roads, forest corridors, reserved-category forests, and *haats* or the local markets where forest usufruct is bartered. There is a clear disjunction in how the department has come to handle forest offences in light of participatory forest management. The forest officials often leave the protection responsibilities and handling of minor forest offences to village communities. The offenders who get apprehended by the foresters are, however, dealt with in the manner of earlier days.

### 3.7 Usufruct Benefits

Apart from access to the forest for fuelwood, the usufructory benefits from JFM provide a share in timber at harvest. Although certain NTFPs such as Sal seeds and Kendu leaves are to be sold to the Large Area Multi-Purpose Society (LAMPS, a farmer cooperative in rural areas) at a fixed rate, the FPC members are eligible to get a share in revenue from timber and from cashew in West Bengal. Also, the members can have 'fallen twigs, grass, fruits, flowers, seeds (excluding cashew) and leaves' (GOWB 1990, 4 (iii) a) at no cost. In Jharkhand, where no actual harvest had taken place in Annagarha, the JFM resolution was supposedly to combine the rights that have already been held by villagers (as recorded in *Khatiyan* II ) (GOB 1994).[37]

The harvest of timber under the JFM arrangement in West Bengal involves the Forest Department at several levels and stages.[38] Microplans are prepared at the beat level to decide the FPCs (and areas of forest) that are marked for harvest

---

[37] The resolution uses the word rightholder (GOB 1990, clause 9 [iii]) indicating the recognition of those villagers who might hold rights through *Khatiyan* II records. The collection of dry, fallen fuelwood is made free of charge for the tenants who are recognized in the *Khatiyan*. Grazing animals that are owned by the recognized tenants is also free of charge (e-mail communication from Sanjay Kumar). However, the right to extract poles for construction of houses and implements (Kumar 1997, 80) is illegal, unless done with the concurrence of the Forest Department's working plans.

[38] The FD is to conduct the harvest in Bengal (GOWB 1990, clause 4 [i] and [ii]) when the FPC attains five years and the crop ten years. It has, however, been pointed out that the JFM contract is not a legal document (Pattnaik and Dutta 1997). The Forest Department has more of a moral responsibility to uphold it.

operation. Next, the Forest Department, Forest Development Corporation, and prospective buyers are involved during the process of harvest. Two FPCs in Bengal's Gopegarh beat, Bhagwati Chowk, and Amratola-Phulapahari, having completed the mandatory five-year period after registration, were given a 25% share in the timber harvest in 1997 and 1998. However, the household share was very different in each FPC (only ten hectares of forest were harvested in each of these villages).[39] Amratola FPC, with 246 members, got a much smaller per household share compared with Bhagwati Chowk FPC, which was to distribute the amount among only 37 members.[40] Admittedly, the FD's infrastructure is stretched to its limit in harvest operations.[41]

In Jharkhand, when the harvest eventually happens, the share in timber over and above what has already been recorded in *Khatiyan* II is going to be even less than the share to a member of an FPC in West Bengal. Hence, most of the VFMPCs do not stand to benefit substantially from harvest returns. Therefore, it is unlikely that actual incentives for most of the village committees to participate in JFM would revolve around the cash share from JFM. Chapters 4 and 5 discuss how the incentives are bound more to the opportunity to secure forest usufruct on a routine basis. The next section, however, states that villagers are keen to involve the FD in larger issues of rural development. The department can capitalize on this and, in turn, bargain for a more sustainable partnership with the people.

### 3.7.1 Rural Development Forestry in JFM

Apart from providing benefits to villagers through forestry works, such as plantation, thinning, and harvest, the Forest Department has, in the past, regularly taken up construction of roads (usually in forest land), earthen dams, ponds, culverts, and so on. The department has also been engaged with external institutions and funding. For example, funds from Jawahar Rozgar Yojana (JRY) and the World Food Programme have paid for afforestation programmes. The department also collaborates with other State departments such as animal

---

[39] Although villagers may decide on the actual plot of forests that can be harvested, Narendra Pandey, the DFO had, considering the infrastructure constraints in carrying out harvest operations in a number of FPCs, limited the area of harvest to ten hectares in each FPC.

[40] Similarly in Bankura south division, in the felling during 1995-96, 19 of the 33 FPCs got less than Rs. 500, and only three FPCs, i.e. less than 10%, got a share of more than Rs. 2,000 (GOWB 1997b).

[41] Branches and twigs that result from the harvest are to be sold to the FD at a fixed price (Rs. 46/cartload in 1997). The villagers in Bhagwati Chowk, however, sold the wood on the open market for a price of Rs. 70-80/cartload, and gave the department the official price. The balance allowed the FPC to build a fund of Rs. 3,000. This is indicative that the FPCs can take on important responsibilities in timber harvest operations, better use market opportunities, and make larger profits.

husbandry, tribal welfare, fisheries, and so on to provide support programmes to forest citizens. JFM has the potential to consolidate this facet of the FD where it can engage in rural development forestry. Although the JFM resolution in Jharkhand expresses interest in rural development, the resolution in West Bengal makes no explicit promise to engage in rural development. Nonetheless, the recent World Bank-sponsored project found the department engaged in several areas, such as construction works, loans, and training programmes.

Beat officers in Gopegarh were asked to prepare microplans to allow villagers to be 'given option to take up projects as per their priority' (GOWB 1997, 61). The microplans are prepared for a five-year period for each FPC using participatory rural appraisal (PRA) tools (data collection is based on such parameters as ranking of wealth, mapping of resources, historicity, and social factors). In practice, the microplan process is a new concept for beat officers and, without sustained and sufficient funding, little has come out of the demands that were made by the villagers. Some of the initial funding to support the projects recommended in JFM microplans came from the West Bengal Forestry Project (funded by the World Bank). The project ended in 1997, drying up the fund that had sustained these microplans. The Forest Department concedes that 'the contribution of the fund in advancement of the JFM concepts cannot be denied' (GOWB 1997, 63). The microplan records that are not implemented nevertheless work as information pools where villages have expressed both their silvicultural preferences (over plantation, harvest), and the nature of development projects they want.

Microplanning in Annagarha, Jharkhand has been used chiefly as a data-gathering tool on types of resources, economic activities in the village, and the pattern of forest use. The Bihar Forestry Project's proposal, however, seeks to include the provisions of *Khatiyan* II in JFM to make 'informed decisions on locations and numbers of VFMPCs to be constituted every year, and [prescribe] forest treatment models' (GOB 1994, Annex 9). Although this is necessary to indicate the surplus of timber that might remain to be distributed as part of JFM, the document limits the purpose of microplans to 'provide villagers with a continuing and improved supply of firewood, timber and NWFP' (GOB 1994, Annex 9, 29). Jharkhand's JFM resolution, on the other hand, states that one third of the cash share from timber harvest (the village fund) is to aid 'social security programmes', such as pensions or help villagers who are in need (GOB 1990). Also, senior foresters from Jharkhand and Bengal, have recognized the role that the Forest Department can play in rural development projects (Mehta and Verdhan 1996).

To the villagers, the Forest Department is arguably the most visible arm of the state or the *sircar*. Indeed many villagers expect the FD to mend many inconveniences that exist in the region and engage in building schools, wells, and roads. In Jharkhand, the villagers had got fewer opportunities to voice their concerns because they rarely met the senior-level bureaucrats and, when they see the officers, 'They rarely talk to us'. The records from the annual general meetings in Gopegarh, West Bengal, on the other hand, describe members frequently demanding training in fisheries and poultry, a Sal-leaf plate-making machine, and irrigation by pipelines. Villagers unfailingly express their expectation that the Forest Department should 'do more'.

### 3.7.2 Discussion

The current forestry operations in Jharkhand and West Bengal, as in most of the country, are based on working plans that are prepared without feedback from local communities. The microplans can be used to provide the Forest Department with necessary information and feedback from the local community, not only about silvicultural decisions but also their expectations and concerns in rural development forestry. The 'stepping out' of forests that the department made by inviting rural communities to participate in forest management could indeed be complete if the Forest Department could engage in issues of rural development.

### 3.8 Conclusion

With the onset of JFM, the state offered decentralization of timber management by suppressing its revenue interests and inviting other institutions to get involved in forest management. On the other hand, the forest bureaucracy has not rid itself from old prejudices, strict hierarchy and conventional objectives. West Bengal was a pioneer in attempting to address the failures of Social Forestry and improvising its own participatory forestry rules. Although the department has made serious and sustained attempts at participatory forestry, it still betrays a conservationist bias and takes a target-oriented approach to JFM, concentrating its efforts in protected-category, mostly degraded forests. Jharkhand's Forest Department, on the other hand, has remained rigidly wedded to the top-down management system. In recent years, despite opening dialogues for participation, it has done little to back the rhetoric and the resolution guidelines. In a recent proposal to overhaul the bureaucracy, Jharkhand's Forest Department admits to many of its failings. The most important lacuna to which the department points, however, is lack of information and funds. Despite reorganization attempts, the forest departments have resisted changes in power-base at the top. Not only the lower officials in the departments but also forest citizens and other ecological institutions continue to feel the insularity of senior bureaucrats.

In both Jharkhand and West Bengal, there is a certain withdrawal in policing of forest resources by the Forest Department. However, the beat officials who are key to JFM have been provided few instructions and little autonomy to respond to JFM. Instead, these lower-level officials, in the absence of explicitly expressed instruction to monitor and enforce participation, have interpreted JFM informally and acknowledged (even sanctioned) many of the community forestry practices that may not follow the JFM rules. The lower-level officers are also instrumental in resolving disputes, particularly between two villages. The beat officer and village leaders emerge as key actors at the intersection of the community forest protection groups and the FD. The beat-level office needs to be strengthened in numbers, have better trained and orientated officers, and offer an attractive remuneration package and fair promotions to staff at this level. There needs to be provision of autonomy where lower-level officials can respond more independently to the field situations. The lower-level foresters have, on the other hand, notoriously suffered from such handicaps as the patronizing attitudes towards villagers, interacting primarily with the village leaders, cases of bribery, and practice of partisanship that is guided by factors such as their relationship with the villages or the status of the village. These issues would need to be addressed while making changes in the structure and power at the lower levels of the forest bureaucracy.

Almost all management decisions in JFM, including formation and annulment of committees, are taken by the Forest Department. Most silvicultural and usufruct distribution decisions are controlled by the Forest Department and rarely take into account market opportunities, individual member's contribution or ways villagers may want to carry out the JFM operations. Finally, the main incentive for villagers to interact with the Forest Department may not be the cash share from the harvest but rather the incentive to be able to secure forest usufruct on a regular basis and have the option to invite the FD into larger projects of rural development. The forest bureaucracy in India will need to take cognizance of these realities if it is to engage more effectively and equitably in participatory forest management.

Chapter 4

# Forest Protection Committees:
# Forestry within the JFM Boundaries

## 4.1 Introduction

Chapter 3 examined the nature of relationship that the Forest Departments have fostered with village communities within the JFM setup. The chapter argued that the Forest Department in West Bengal has made several innovations to align itself with the needs and structure of villages. The Jharkhand Forest Department's attempts at participatory forestry, despite having expressed similar sentiments in policy guidelines, on the other hand, have been modest, erratic, and seldom sustained. Moreover, although the higher offices of the FD in both States show a conservationist approach and an inclination towards a top-down management style, the junior officials have made several adjustments in their functional styles in face of the involvement of the rural communities in forest management.

The next two chapters re-situate forestry practices within the village setup. Chapter 5 focuses on the inherent characters of community forestry practices and discusses, particularly, the voluntary forest protection groups in Jharkhand. This chapter, however, discusses the forest management in the villages that are registered under the Joint Forest Management agreement. The villages are Bhagwati Chowk and Amratola-Phulpahari in West Bengal, and Maheshpur and Nawagarh in Jharkhand. The chapter discusses the population composition, the (mainly, oral) history of local forests, the degree of dependence on forest, management patterns, local leadership, and how villagers have responded to JFM in each of four forest protection committees. A number of features are found common to the community forest management in West Bengal and Jharkhand. The protection mechanism is the most robust in the villages that have substantial dependence on forest. On the other hand, in instances where there is a less significant dependence on forest, the resource is often compromised in face of external pressure or lucrative incentives. The chapter illustrates the essential disjunction that exists between the village polity and forest politics. It also discusses intervillage contests over forest usufruct. Also, in each case, it is demonstrated that village leadership plays a unique role in guiding forestry practices within a village and in giving shape to the relationship with neighbouring villages and the officials of the Forest Department.

### 4.2 Forests in Gopegarh and Annagarha: Oral History of Local Forests

In both Jharkhand and West Bengal, the forest land shares a history of colonial acquisition,[1] conflicts between the state and peasants and, at Independence, the management of forests by the State Forest Departments (GOB 1994; GOWB undated). Both regions have, in recent times, witnessed increased agricultural intensification, anthropogenic pressure and depletion of forest resources (Krishnaswamy 1995; Beck and Ghosh 2000). Within the microcosm of peasant-foresters relationship, there has been a certain breakdown of *fear* that dominated the earlier management style (Palit 1993) and has been replaced by indifference or, in better situations, a camaraderie shown by the foresters towards the forest citizens (Vasan 2000).

The forests and their politics in Gopegarh, Bengal are, nevertheless, different in several ways from those in Annagarha. First, the forests in Gopegarh are typical of the forests in southwest Bengal, consisting of patchy islands of Sal and eucalyptus trees with human habitation surrounding them. In Annagarha, on the other hand, the forests are expansive and present in large continuous clusters, most of which are located along the *Paina* hills (see Map 5.1). Second, in Gopegarh, the descendants of the former-landlords are no longer residents of the village. The Manaki-munda family of Nawagarh village who held titles to most of the forest land, on the other hand, are still residents in Annagarha and influence the rural polity of the area. Third, the relationship between the Forest Department (see chapter 3) and the *panchayat* (see chapter 5, also Tiwary 2003) and local residents has taken different courses in two States.

### 4.2.1 Forests in Gopegarh

The forest in southwest Bengal was brought under the British rule by about 1800 A.D. (Malhotra et al. 1993), although the forests in Gopegarh remained under the management of the *zamindar*. Until the 1930s, vast areas of southwest Bengal had luxuriant forests of Sal (Shorea *robusta*) (ibid.). However, owing to several factors such as an increased logging of timber by the state, reckless felling by the *zamindars*, greater population pressure, and failures of the Forest Departments' methods of management, the forests were in a state of degraded Sal bushes and denuded wastelands by the 1960s (ibid.). The elderly residents in Gopegarh concur that in the period immediately after the abolition of *zamindari*, the felling of trees was high. The forest cover was sharply in decline as early as 1962, and villagers faced a scarcity of fuelwood. It is commonly accepted by the villagers that, by the late 1970s, the forests, not unlike most of southwest Bengal, were highly degraded and resource poor in the Gopegarh forest beat. The Forest Department faced universal distrust. The relationship between the two, as remembered by a villager,

---

[1] Also, in the context of Gopegarh and Annagarha, forests were managed by landlords.

was one between 'a tiger and a cow' (the roles would often be reversed when villagers resorted to violent protests against the repressions of the forest bureaucracy).

Villagers recall that the period of Social Forestry programmes brought a definitive change in the relationship between the villagers and the FD. Also, the period saw the engagement of the *panchayat* (particularly when *Ban-O-Bhumi samitis* were constituted in 1981) with the Forest Department.[2] In its monthly meetings, the *panchayat* would discuss forest issues including employment opportunities and development projects with the FD. What was of importance in the context of many villages in Gopegarh was the sympathetic attitude of the then forest beat officer, Binoy Biswas. During his tenure as the beat officer, Biswas gained the confidence of the villagers and their leaders. He would regularly attend the *panchayat* meetings and be tactful while handling forest offences (he would, for example, punish young villagers over minor offences by making them do sit-ups in front of the villagers and ask the children to clap).

A combination of a gentler role of the Forest Department officials and the involvement of the *panchayat* in forest issues typically underscores the forestry-related practices in Gopegarh. This attitude has continued with JFM despite the fact that the forest interests of villagers are supposed to be represented by a specialized institution, the Forest Protection Committees.

### 4.2.2 Forests in Annagarha

The villages in Annagarha are found along the road to the Hundru waterfall. Maheshpur is next to the Ranchi-Purulia highway and stands at the entrance to the road to the fall. As one makes one's way to the waterfall, the road ahead, starting from Maheshpur, branches out at Getalsut, Vanadag, Nawagarh, Ober, and finally there are the villages of Bisa and Hundru (see Map 4.1).

The forests in Annagarha were under the management of Manaki-munda landlords. Most of the land, however, got vested with the state soon after Indian Independence. The voluntary protection that characterizes Jharkhand is linked with the poor state of forests since the late 1970s and the realization among the villagers, particularly the tribal population, that unless local forests are protected from various pressures, the villagers will be deprived of getting to meet the essential forest-based needs. Although the tribal population in Jharkhand has

---

[2] It may be noted that the *panchayats* did not always have a presence or the command they have now, nor did they enjoy the confidence of rural communities. Villagers recall that from 1975 to 1977, during the Emergency period, the *panchayat* was used as a vicious agent of the state to victimize people. The relationship of villagers with the Forest Department in that period was particularly bad. A respondent said that the FD's working rule was *pakarna, dhakarna, marna* (to catch, detain, and beat people).

depended on agriculture (Panangatt 1983) as their main source of income, forests remain a prime source of sustenance in an economic and cultural sense. However, the incessant failure of the Forest Department in Jharkhand to ensure an equitable distribution of the villagers' rightful share in forest, and the exploitative attitude that the Department has frequently adopted, has made the villagers turn to indigenous management methods.

Most of the villages in Annagarha have rights to extract fuelwood and share timber on harvests. The rights recorded in village registers, *Khatiyan* part II, predate the department's acquisition of forest land.[3] Upon getting management responsibility, the department agreed to recognize these rights. However, in practice, the villagers received a shoddy deal. They recount constant harassment by the lower-level officials over extraction of forest produce from the forests. They recall that the patrolling staff of the Forest Department would frequently target the headloaders and harass them with accusations of cutting green trees for selling. Moreover, the timber share the villagers received was seldom satisfactory. The department rarely followed the *Khatiyan* records strictly when carrying out the harvest operations. Typically, they would divide a forest into two halves and allow the villagers to choose their share. However, the tribal villagers complain that the process put them in a disadvantageous position. During the felling operation, the villagers were required to either mark trees in advance or literally hug the trees (an ironical reference to the *Chipko* [literally, to stick to or to hug] movement cannot go amiss, where villagers had hugged trees to prevent them from being cut) to indicate they wanted the tree as part of their share. However, in such cases, not only would this preclude villagers who arrived late or were absent during the operation from getting timber, but residents who were better equipped with information on dates of felling or lived next to the forest got a better deal. Also, the felling operations were often coupled with malpractices, such as private contractors who cut away a large number of trees without the authority to do so and smuggled them out. Many respondents agreed to the sentiment that forests had become depleted because of the combination of the 'coupe system and private contractors'.[4]

Dependence on forest coupled with the insecurity in procuring essential forest usufruct, such as fuelwood, Sal poles, and fodder are, arguably, the main reasons

---

[3] See Kumar (1996) for an exhaustive discussion on land tenancy and forest tenurial regulations in Jharkhand.

[4] Kumar (1996, 62) also blames *panchayat* leaders who colluded with the contractors during harvest operations allowing little time for villagers who had rights to log trees that were part of their share. It should be noted that the private contractors were not allowed to work on forest land from 1977. Since 1983, there has been no forest coupe carried out by Bihar's Forest Department. (Coupe system refers to large-scale timber harvest carried out at the initiative of the Forest Department.)

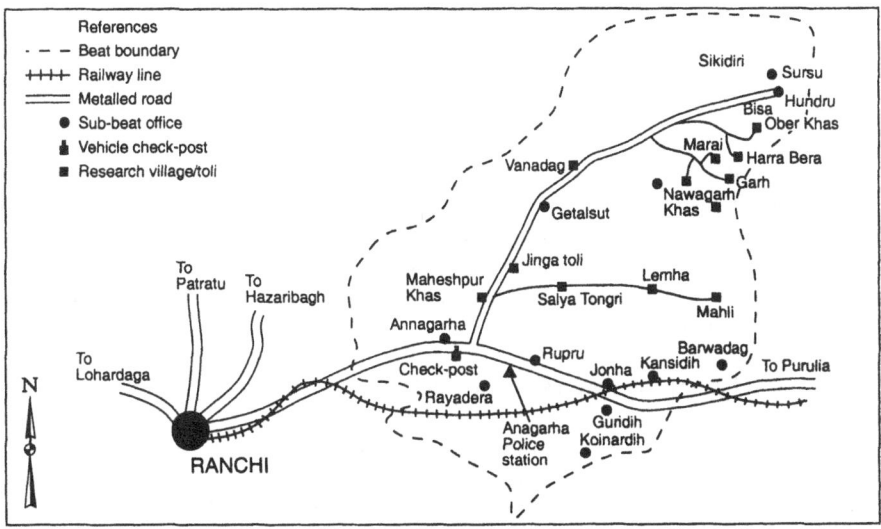

**Map 4.1 Layout of Research Villages and *Tolis* in Annagarha Forest Beat**
*Source*: Ranchi East Forest Division Office

that many self-initiated protection groups were nursed and sustained by the villagers. The positive results these voluntary groups achieved helped encourage such methods of protection. The elderly villagers agree that forests today are far better than what they were a decade ago.[5] The onset of Joint Forest Management, if

---

[5] However, some added that the quality of forest cover is still far behind what the forest had 30 or 40 years ago. To illustrate the point, one villager pointed out that, although the rejuvenated forest meets most of the needs of the villagers, they still cannot supply the *bang*, the thick Sal pole needed to support a house's roof.

anything, has only strengthened the opinion already held by the villagers that community protection is necessary to secure their forest-based needs.[6]

### 4.3 Joint Forest Management in Gopegarh Forest Beat, West Bengal

This section discusses the forestry practices in Bhagwati Chowk and Amratola-Phulpahari Forest Protection Committees (FPC). Bhagwati Chowk FPC has enjoyed good forest cover and a coherent forest management. The protection of the forest has been achieved mainly through the knowledge that the forest belongs to them and 'improved' behaviour such as restraint in cutting trees and practically excluding outsiders from their village forests. Patrolling of forest is, however, absent in any active sense because the villagers are unprepared to do it unwaged. The case of Amratola-Phulpahari FPC, on the other hand, presents a contrast in how a lower dependence and an indifferent leadership influence the forest management in villages.

### 4.3.1 The Case of Bhagwati Chowk FPC

Bhagwati Chowk is roughly at the centre of Gopegarh forest beat (see Map 4.2). The village, on its registration as an FPC, was assigned with 150 hectares of forest land that lies adjacent to the village. Nearly half of this is made up of Sal trees; the other half is eucalyptus plantation. The villagers have been involved in forest protection (mainly by restraining from cutting trees) since the Social Forestry period, when they had faced an acute shortage of fuelwood and supply of poles. They have also maintained a harmonious relationship with the FD.

These characteristics got a boost when the village was formally registered under the JFM agreement. In effect, the protection mechanism of the villagers was consolidated under the FPC, with the FD (and even the *panchayat*) having the obligation to support them in the management of the local forest. However, Bhagwati Chowk, like other FPCs, has six members enlisted in its executive

---

[6] That *adivasis* or the tribal communities have forest protection implicit in their cultural elements and religious practices has been widely noted (Shepherd 1997). Indigenous protection to forests is witnessed in the form of sacred groves, temple forests, sacred corridors, protected (or taboo) tree species (Pandey and Singh 1995; Pandey 1999), etc. In Chotanagpur (and Annagarha), it is common to find sacred groves, usually a portion of the local forests, called *sarna*. A ring of ancient trees (indeed reflecting the protection status they get from the community) houses the principal deity and is sacred to the community. The tribal customs prohibit felling of trees or lopping of branches in the sacred grove. One of the most evident aspects of the sociocultural/religious importance of forests is the celebration of *Sarhul*, or the festival of flowers. In Nawagarh village, for example, *Sarhul* had the community gather around the village-*sarna* for a day-long celebration (also considered as a post-harvest dance). Later on, the village priest, the *Pahan*, went into the village with Sal flowers to bless the householders.

committee[7] to lead the committee. In practice, however, there are only three leaders whom villagers recognize as 'forest leaders' and who are actively involved with the formal activities, such as bookkeeping and attending JFM-related meetings, and to whom, as noted in chapter 3, the foresters usually talk when they are in the village. Of these leaders, Poltu Singh is the most visible member of the committee. Singh represents the village on several issues, but since he is no longer a member of the *panchayat*, he is most vocal on forest politics.

### 4.3.1.1 Forest Patrols and Protection Mechanisms

Most villagers in Bhagwati Chowk, including women, are familiar with the JFM agreement. They are conscious of the protection responsibilities the membership requires and the usufruct benefits they derive in return. The villagers understand that the forest has to be guarded against felling and other forest offences. A typical response by the villagers in Bhagwati Chowk, during the initial round of interviews, was that they patrol forest on a rotational basis, where members of households take turns to roam forests. When it was pointed out that such an active form of forest patrolling was hardly visible, the villagers reasoned that the slack in guarding is mainly during the peak agricultural seasons (this discussion coincided with the paddy plantation season). However, on further inquiry, it was clear that there is no strict guarding system on any regular basis except during the timber harvests when the Forest Department pays the villagers to keep vigilance.[8] On normal days, guarding of forest can be visualized more as an extension of the routine activities of villagers.

For example, the villagers who are in and around forests to collect fuelwood or are with their livestock 'keep an eye' for outsiders.[9] The method nonetheless is effective because, due to high dependence, not only is the protection of the local forest necessary, but villagers also foray into the forest regularly for various forest-based needs. In addition, the house of the village leader, Poltu Singh, is next to the forest. He remarked that the proximity to the forest makes it easy for him to detect the presence of 'unwanted' people in the forest. Arguably, what works most effectively in protection of their forest is, however, the mutual agreement among the villagers not to cut Sal trees. As a result, although there are still cases of 'thinning and lopping' of trees for fuelwood (when dry fallen twigs are not

---

[7] The JFM resolution in West Bengal suggests not exceeding 'six elected representatives of the beneficiaries' (GOWB 1990, clause 1 [v]) to be part of the executive committee.

[8] Villagers are employed by the FD for felling, storage, and transport activities. During the harvest period, Rs. 200/ha is given to the community for keeping a night watch.

[9] This does not mean that the protection of their forest is offence-proof. A few young residents in Phulpahari village admitted candidly that they always manage to sneak into Bhagwati Chowk forest and bring back a Sal pole in a matter of an hour, 'If there are people present in one corner of the forest, one can always cut trees at the other end'.

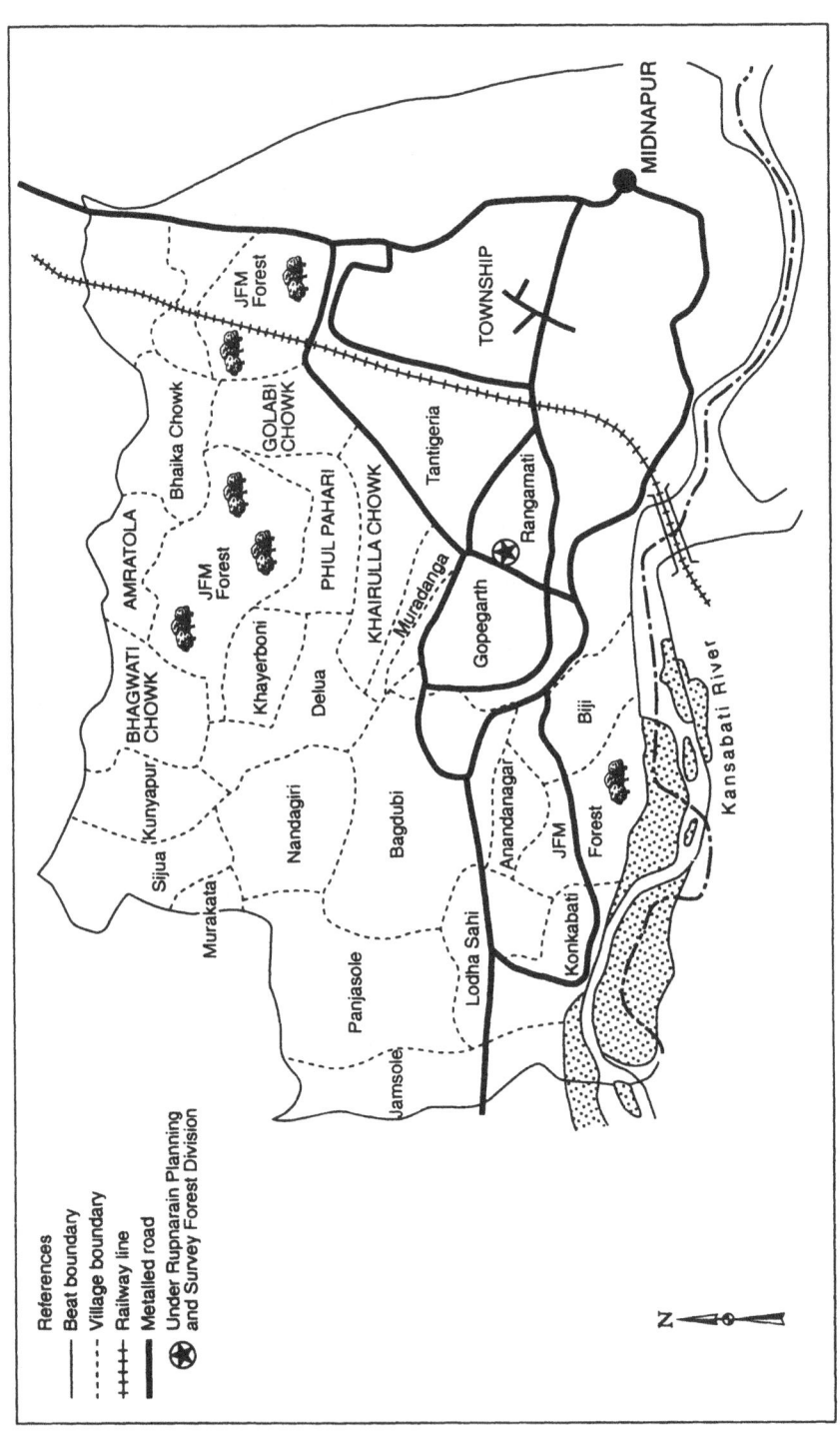

**Map 4.2 Resource Map of Gopegarh Forest Beat**
*Source*: Midnapore East Forest Division Office

available),[10] villagers at large respect the verdict of no clear felling of mature Sal trees. The consensus within the village not to fell trees brings the villagers to their most potent protection mechanism, to exclude villagers from outside Bhagwati Chowk from using the forest that they have identified to be under their protection. In effect, the forest of Bhagwati Chowk is practically out of bounds for outsiders. The villagers have asserted their control in no uncertain terms and have taken up fights with villagers from outside.

### 4.3.1.2 Usufruct Extraction

Bhagwati Chowk has a healthy forest cover and a high forest land to household ratio compared with the neighbouring FPCs. The relatively larger forest land ensures a secure supply of fuelwood and other usufruct, notably Sal leaves to the villagers. Almost all the households collect wood from the village forest to use as cooking fuel, although a few supplement their fuel requirement with kerosene oil and dung cakes.[11] The factor that makes the presence of Sal forest particularly crucial for villagers is that nearly 15 of the 37 households in Bhagwati Chowk have one or more members of the family involved in the business of making plates from Sal leaves. Women supplement their household income from sale of Sal-leaf plates in the nearby Midnapore town.[12] Apart from the routine benefits from their forest (such as fuelwood, fruits, mushrooms), the villagers have twice received shares from harvest that was carried out by the FD as a part of the JFM agreement.[13] In

---

[10] Villagers are expected to consult with the FD to conduct thinning operations once the timber stock that comes from harvest has finished.

[11] Fuelwood for household use comprises of a number of species including *atang, kurchi, mohul, parasi,* and dry Sal twigs and branches. While collecting fuelwood, many villagers also collect *kukri, chaatu, and karani* mushrooms, and young Sal leaves to make dishes.

[12] Making plates and cups from Sal leaves is a highly labour-intensive work, and the opportunity costs are low (Pachauri undated). Mostly women are involved in collection and making the plates, although occasionally men join in to sell the plates in Midnapore town. The villagers are particular about the kind of leaves they pluck to make Sal-leaf plates. Newer leaves are better for the purpose, and villagers admit a preference for leaves from younger trees. A villager in Maheshpur, for example, pointed out that, due to the village protection, the Sal trees have grown taller, and they have to use *hansuli*, a sickle tied to poles, to reach the young leaves that are high on the Sal trees. Sal-leaf plates can fetch from Rs. 30-70 per 1000 plates, and a family earns up to Rs. 400/month from selling Sal-leaf plates and cups.

[13] On both occasions, eucalyptus plantation was chosen for felling (this was according to the wishes of Chowk's villagers who wanted to wait longer for Sal, so that they could reap a more valuable Sal crop). Many respondents spent the JFM money on essential purchases, such as food. However, a few utilized their share to buy oxen-calves, and another respondent bought back a piece of land that he had mortgaged a few years before to override financial hardship he was facing then.

1997, each household received Rs. 1,248 as their share from the harvest. The harvest also yielded a share in timber from thinning operations (mostly twigs and branches). As noted earlier, the villagers were allowed to sell the FD's share of timber at a higher market price and give the official price to the FD, pocketing the difference for the village 'FPC fund'.

### 4.3.2 The Case of Amratola-Phulpahari FPC

Amratola village has 246 households of which 170 households are from schedule caste (mainly Bawri and Bhuyian castes) and 13 are from schedule tribe (mainly Khriya and Lodha). Phulpahari, on the other hand, has 80 families all of whom belong to schedule caste. The forest in Amratola-Phulaphari was formalized under the JFM agreement in 1991. The villages were entrusted with approximately 240 hectares of forest land comprised mostly of eucalyptus plantation that was brought up during the Social Forestry period. The villages border the forest land on two sides (see Map 4.2) and were registered as one FPC.[14] The forest management in Amratola-Phulpahari has remained troubled for several years. The forest has often been subject to both minor offences and large-scale felling. The plantation (already a sign of degraded natural forests) that started as part of the Social Forestry schemes has been cut down several times since. The forest was completely cut down during the regional elections in 1998 (during my research period, the vast forest land, except for shrubs and bushes, was barren; the situation was summed up by a resident, 'We have to keep stool in our stomach, there is no forest to even go for that').

### 4.3.2.1 Forest Dependence

This section discusses the recent history of the forest that was allotted to Amratola-Phulpahari FPC, the nature of dependence on forest among the members of the FPC, and the relationship to their leaders. Amratola, a relatively large village, is spread along the forest, and although there is no distinct *para*-wise distribution of population,[15] it is discernible that the Hindu Chawlia population lives on one side of the village, and the members of schedule tribes reside on the other side. Most households own agricultural land and, in many cases, one or more members are employed in town-based business (relatively better-off households) or in town labour (the poorer households).

---

[14] Residents from both villages have used the forest land for a long time, and the Forest Department did not find it reasonable to divide this forest (through fencing, for example).

[15] *Para* is the Bengali equivalent of *tola*. In Phulpahari, the houses, based on ethnicity, are located in clusters called *paras*: Lodha *para*, Singh *para*, Bhumij *para*, and so on (Maity 1997).

A number of residents in Amratola, mainly the well-off Hindu population, do not enter the forest for fuelwood or timber extraction. Instead, they purchase wood from the villagers from Salboni (village) who go about selling fuelwood to Amratola and other villages. Being able to afford fuelwood is not the only reason the women from this group do not enter the forest. Many respondents among Hindu households stated that they do not let their women go to collect fuelwood in forests. Another respondent reasoned, 'People who are educated feel ashamed to go into the forest and cut trees'. Some of these households pointed at their homestead trees that supplement some of their fuelwood needs. They also use dung cakes and kerosene oil for cooking purposes. The poorer households (including those in Phulpahari), on the other hand, have habitually extracted wood from the forest around the villages. However, since the large-scale felling of the village forest, these villagers either walk to farther villages to fetch fuelwood or are forced to buy fuelwood like the others in Amratola.[16]

There are, hence, two distinct dependence patterns in the village: the elites who do not usually enter forests and fulfill their fuel needs from other sources, and the poorer households who, in the absence of local forest, travel farther to collect fuelwood. The local forests hold modest incentives for the majority of the villagers to become involved in forest protection. Among the poorer households, the business in Sal-leaf plates or other forest-based products is not as visible and organized as in Bhagwati Chowk. The forest was harvested under the JFM for the first time in 1997. However, unlike Bhagwati Chowk where the harvest yielded substantial sums of money, the share in Amratola-Phulpahari FPC was so meagre (Rs. 65 per household), that many villagers do not even recall getting a share.

### 4.3.2.2 Village Leadership

The politics of Gopegarh area, since 1977, have been dominated by the left politics of the Communist Party of India - Marxist, CPI (M). This plays an important role in the case of Amratola in that the village is the epicentre for *panchayat* politics and the headquarters of the CPI (M) in Gopegarh. The leadership in Amratola is divided between the CPI (M) party secretary, Ranjit Pandit, a Hindu resident, and Madhuri Chalak (from schedule caste), the new *panchayat* representative for the village. The division, however, is more of a necessity than anything inherent to the village. Amratola is under the 'scheduled' list, which requires *panchayat* representatives to belong to schedule caste or tribe. The village, hence, is obliged to nominate members from schedule caste (hence, the selection of Madhuri Chalak). Nevertheless, the actual line of command in the village is unaltered. Madhuri Chalak confessed that she has never been involved with 'party politics'

---

[16] One can buy a cartload of fuelwood for Rs. 70. Alternatively, villagers walk to neighbouring villages such as Gaighat, Khorikasole, Susnibari, Patharkumkumi and Salboni to fetch fuelwood.

and was nominated by the CPI (M) while the *rest* (the election campaign, for example) was done by the 'party bosses'.[17]

What is remarkable, however, is that none of the key village leaders including the CPI (M) leader, Ranjit Pandit, or the *panchayat* leaders, Madhuri Chalak and Brati Chalak (former *panchayat* leader), demonstrate intimate interest in conservation of the forest. Although the villagers concurred that the former *panchayat* leader had been catalytic in bringing a few development projects into the village (electricity, for example) or had helped with granting loans, they said that, vis-à-vis forest, her attitude had been reckless. Her son, for example, had regularly cut trees and done petty business in selling the forest timber. With this background, the villagers argued, she could hardly stop others. However, this does not affect Brati's reputation in Amratola. The villagers (mainly tribals) who confessed of having defected to vote for the Trinamool Mamta Congress (TMC) in the 1998 election, for example, expressed their discontent with CPI (M) leaders not on count of access to or distribution of forest usufruct but because of partisanship shown by the CPI (M) leaders in access to *panchayat's* development schemes.

Phulpahari village, on the other hand, is 'without leaders'. The *panchayat* leaders who represent Phulpahari are not residents of the village. Instead they live in the neighbouring village, Golabichowk.[18] Although this village too has been a bastion for CPI (M), it shares little with Amratola's village polity. For example, Ranjit Pandit of Amratola has never conducted election campaigns in Phulpahari and showed little interest in or knowledge of Phulpahari residents. This, however, is tragic as far as forest management is concerned. There is but slight communication between the village leaders on forest offences and little coordination or agreement to safeguard the forest from frequent felling.

### 4.3.2.3 Election-time Forest Felling in Amratola-Phulpahari

As mentioned earlier, the entire forest in Amratola-Phulpahari was cut away during the 1998 election. A number of responses were given by the villagers and the forest guards. Some opined that the poor state of the forest in their villages was a result of the constant pressure that is made for timber from the nearby town, Midnapore. A

---

[17] This is not to indicate that Madhuri Chalak is not an able *panchayat* leader. In one of the first meetings after the *panchayat* election, Ms. Chalak ably presented her credentials to the *panchayat* officer and went on to discuss the agenda for the coming months. However, the control of the CPI (M) representative over *panchayat* politics is clear. For example, the CPI (M) office of Amratola houses all the village's *panchayat* records, and the oft-quoted slogan was repeated here, 'the party (CPI [M]) is *panchayat*'. Of late, of course, the CPI (M) dominance has been challenged by the supporters of the Trinamool Mamta Congress (TMC) party.

[18] The *panchayat* leaders, Alpana Mandal (the new *panchayat* representative) and Dhiren Malik (former representative, 1993–1998) are both from Golabichowk village.

respondent was of the opinion that, 'You just can't protect a forest that is near a town'. Indeed, the presence of a local town has meant an easy access to market for the forest timber. This, however, can be only a partial explanation, because similar pressures are true for forest in Bhagwati Chowk. The villagers in Amratola–Phulpahari concede there has been little direct involvement of private contractors from Midnapore who pressurize villagers to cut the forest down. It is likely that most of the felling was carried out by the Amratola-Phulpahari villagers themselves. In the context of the villagers being the defaulters, the blame for cutting down the plantation shifts among three groups: the resident tribal villagers (blamed by the Hindu residents), the villagers from Khairulla Chowk, and Amratola residents blaming the Phulpahari residents and vice versa. (As noted in chapter 3, the foresters felt that a large responsibility was with the Khairulla Chowk residents.)

A consensus among the caste-Hindu villagers is that the members of schedule caste and tribes cut the jungle down for sale during the election because the party would not discourage the practice. Once the felling was under way, the residents were joined by Khairulla Chowk people to 'finish the job'. Apparently, felling of forests during elections is not a new thing to the Amratola-Phulpahari forest or, for that matter, in southwest Bengal. Many agreed that 'during an election, no one stops villagers from cutting forest'. Another atypical but plausible reason came from a respondent who felt that, 'during elections the politics obsessed people do little work outside their villages and just *sit* and cut forests'. The Forest Department staff said that it is difficult to communicate with the village representatives during this period; the election means a potential change in the leadership and, in such period of uncertainties, the leaders are unwilling to have their attention diverted to forest issues. Senior forest officials, on the other hand, mentioned that the use of the Forest Department officials for election duties means that they work out-of-station, providing ample opportunities for villagers to cut forests.

It must be noted that forest leaders of Amratola do not necessarily portray forest control or use of forest as the chief agenda during elections. The forest usufruct instead is used mostly to gain an edge in electoral politics. A villager in Amratola said that a former *panchayat* leader had an election slogan during the final days of campaign, 'Stop the TMC people from getting forest timber, but let the CPI (M) supporters cut forests'. The factions in the village between the supporters of TMC and CPI (M) supporters have only worsened the situation. For example, when a meeting is called in the village (over forestry or otherwise), people who attend meetings are invariably affiliated to one of the two parties. Finally, because of the poor communication between Amratola and Phulpahari, the accusation over forest felling that shifts between them has never been resolved.

### 4.3.3 Intervillage Conflicts

The earlier sections discussed successful and troubled management of forest within Bhagwati Chowk and Amratola-Phulpahari FPCs respectively. This section discusses the conflicts that arise between villages over control and use of forests. The conflicts often are a result of resistance put up by villagers who have used a forest for a long period but, since the onset of JFM, have found the resource claimed for exclusive use by the members of a particular FPC. For example, although villagers from Amratola, Phulpahari, and Khairulla Chowk feel at liberty to venture 'up to the boundary of Bhagwati Chowk', they are reluctant to enter the Bhagwati Chowk's forest. They no longer feel welcome in the land that is recognized as property that belongs exclusively to Bhagwati Chowk. Indeed, these conflicts are one of the most visible outcomes of Joint Forest Management.

### 4.3.3.1 The Bhagwati Chowk Fight

In a much publicized *gondgol* or a messy incident in 1998, five women from Amratola ventured into Bhagwati Chowk forest to fetch fuelwood. They had, allegedly, started to cut young Sal poles when they were apprehended by women from the Bhagwati Chowk village. The Amratola women were verbally abused and detained for the better part of the day. Finally, when they were let go, one of them was stripped of her *sari*. The incident initiated a number of infuriated arguments between the two villages. Finally, Ranjit Pandit went down to Bhagwati Chowk to resolve the dispute with Poltu Singh. Singh, though assuaged, would settle for nothing less than discussion of the issue at meetings at the *panchayat* and the forest-beat level. In the meetings that followed, it was agreed with the *panchayat pradhan* (village council leader) that Bhagwati Chowk would allow neighbouring villagers to collect mushrooms, but fuelwood would remain exclusively for the use of Bhagwati Chowk residents.

Although many respondents in Amratola expressed their anger over the incident, few lamented the protection methods of Bhagwati Chowk. One of them conceded that, 'It is a shame that our forest is cut under our very own nose'. The presence of the *panchayat* and a sympathetic beat officer meant that the fight did not escalate beyond a point and lent legitimacy to the adopted forest protection methods of the village. The conflict and its outcome sent a clear message to the neighbouring villages that Chowk's forest was out of bounds for outsiders.

### 4.3.3.2 Khairulla Chowk: A Sore in the Eye

The village of Khairulla Chowk has been blamed for reckless felling not only by the neighbouring villagers but also by Gopegarh foresters. Unlike Bhagwati Chowk and Amratola-Phulpahari, this village is yet to be formally allotted forest land or registered under the JFM agreement. The Forest Department reasons that there have been too many offences by Khairulla Chowk villagers for the village to be recommended for JFM. The residents, on the other hand, are disillusioned by the attitude adopted by the department. Khairulla Chowk is made up of immigrants from Bangladesh,[19] and the village is, to some degree, a target for the blame for forest offences because of 'local' prejudice. Jeevan Pandit, the village leader and a member of the *panchayat* for the past three consecutive terms, said that the Khairulla villagers had come penniless but, with time, they have done well, and so the rest are jealous. Although the village has no history of involvement with conservation of forests (such as restraint towards felling trees, as in Bhagwati Chowk), there is a markedly lower dependence on the immediate forest, and the village leadership, as in Amratola, is indifferent to forest conservation.[20] If anything, those Khairulla residents who are in the business of Sal-leaf plates and cups buy Sal leaves and even unfinished plates from the sellers from Salboni village and use Sal-leaf pressing machines for making polythene-coated plates. They also have a better network to sell the plates in markets.

Jeevan Pandit remarked that the FD officials are unsympathetic to Khairulla's residents or to their occasional (if they ever tried) efforts to assist in forest conservation. He cited an example that, in May 1989, the villagers handed over to the FD approximately 500 trees that had got uprooted in a storm. The department had, he said, in return promised to give one third of the poles back to the villagers but, in the end, nothing came of it.[21] Another resident alleged that the forest officials seldom interact with the villagers and are indifferent to the forest that lies next to their village. He was of the opinion that constant felling meant repeated plantation by the department that yielded petty commissions to be pocketed by the lower-level foresters.

### 4.3.4 Discussion

The JFM agreement has produced mixed results in Gopegarh forest beat. Although most respondents show some form of accountability to forest protection, the villages have responded in varying degrees to JFM. JFM in Bhagwati Chowk has several successful indicators including good forest cover, high awareness, minimal forest offences, forest-harvest operations, and a positive villager-Forest Department relationship. This is despite the fact that villagers have not followed the JFM rules by the book. The success, instead, is embedded in the fact that there is high dependence on forest that provides a supply of essential usufructs, a cash income, and Sal leaves for business. A strong cohesion within the small

---

[19] The villagers came in two *waves* of migration, one in 1951 and another after 1981.

[20] Jeevan Pandit interacts with the FD officials mostly when there is a problem, for example, to rescue a resident if he/she has been apprehended by the FD; otherwise, he said, he would 'lose face' with his people.

[21] The claim could not be verified. It is likely that one of the lower-level officials had informally committed to reward.

community and an able leadership have been able to establish effective forest management through consensus.

In Amratola-Phulpahari, forest occupies a relatively marginal status in the overall village polity. The local leaders play an insignificant role in forest conservation. Although poorer households continue to depend on forest for household use, in the absence of cohesion and a less intensive forest-based business, they have not expressed their opinions for forestry purposes.

In an intervillage framework, one notices partisanship and contested claims by villagers vis-à-vis management of forests. The nature of dependence on forest and leadership in Khairulla Chowk, for example, is not different from in the Amratola-Phulpahari FPC. But the local prejudice keeps mutual distrust alive between the villages and also the FD. On the other hand, forest contests demonstrate that forests that are assigned to FPCs do not necessarily reflect the history of use by local residents. (Knowing history helps; it determines the relationship villagers have had with the local forests. For example, the committees that perform well in JFM usually have had a concern for protecting local forests before the JFM came into place.) The villages adjacent to forest are placed in an advantageous position compared with villages in the hinterland who also may have similar needs from the forest. The resultant contests are often the testing grounds for the mechanism that villagers employ and the support they could get from the larger institutions such as the FD and the *panchayat*.

### 4.4 Joint Forest Management in Annagarha Forest Beat, Jharkhand

The sections below discuss two Village Forest Management and Protection Committees (VFMPCs) in Annagarha forest beat, Maheshpur and Nawagarh. In both cases, self-initiated forest protection had existed before registration under the JFM agreement. In the case of Maheshpur village, the Forest Department reorientated the forest management by taking forest management responsibilities away from the tribal leaders and formalizing the management under an all-woman committee with an elderly Muslim woman from Maheshpur *khas tola* of the village, as the leader. The effort was radical, particularly because the JFM resolution in Jharkhand precludes an all-woman protection committee. There was, apparently, also an effort to seek participation from the villagers of Maheshpur *khas tola* who are notorious for forest offences. The all-woman committee, however, soon became defunct and, on the other hand, the tribal protection was never revived.

In Nawagarh, the Forest Department registered the VFMPC under its village leader, Kamakhya Munda Shahi, who is also the *panchayat* representative and a member of the landlord family that managed the village forests before 1951. The registration of the village, however, has made little difference to the protection characteristics that existed in Nawagarh in the pre-JFM period. Villagers, however, are conscious of the boundaries to the forest that have been allotted to their VFMPC.

### 4.4.1 The Case of Maheshpur VFMPC

Maheshpur is a relatively large village and the allotted forest land amounts to 172 hectares. Six *tolas* that make up the village contain different population groups such as Khans, Naiks, Mahali, Mundas, and Oraons. The village polity is, however, dominated by the muslim (Khan) and the tribal Munda population. The forest management in recent years has changed hands from the Munda villagers to the Forest Department-sponsored management by women from the Muslim community in Maheshpur *khas*.

#### 4.4.1.1 The Voluntary Forest Protection Group

The forest protection in Maheshpur *panchayat*, like other areas in Annagarha, started at the villagers' initiative and was headed by Sardyal Munda, an elderly member of the Munda tribe from Jinga *tola*. Sardyal Munda sought assistance from Rameshwar Mahto who was a veteran leader in the Maheshpur *panchayat*. In 1982, they constituted *Van Raksha Samiti* or Forest Protection Committee. Later on, the leadership was taken up by Saubhagya Munda, and protection fell into the usual pattern of meetings, patrolling, warnings being sent out to offenders, and inviting foresters to inspect their initiatives. Saubhagya Munda recounts that numerous people were caught, and volunteers from the village even took to stopping women and guarding forests during nights. Munda, however, concedes that, with the passing of the years, this protection went into decline; the two veteran leaders became incapacitated due to poor health, and the 'new generation' was less interested in forest issues.

The protection had sanction from the Muslim population from Maheshpur *Khas*, and good relations were maintained between the forest leaders and the political leaders of the Maheshpur *khas tola*. The Muslim leaders still hold Saubhagya Munda in respect. They remarked that the formation of an all-woman committee was altogether an initiative of the Forest Department that had shifted the protection of village forests from the tribal leaders to Maheshpur *khas* residents. The formalization of forest management under a new committee shattered the hopes for Saubhagya Munda to revive his own protection committee.

#### 4.4.1.2 The All-Woman VFMPC: A Forest Department's Initiative

During the phase of recording villages under the JFM agreement, the Forest Department followed the standard procedure of inviting all the villagers to a public meeting and appointing the village leader to head the VFMPC. In Maheshpur, however, the department went on to form an all-woman VFMPC (Adhikari et al.

1991).[22] This was, as a lower-level forestry staff member argued, prompted by the 'bad' record that Maheshpur *khas* had in forestry; there were regular incidents of forest offences (mostly felling, but also, at times, large-scale timber smuggling) by the residents of the Maheshpur *khas*. It was hoped that having a protection committee in the heart of the village would help bring the forest offences under control. The reason to appoint an all-woman committee, apparently, was also to experiment in Jharkhand with what had gained momentum in participatory forestry elsewhere: the inclusion of women in forest protection and management. It assumed that because women forage forests the most, having them as prime beneficiaries would increase the efficiency of forest management and better reward their opportunity costs. Interestingly, lower-level forest officials are aware of the sentiment that 'a woman can pressurize fellow women collectors more effectively than men'. Also, an incident prompted the foresters to recommend Maheshpur to be picked as an all-woman FPC. A woman leader, Baratan Khatoon, frustrated by the scarcity of fuelwood, had taken out a *juloos*, a procession in the village to protest frequent felling of timber. The *panchayat sarpanch* (judicial officer) had, resultantly, recommended Baratan to head an all-woman committee if one were formed. The villagers of Maheshpur were registered as members of a VFMPC in November 1991 and, for several months, the committee functioned well. There were several village meetings, and forest patrols were the order of the day. Women of neighbouring Lemha and Jinga *tolas* remember being vigilant and feeling a part of the larger Maheshpur forest protection machinery. They also remember going to meetings and contributing money to the VFMPC's fund. Baratan recounts that women would not only patrol forests but also raid houses to recover stolen wood. There was also a provision to fine the offenders.[23] However, the entire range of activities became dysfunctional in a year or so. The residents of Lemha *tola*, when asked about the VFMPC, responded, 'Isn't that all finished?' Currently, meetings are no longer held and there are no forest patrols. Baratan claims that she would still protest if someone cut a *green* tree, but she no longer feels responsible for the forest management on a day-to-day basis.[24]

---

[22] The paper presents a highly simplistic account of the role of Maheshpur women in forest protection. It acclaims the 'involvement of the Forest Department' in finding the 'hidden' gem, an all-woman forest protection group. The paper recommends that the two existing self-initiated forest protection groups (based in two *tolas* in Maheshpur) should be merged into one large VFMPC for an even better performance (as advised by the FD). These are counter to my findings.

[23] They had collected nearly Rs. 1,500 from fines and payments for non-attendance at the meetings, but all this came to nothing.

[24] Baratan Khatoon lost a son and since has been uninterested in public life. Her son was of immense help to her in forest management. Baratan herself is an illiterate woman and depended on him for keeping VFMPC's records, for example.

Baratan Khatoon ascribes the failure of the committee to the lack of support from the Forest Department. The registration of Maheshpur VFMPC was a publicized event in Annagarha, and Baratan had expected constant support from the Forest Department. She once confiscated a large amount of timber that was being smuggled out of Maheshpur in a vehicle and handed it over to the FD. She did so despite facing resistance both from owners and the villagers. The Forest Department, she complained, did little however other than 'confiscate the timber, stamp it with the FD seal, and send it to the headquarters in their usual way'. There were no 'rewards', she remarked. Moreover, she had requested light torches from the FD to help the members move around the forest area in evenings and during the night. None, however, were provided.

Baratan Khatoon had the making of a village leader. She said, 'It is difficult for the residents of Maheshpur *khas* to cross me; more than 100 households would come in my relations alone'. Due to her stature and age, she is referred to in respectful terms, such as *Sadar saab* or *Bhauji saab* by the villagers. Nevertheless, Baratan, as a woman from a conservative Muslim background, worked with limitations. She confessed, 'I would not usually roam in the forest myself, but send others'. Despite this, a few younger residents remarked that they would never have allowed their womenfolk to go into the forest without a *purdah*, the veil, and Baratan was shameless in doing so. Apart from these limitations, Baratan also betrayed little understanding of the needs of the neighbouring *tolas*. The principles of forest management, to her, were simple: not to allow outsiders into Maheshpur's forest and not to permit felling of timber by any resident. This attitude, however, does not permit a plan in which VFMPC members can use the forest in a manner that meets their essential needs (including that of poles) nor does it conform to working methods followed by leaders of successful village-based forest committees who respect and concede to routine extraction by fellow villagers. Baratan also remained on the margin as far as the larger village leadership was concerned. The political leaders of Maheshpur *khas* include the *panchayat* (which was defunct) representative, the *sarpanch*, or the council's judicial officer, Ali Baksh Khan, and Qutubuddin Khan, a private contractor who is also into local politics and holds the post of the district secretary of Rashtriya Janta Dal. Both leaders, not unlike the leaders in Amratola in Bengal, are unsympathetic to forest conservation.[25]

---

[25] Both the leaders are relatively affluent and, like many other residents in Maheshpur *khas*, have little direct dependence on forest. Mr. Ali Baksh Khan was even implicated and imprisoned for a forest offence that his son had committed, but for which Mr. Khan, to save the boy, took the blame. Since the dissolution of *panchayat* in 1997, Ali Baksh has kept a low profile. Interestingly, Aspand Khan, the founder of the NGO, Agrarian Trust (see chapter 7), is a resident of Maheshpur. Although he is involved with the issue of forest conservation in the tribal villages, he is not involved with forest management in his own village.

### 4.4.1.3 JFM and Access Patterns in Maheshpur Forests

Maheshpur VFMPC has members from all of its six *tolas*. However, the village as a unit of management does not reflect the pattern of forest use nor the basis on which self-initiated committees are formed or function in Annagarha. Villagers depend most directly on forests that are adjacent to their *tolas* and seldom, for example, interact with the users from other *tolas*. A respondent from Lemha *tola* explained, 'Why would villagers from other *tolas* come to forests here? They have their own forests to go to'. Also, the perception of jungle for villagers in Maheshpur *khas tola* is clearly different from those in nearby Lemha or Jinga *tola*. In Maheshpur *khas*, many villagers have limited dependence on firewood, and many, as in Khairulla or Amratola in West Bengal, buy fuelwood from tribals or from *haat*, the weekly village markets. For some of these well-off villagers, forests hold interest because of their aesthetics ('*achha lagta hai*, it feels good to have them around'), whereas others, as reflected in the high number of forest offences and oral reports, have not hesitated to provide access to timber for money. (Maheshpur *khas* has, in the past, allegedly served as an entry point for the timber mafia and private contractors.)

### 4.4.2 The Case of Nawagarh VFMPC

Nawagarh is responsible for 172.76 hectares of mainly Sal forest, although an ample number of associate species are found in the forest. The village was registered under the JFM agreement on 28 September 1993.[26] Most of the residents in Nawagarh are dependent on agriculture and their own livestock. Forest is important to the residents in several ways. It provides fuelwood, fodder for livestock gazing, and poles for construction and repair of houses and agricultural implements. There are also households that depend on forests for business and drought relief.

In Nawagarh, voluntary protection never had the intensity it had in Ober or Vanadag (see chapter 5). There was, nonetheless, self-regulation and restraint over use of the forest since the early 1980s. These characteristics continue in current forest management practices. As a result, there is no system of village meetings or forest patrols to manage forest. The restraint to cut trees is fairly lax when it comes to meeting the essential needs such as fuelwood and poles for houses and agricultural implements. A respondent stated that, 'When there is no dry wood, we lop the branches or cut young trees for fuelwood'. The residents maintain an egalitarian attitude towards neighbouring villagers for collection of fuelwood, 'We don't stop if some one picks dry wood'. A clear impact of JFM, however, is that the villagers are familiar with the boundaries of forests that are allotted to Nawagarh VFMPC. This is not only because of formalities on paper, but also

---

[26] It is likely that formalization of Nawagarh took place because of the presence of the *panchayat* leaders and the influential Manaki-munda clan.

because the neighbouring villages of Ober (and Vanadag) have asserted their control over their local forests.

The village is headed by Kamakhya Narain Sahi who is from the landlord Munda family and has been the *panchayat* representative for the area.[27] On registration, Sahi was nominated to head the VFMPC as its secretary. Like other villages in the Annagarha forest beat, Nawagarh too is made up of smaller units, or *tolis*.[28] Most of the resident population, however, are members of the Munda clan (they are further divided into Manaki munda, and *Khas* munda; the former are related to the landlord family). However, there are also a few Bediya, Oraon, and Hindu households. Kamakhya Sahi recounts that during the *zamindari* period, villagers would not cut forest because guards were employed for protection purposes. Although the essential needs, such as fuelwood and forest usufruct were provided free of cost to the villagers (who were usually *raiyats* or tenants to the landlord, paid agriculture tax, and were exempt for consumption of basic forest usufruct), extraction of timber required payment of royalties, such as a portion of the crop or in kind (goats, chickens, etc.). A majority of the Munda population remains loyal to the Sahi family. They complain of the takeover of control of the forests by the state and by the *dikus* or the outsiders, particularly the 'private contractors and smugglers' who have eroded the sovereignty that the villagers enjoyed over the forests.

Kamakhya Sahi has not cared to maintain any logbook for VFMPC activity in the village. This contrasts with the vast amount of records he maintained as the *panchayat* leader (many are related to timber felling, although mainly those from homestead lands). He commented that little has changed due to the registration of the village under JFM. The executive body, for example, has been given little power to enforce the management decisions. As the *panchayat* representative, he has arbitrated various village issues and made decisions that were enforceable by law. On the other hand, he feels that he can give few directions to fellow villagers on what to do with forest offences. As the head of his village, he is not interested in taking up 'illegal' fights, he said. In the few instances when Nawagarh residents withheld forest offenders, he asked them to deposit the timber and let them go: 'With what authority can I stop them?' Sahi reasoned. On the other hand, the residents are not interested in active patrolling. One of the respondents tried to sum

---

[27] Sahi's family belongs to a Manaki-munda clan, and many of their rituals have been influenced by Hindu customs. They continue to have munda rituals like *sarana*, or nature worship, carried out by the tribal priest, the *Pahan*. However, they also follow Hindu rituals and employ Hindu Brahmins for rituals like marriages. Also, women members from their household, unlike other tribal populations, do not go to forests to collect fuelwood.

[28] The present site of Nawagarh village is removed from the old site. They were originally living one kilometre away in Garhtoli (literally, the fortified village). After conflict with the British and the resultant destruction, they moved to the current location, Nawagarh (literally, the new fort).

up the attitude of Nawagarh villagers towards forest protection: 'Nawagarh is a *raja* village, a village of landlords. It is too much to expect of villagers to patrol forests on a daily basis'.

### 4.4.2.1 Access to Village Forests

As pointed out earlier, Nawagarh residents display an ease about villagers taking out forest products, even Sal poles, to meet essential requirements. 'If we can't get usufruct to fulfill our needs then what is the use in protecting the forest?', one respondent explained. This access, however, is not without qualification. It depends on ethnicity and the quantity of extraction a household carries out. Registration of several other villages under the JFM agreement has made the residents in Nawagarh, like other village forest committees, aware of the forest area that belongs to them and that the neighboring villagers are essentially 'outsiders'.

Many senior Munda villagers alleged that a few Bediya and Oraon families in the village were involved in wood-based businesses, such as making furniture. A Bediya resident, on the other hand, remarked that wood artisanship is their family business. Although in normal circumstances they purchase homestead trees for their business, in many instances (often hardship) they have to cut trees from forest land. However, they added that the newly rejuvenated forests do not provide them with the quality of timber they require for the business. They also alleged that Mundas have looked down upon them, and in any case, they feel excommunicated from the rest of the village.[29] Another resident, who sells fuelwood in markets, insisted that the money he earns is enough only for *namak-tel*, literally salt and oil, or it only supplements the household income, and does not replace it. Despite the complaints that Munda residents made against other groups in the village, they have rarely reported forest offences to the Forest Department (a 'quiet' village in the words of an FD official). In part, this is because the good forest cover allows the villagers an amount of latitude for those who extract forest usufruct (timber particularly) more than others. The attitude of the leader who, unless he has real powers, does not want to get involved with informal forest politics also makes this a quiet village. It was the consensus among several residents that only a few depend on the forest for a livelihood; the rest use the forest to fulfill essential needs and occasionally help subsistence.

### 4.4.3 Discussion

Maheshpur represents a failure of expectations both for the villagers and the forest department. The women representatives of the committee read too much into the JFM agreement and felt cheated. The Forest Department, on the other hand, could

---

[29] An Oraon elder similarly remembered the time of Munda *zamindars* as one of exploitation when their land would be put up for sale on non-payment of taxes. He also blamed non-tribal Khan for cutting away forests.

never consolidate its well-meaning initiatives that started on a promising note. Because of lack of support from the political leadership in Maheshpur and from villagers in general, the all-woman committee produced little difference in the forest management in the village.

The villagers in Nawagarh practise restraint in cutting trees, although they allow fellow villagers including residenlts of neighbouring villages to collect minor forest usufructs. The onset of JFM has brought home the reality that certain forest land is allotted to them for forest management as well as any excesses that are done by fellow or neighbouring villagers. Nonetheless, Nawagarh villagers remain uninterested in patrolling forest or taking into account every minor offence. The VFMPC leader belongs to the landlord family and has led the village through his involvement with the *panchayat*. He feels dissatisfied with the modest amount of formal power that the JFM has vested in him.

## 4.5 Conclusion

This chapter combined oral history with villagers' accounts of contemporary forestry practices. Although similarities were drawn between the forests in Gopegarh (West Bengal) and Annagarha (Jharkhand), several differences, including the nature of forest distribution, history of management, and presence of voluntary forest protection committees (in Jharkhand) were noted. It was suggested that the degree of dependence, homogeneity, and size of the population play significant roles in the management of forest. Leaders play key roles in determining forest management and providing interpretation of JFM and bridges between other villages, the FD, and *panchayats*.

In the case of West Bengal, it was noted that Social Forestry and the subsequent involvement of *panchayats* with forestry activities created a hospitable environment for JFM. Nonetheless, JFM has produced mixed results in the area. Bhagwati Chowk has successfully combined many of the provisions in JFM for its own needs and attitudes to provide successful management of its forest. The villagers in Amratola-Phulpahari do not share the same consensus over protection of forest. There is disjunction between village polity and forest politics and, as a result, the forest is often compromised. Villages who do not enjoin forest or villagers who do not agree with the forest demarcation results in intervillage conflicts. It was argued that such territorialization of forest resources and resultant contestations are the key outcomes of JFM.

In Jharkhand, several villages in Annagarha had started managing forest on their own due to the hardship from denuded forest cover. Through these initiatives, the villagers tried to protect local forests and legitimize their perception of rights over forests. The villagers still carry the memory of the unjust distribution of timber by the FD and the patronizing exploitative attitude of the *dikus*, the private contractors. With the onset of JFM, and despite being registered as VFMPCs, villages have not received support from the FD as is the case in West Bengal. Despite the department's lacklustre involvement, villagers have identified themselves with individual patches of forest.

Chapter 5 discusses the nature of the inherent characteristics of community forest management. It is noted that several features are shared between the villages that were formalized under the JFM agreement and the self-initiated forest protection groups. I also argue that a dichomotization cannot be held between forestry and other rural development issues.

Chapter 5

# Voluntary Forest Protection Groups: Indigenous Beliefs, Autogenous Management

## 5.1 Introduction

This chapter examines the notions, beliefs, and elements in the forest-peasant dynamics that inform many of the inherent characteristics of forestry practices in rural communities. It discusses the voluntary forest protection groups in Jharkhand and compares them with the Forest Protection Committees (FPCs) in West Bengal. In doing so, the chapter puts Jharkhand and Bengal on a similar footing by arguing that, given similar characteristics within a community, villagers demonstrate analogous forestry practices. The chapter, however, also argues that an inherent instability remains in such specialized systems and suggests that forestry initiatives do not exist in a political and social vacuum. The villagers constantly seek support from other stakeholders of JFM such as the Forest Department, *panchayats*, and NGOs not only to bolster their initiatives in forest management, but also in other aspects of rural life.

The chapter is divided into four sections. The first section discusses the peasant-forest interrelationship and the influences of forests on community forestry practices. It is argued that spatial and temporal factors of forests have important influences on the forestry practices of communities situated nearby.[1] The next section notes how the villagers secure forests for use and management by creating 'zones of exclusion'. The section that follows discusses the methods that the villagers use to protect forest and extract usufruct, and the ways these are not in consonance with the allowances in the JFM agreement. The final section studies the records from the meetings held by the villagers in Jharkhand and Bengal. It evaluates the strength of the forest democracy and tests the degree and nature of the homogeneity of interests, opinions, and functions. It is noted that the forest forums are male-dominated, and the village communities talk over various issues including development work during such gatherings rather than separating forestry concerns from other facets of rural life.

---

[1] Also see Jewitt (1995) who, on the other hand, finds that the historical sense of place and identity that the tribal population in Jharkhand has, are important factors in mobilizing interest for forest protection and management.

## 5.2 Forest-Peasant Relations: Forest-guided Influences

Political ecology studies have chiefly been concerned with the effects of human activities on the physical environment; to examine the subject the other way round opens a plethora of perspectives. This section, as a prelude to an examination of the characteristics that are inherent in community forest management, considers influences that forests have on human activities. It is argued that many key characteristics of forest management can be addressed by shifting the peasant-state locus to one between the resource (forest) and the peasants. This section argues that the nature of forests influences the *modus operandi* of the forestry practices of the peasants who live next to them. Although some of the forest influences are generalizeable, others demand an appreciation of the unique set of factors that make up each of the forest-peasant environments.

Based on the proximity and usefulness to the village communities, the forests influence the setting of hamlets and agricultural fields, the patterns of forest use, the leadership, and even the encroachment on forest land. Often the knowledge or the access exercised by peasants vis-à-vis forests do not reflect the government policies or legally established property rights over the forest land and its usufruct, and instead are informed by the flow of 'information' between the forest and the dependent peasantry. This section assigns weight to such influences that emanate from forest resources to the dependent rural population. It does so by looking into temporal and spatial factors.

### 5.2.1 Temporal Factors

Temporally, forests' influences on peasants' lives are wide-ranging. The productivity of forests occurs in seasonal and even monthly cycles.[2] The summer months in east India, for example, often coincide with a lean agricultural period. During this period, the forests 'step in' in a crucial manner as a source of drought food. They provide the farmers with a number of non-timber products for barter, sale, and consumption. Those peasants who are economically marginalized consider this resource insurance against abject penury and starvation. Trees are usually logged during low periods of agricultural activity; therefore, midsummer often coincides with the time when the menfolk fetch Sal poles from the forests for timber-related purposes. Nearly half of the households in Bhagwati Chowk in Bengal, for example, are in the business of making plates and cups from Sal leaves. This business is particularly intense in the months of *Baisakh* and *Chaith* (April-June); the families can, however, find themselves engaged in Sal business from 6-12 months in a year (Pachauri undated). Such dependence has a marked impact on forest management. Not only does the protection of forest during these months

---

[2] The food calendar in Bengal, for example, indicates that the forest work is available for the poor from mid-November to mid-December, when both men and women can find employment. The next month provides work mostly for men. In February and March, the villagers sell firewood to support their livelihood (Mukherjee 1995).

become necessary, but also the defence is strong and constant. Groups of women who collect fuelwood and Sal leaves are on the lookout for outsiders (see chapter 4).[3]

The forest-peasant interrelationship taken on a larger temporal scale unlocks another set of issues. For example, in the last fifty years the structure of forests and the peasant population has changed dramatically. Although some areas in *Jharkhand* still contain vast expanses of forests, the majority of the forests in southwest Bengal are located in isolated, patchy pockets with a long history of institutional management. The changing sociopolitical conditions that have occurred with time have had considerable impact on how forests are perceived and managed. There are, for example, several instances where, within villages, such as Amratola (West Bengal) and Maheshpur (Jharkhand), the population make-up and economic conditions have become diverse and so have the forestry practices. There are clusters of households that are better off than the rest of the population, their womenfolk do not go to the forest for collection of fuelwood and buy it instead from other villagers or in the local markets.

## 5.2.2 Spatial Influences

The spatial location of forests also demonstrates a definitive, albeit subtle, influence on peasants' lives. The landscape gradation, particularly in the Annagarha forest beat, shows that the forests are followed by agricultural land and finally by clusters of homesteads. This is, however, not generalizable beyond a point. On the other hand, within these protected zones in the forest, the land that is next to an individual farmer's *raiyati* (also referred to as *jote*) or private land is understood by the fellow villager to be under the protection of that individual. The fauna on this piece of forest land is usually held by him as a resource that could be used at a time when forest usufruct is unavailable from elsewhere in the forest or from the *rakhat*, the community forest. Not surprisingly, encroachment of forest land is often by villagers who have agriculture land next to this forest land.[4] Thus, a circle of influence, from community to individuals, is not uncommon in forestry practice.

---

[3] Changes can also be seen in usufructs (both in quality and quantity) that are taken to weekly-held rural markets, the *haats*, at different times of the year.

[4] There are also regular encroachments on forest land by villagers, mainly for agricultural purposes. Although many of the encroachments, understandably, existed before the JFM was implemented, with the current management practice, the FD (particularly so in West Bengal) finds it difficult to wrest the land from these villagers. The encroachment is committed often by people who have leverage within the village community and are active members of the Forest Protection Committee.

## 5.2.3 Discussion

The villagers use the forest not only for different purposes (Rangarajan 1996, 61) but also in different manners depending on the temporal and spatial characteristics of their forests and their own socio-economic condition. These issues are rarely reflected in the Joint Forest Management resolution where, for example, a universal membership is provided for and a uniform set of rights and duties is called for from all members all year round. However, the forest-centred discourses are not without limitations. Although they can bring incisive insights into forestry behaviour in local set ups, the potential cannot be overestimated. Noteworthy is the limitation of the nature and intensity of the role that the forest can play in community-based forest management. Often, a uniform, small FPC, with members with great incentive to save the forest, performs well. Others with low forest interaction have little to gain from the forest and, as noted in earlier chapters, forests in such cases are bartered in exchange for better alternatives. More importantly, this microlevel analysis, taken on its own, precludes consideration of interaction, obligations, incentives, and pressures that arise from compelling institutions like the Forest Department, *panchayats*, and the development NGOs.

## 5.3 Zones of Exclusion

The most telling impact of the forest-peasant interaction in the context of JFM is found in the key management practice of the communities. FPC members create exclusion zones in their proximate forest that are declared out of bounds for people outside their community and, if violated, fights are started with the infiltrators. Notably, the boundaries that constitute these zones are not always the ones that have been delineated by the Forest Department but the ones that villagers perceive as forests under their influence and for their exclusive use.

### 5.3.1 Zones of Exclusion and 'Rules' of Forest Engagement in Jharkhand

In Jharkhand, the voluntary forest protection groups mark out an area in the forests as *rakhat*, the land that is under protection. *Rakhat*,[5] like *toli*, are informal in demarcation and not necessarily what are or might be carved out as official boundaries by the FD for management by a VFMPC. They instead reflect an area in the forest that has been used by or held under the influence of the villagers over a long period of time. The *rakhat* could be marked out literally, as in Ober (see below), or be held conceptually, as in Nawagarh and Vanadag. These protected zones are the core area where villagers practise their management methods, mainly

---

[5] The term *rakhat* was used in the case of *zamindari* forests in the pre-Independence period (Kumar 1997, 81). The rights to such forest land (*rakhat*) was exclusively held by the landlords. This contrasts with *katat* forests where the customary rights were freely used by the tenant population (ibid.).

through protection and by excluding outsiders. Oft-repeated advice in Ober is, '*Rakhat se mat lao; rakhat ke bahar se lao*'. [Don't bring wood from the protected part of the forest; do so from outside of it.]

Within the community setting there may, however, be a noteworthy egalitarianism: not only do the villagers maintain an understanding about extraction of fuelwood (usually of fallen twigs, branches, and green shrubs, although, at times, also young trees and branches, which the villagers lop from trees), but there also exists a consent for extraction of timber for meeting essential needs like construction and repair of houses and agricultural implements. These activities generally need a 'clearance' from the forum or carry the understanding of the local leader.[6]

### 5.3.2 The Case of Ober Voluntary Protection Group

The village of Ober falls within the jurisdiction of the Nawagarh *panchayat*.[7] The Bediyas that make up the Ober village are principally agriculturists with small per capita landholdings. They depend on forests for vital necessities such as fuelwood, Sal poles for construction of houses and ploughs, and also as a source of food in case of droughts. As a result, the villagers in Ober have, as a matter of routine, taken out usufruct from the forest adjacent to the village and remained in contest with the patrolling staff from the Forest Department. However, with the initiation of a voluntary forest protection group, the villagers have used the forum to legitimize their perception of rights and practices in the forest land.

Traditionally, the leadership in Ober was provided by the religious headman, Puran Mahto. After 1976, however, a resident from Ober's *Neeche toli*, Lahru Bediya, became involved in 'social service'. A secondary school graduate, he left a lower-ranking government job to work for the village's welfare. Interestingly, from the beginning, Lahru addressed forest conservation as a priority. The period after 1976 had coincided with large-scale forest felling by the FD with the help of the private contractors. The period exposed the villagers to the commercial value of timber and moreover eroded the 'logic of conservation' that the Forest Department had until then advocated to these villagers. According to Lahru, the villagers in Ober had fallen into the practice of indiscriminate felling and often collaborated

---

[6] The egalitarianism, however, needs to be qualified. For example, in a highly regulated village like Vanadag in Jharkhand, the community leader keeps the forest 'closed' for extended periods and demands even minor extraction is from outside the *rakhat* forest. In other villages, the extraction of fuelwood is acceptable. Moreover, in villages with large forest resources and/or weaker management (as in Nawagarh, Jharkhand) fuelwood could have a 'noncompetitive' label, where outsiders too have access to *rakhat* forest to collect firewood (although not cut away timber poles).

[7] Spatially, the village of Ober is made up of 2 *tolis*: Ober *khas* and Harra Bera. Ober *khas*, further, has sub-*tolis*: the one higher up is *Upar toli* and the lower one is *Neeche toil* (see Map 5.1).

with the contractors. The forest acquired an open access resource image: one which could provide the people with a source of quick revenue with little accountability.

It was during this period of open-access attitude that Lahru Bediya closed ranks with other like-minded villagers. They delineated an area in the forest that would be out of bounds for outsiders. In effect, they marked out an area, the *rakhat*, that would be under the management of the Ober *khas toli*. The first major fight that Lahru Bediya took up with outsiders was in 1981. The villagers from the neighbouring village of Sringeri regularly felled trees in the forests of Ober *khas toli*. Lahru's fight was against the wishes of the headman, Mahto, although it was resolved in Lahru's favour by the officials at Sringeri and the Munda *panchayat* leader at Nawagarh. By 1984, Lahru had established boundaries in the forest of Ober[8] and initiated the practice of keeping a logbook that would record the minutes of various meetings (discussed below). With increased acceptance in the community, Lahru became active in other areas of Ober's routine life. Within a year, the meetings arbitrated the social and moral issues of the Ober *khas* community. In 1992, Lahru Bediya challenged the leadership of the religious headman, Puran Mahto. He accused Mahto of being unable to bring development into the village. He also accused Mahto of theft and his son of immoral conducts, and proposed the name of Balsu Bediya, a resident of his *toli*, as the new religious head of the village.

The success of Lahru's initiatives has spatial connotations. First, it was easy to organize support for the defence of a forest that was in the immediate environment. Second, he could offer himself as a proximate alternative to the leadership for development and resolution of disputes – the other alternative was the unsympathetic *panchayat* leader of the Nawagarh village. Third, Lahru, a resident of *Neeche toli*, enjoyed a loyal following from his own *toli*. The Mahto leadership, on the other hand, in *Upar toli* fought against Lahru's agenda, and it took three years for the new Mahto, Balsu Bediya, to replace the old one.

However, the vulnerability of Lahru's methods was exposed in October 1987 when Lahru Bediya was absent for eight days in a nearby town. He found on his return that most of the *rakhat* forest had been cut down by the villagers. In his absence, the villagers could neither stop the outsiders nor curb their own temptation to cut down the forest for quick revenue. After a gap of five years of protection, the villagers wanted returns for their labour and patience. They viewed Lahru's attitude towards the forest as autocratic and dictated by a personal agenda. Moreover, in 1992, an NGO, Ram Krishna Mission (RKM), that had been operating in a few nearby villages became involved with Ober and chose a young

---

[8] The demarcation of the *rakhat* forest was done by clearing the shrubs and bushes in a straight line on the two sides of the forests. Although Ober *toli* itself is in front of the demarcated forest, the *Paina* hills in the back formed the other natural boundary to the forest resource (see Map 5.1).

resident of *Upar toli*, Sanichar Bediya, to head the NGO's activities in the village. This external force with more potent incentives challenged and marginalized Lahru's leadership even more.

RKM was (and still is) involved in tribal development, mainly through mobilization of government and private funds and by institutionalizing norms, such as training, meetings, gifts of labour for development schemes, pooling funds, in the villages (discussed at length in chapter 7). Although the NGO-sponsored forum in Ober is focused primarily on issues of agriculture, health, and education, the increasing membership brought forestry issues into its purview. The new leadership, in turn took a populist approach to the forests. For example, it did not demand forest guard duties of its members and asked a nominal fee of five Rupees for each pole a member extracted from the forest.

The final test for Lahru Bediya's claims to leadership came in 1993, when the village was formally registered under the JFM arrangement and Lahru was made the secretary. However, with the subsequent lack of support from the FD and despite Lahru's approach to the lower-level officials on several occasions (see chapter 3), Lahru was left a leader on paper only. The recent installation of lift irrigation by the NGO was the last straw. To benefit from the irrigation scheme, the staunchest of Lahru's supporters *migrated* and joined the *Upar toli*-run club membership.

### 5.3.3 'Zones of Exclusion' in the Forests of Gopegarh, Bengal

As noted in chapter 4, similar zones of exclusion are visible in southwest Bengal. In the Gopegarh forest beat, the presence of patchy and isolated forests makes it easier for the members of the FPCs to identify with and secure the forest lands that are allotted by the FD. On the other hand, villagers have contested the 'artificial' demarcation of forest boundary by the Forest Department because it does not agree with their original area of influence and activity.

### 5.3.4 Discussion

Typically, the way villagers engage in forest protection is to keep outsiders away from the area they recognize as the forest under village protection or *rakhat*, as it is called in Jharkhand. This area may or may not correspond with areas that have been officially allotted by the Forest Department, and can often be a reason for contestation. Yet, as seen in the case of Ober village, the forest-dominated influences are not without limitations. The associations, norms of reciprocity, and attitude generated through these resources are dynamic in nature, and choices are made by individuals in such a manner as to maximize benefits to themselves. The villagers seize upon new opportunities and do not mind risking breaking the established conventions (e.g. the crossover of 'spatial and temporal loyalty' in Ober or the forest sell-out during the elections in Amratola). In Bengal, similar territorialization and contestation may be witnessed.

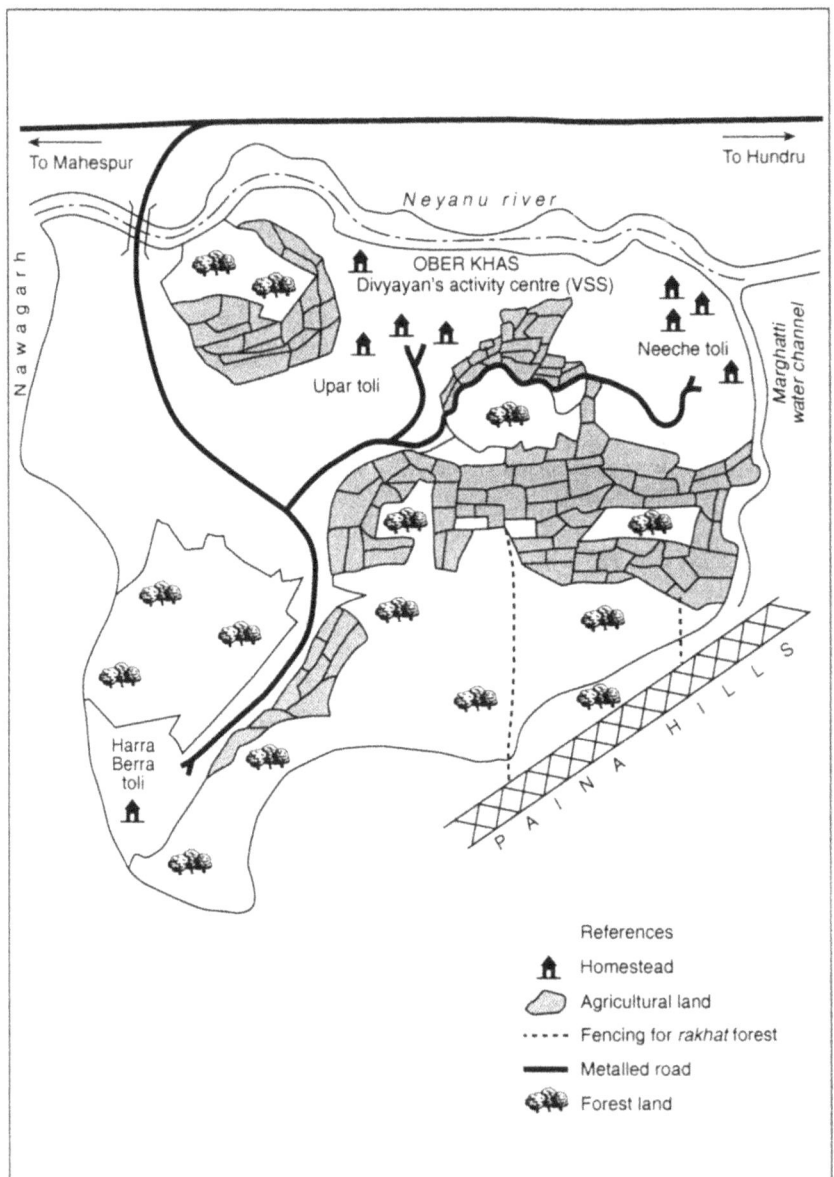

**Map 5.1 Spatial Setting of *Tolis* in Ober Village and the Demarcation of**
**          *Rakhat* Forest by the Lahru Bediya Group**
(Adapted from land classification maps of Ober village; Map Section, Ranchi East Forest
Division Office)

## 5.4 'Fluid' Boundaries of India's Forests: Informal Niches in JFM[9]

The earlier section discussed how the forest-peasant relationship, despite limitations, has a certain definitive element to influence forest management. Similarities were drawn across the States to illustrate how community forest protection groups create zones that mark out areas, literally or conceptually, in the forest to protect them from reckless use and felling. This section further closes the gap between the JFM-sponsored committees and voluntary forest protection groups. It is argued that methods and practices in community forestry management such as protection, usufruct extraction, and nature of contest are similar across the States.

### 5.4.1 Protection Mechanisms

The recent forest management methods in both Jharkhand and West Bengal are characterized by a *withdrawal* of the Forest Department staff from patrolling resource areas around villages (see chapter 3). This has prompted many inherent, albeit veiled, activities of the rural population to come to the fore. The forest bureaucracy is no longer seen as a common foe against which the village communities need to unite, and turn forest land into 'open access resources'. Instead, villagers are identifying more solidly with isolated forest patches that lie under the jurisdiction of village Forest Protection Committees. Forest lands are now demarcated and governed (for protection and usufruct extraction) by JFM-sponsored committees and voluntary forest protection groups.

The protection mechanism used by the villagers often replicates the policing methods of the FD through forest patrols, exclusion, and fines. To 'catch and punish the erring villagers' frequently forms the basis for protection of forests and establishment of norms for villagers. Informed by the Forest Department's policing methods, villagers exclude members outside their community through force and monetary penalties. One of the residents in Maheshpur complained that they should be supplied with *lathis* or batons to effectively guard the forest. The manner of patrol that is advocated in less successful forest committees is similar. Villagers opine that effective protection involved groups of four to five men making rounds of their *rakhat* forest on a rotation basis. A record of forest guard duties is often advocated. Yet, there is a notable difference – villagers do not persecute fellow villagers beyond a point and seldom report them to the FD. Despite having little arbitration powers, the committees decide on the exclusion of neighbouring village-communities from use of the forests they mark out as under protection. The gradient of protection is such that the exclusion from the forest is first for the

---

[9] It is important to note that forestry activities are termed informal only when seen against the norms and rules that are laid out in the Joint Forest Management agreement. Many practices are not only essential to villagers' day-to-day needs but have been in practice (noticed or disguised, contested or informally recognised by the FD) for a long period of time.

outsiders (from villagers who are outside their villages, but also who are not from their community) and then for the members of community forest protection groups.

### 5.4.1.1 Non-participation in Forest Management

The most common complaint by those villagers who are involved with care of the local forests is against those villagers who abstain (or defy) the village's forest protection machinery. The meeting records in Vanadag constantly remind and even threaten male members who do not take their turns to protect the local forest. In Bhagwati Chowk and Jinga *tola* (part of Maheshpur village), the leaders, on the other hand, complain of the conflict that exists between their ideologies and the younger generation who are not interested enough in protection of forests. In Nawagarh, the complaint takes an ethnic slant in which Munda villagers complain about the practices of a few Oraon families who are woodcutters by profession.[10] Finally, in Amratola-Phulpahari and Ober, there is conflict due to divided loyalty (based on affiliation with a political party or leader).

Villagers who do not show up for regular meetings or forest patrol, for their part, stated that either they have other work to do, the meetings are too frequent, or they have little interest in the forest. These villagers have to fulfill their needs without being in tandem with the rest of the villagers. In Lemha there is, for example, a member of the Dang community married to an Oraon woman who communicates little with other villagers. When Sal poles are needed for house repair, he goes to a 'farther' corner of forest away from household settlement (effectively away from *rakhat* forest) so that no one objects.

### 5.4.2 Usufruct Extraction

The community forest protection groups indulge in forestry practices without adhering to the boundaries (that mark concessions and rights) that the JFM agreement has prescribed.  To be sure, a range of concessions allowing collection of fuelwood and minor forest produce has existed, predating the current participatory forestry in both States. The forest citizens in south Jharkhand also enjoy a larger number of rights over forest use than the residents in southwest Bengal. For example, in Jharkhand, there is no fee for grazing livestock.[11] Moreover, the population living next to the protected-category forest is also entitled to share timber at harvests. There is, however, no provision (including that in a JFM scenario) in either State that allows felling trees other than that announced through government circulars that are sanctioned through official

---

[10] Mundas from Nawagarh also blamed the Hindu Pandey and Rajwaar households for cutting trees.

[11] In West Bengal, there is a fee to graze livestock in the forest, the amount of which was fixed in the pre-Independence period. The amount is so nominal that the cost of collection would easily exceed the actual revenue, and hence, is seldom collected.

working plans or working schemes, and carried out at the initiative of the Forest Departments. The use of forest, nevertheless, is not limited to what is prescribed within the JFM agreement, which allows collection of fuelwood and a share of usufruct (including cash) at harvest. Villagers regularly extract poles and green trees by lopping, thinning, or felling from the forest to fulfill various household needs and for sale in markets. This is the case in both 'good' forest protection groups (registered or voluntary), such as Bhagwati Chowk in Bengal and Vanadag in Jharkhand, and in 'weaker' committees such as Amratola-Phulpahari and Maheshpur and Ober. The poles that the villagers need are at intervals that are more frequent than the harvest operation of the FD can promise and, in these cases, villagers feel obliged to extract timber to meet their needs.

In Jharkhand, the villagers' understanding of Joint Forest Management systems is, at best, vague, and their forestry practices, in the assumed participatory atmosphere, are instead informed through their own interpretations. Although the villagers are aware of their responsibility to protect forests through informal patrols and self-restraint, the nature of rights they are to have in return is uncertain. In Bengal, the villagers in general have been briefed for a longer period and are in touch with the FD. They understand the duties and usufruct return that has been guaranteed to them as part of the JFM agreement. Nonetheless, in both States, it is commonly understood that forests are not open to indiscriminate logging, but would provide fuel and timber to cover essential needs.[12] Villagers use the insularity derived from the power and legitimacy of the community forest protection committee to extract timber and non-timber forest products (NTFPs) for household and commercial purposes.

Although villagers sympathize with the need to collect fuelwood and extract Sal poles for essential household needs, providing a source for forest-based business draws mixed results in different villages. In Bhagwati Chowk, a large number of households collect Sal leaves and sell them in Midnapore. This is also the case in Lemha *toli* (a part of Maheshpur village) in Jharkhand,[13] and villagers are accommodating of the situation. On the other hand, in Nawagarh, the Mundas complain of the Oraons extracting timber that is more than their share. In Vanadag, timber-based businesses and offences are more strongly frowned upon.

---

[12] Construction of a new house may require as many as 200 Sal poles, of which 10-12 need to be *kandis* or *bang*, poles with substantial age and girth. In routine cases, a household, however, would usually need 10-12 poles each year for repair purposes. Sal trees are usually cut six inches above the roots so that saplings can resprout. The time needed to cut a Sal tree could vary from a few minutes to a couple of hours.

[13] Bobby Devi, a resident of Lemha *toli* (a part of Maheshpur village), collects Sal leaves three days a week and every fourth day goes to the Ranchi to sell the plates. Unlike Midnapore, the group from Lemha has to take a two-hour journey on a bus to reach the market place. A Sal-leaf plate needs a dozen leaves and is sold at a minimum of 50 *paise* a dozen. There are months, such as *Jeth* (June), when the leaves are not available.

Finally, the incentive of cash returns, the principal way in which the JFM has departed from previous participatory initiatives, has produced mixed results. In Bhagwati Chowk, with 37 households and nearly 150 hectares of forest under the FPC's jurisdiction, the two annual harvests carried out by the FD have fetched each of the households a significant amount of cash. This has rarely been the case in other situations. Amratola, the neigbouring FPC with 240 hectares of forest and 246 households, has a much lower forest to household ratio, and the cash return on the harvest is hardly an incentive for them to institutionalize JFM practices. Jharkhand, on the other hand, has yet to carry out its first harvest under the JFM agreement. As noted in chapter 4, the villagers are unsure that the FD will bring fair results at harvest operations. Here, and in instances where the cash incentive is insufficient, the reason for involvement by the villagers in forest management lies more in the actual control of the resource to ensure availability of usufructs for household and business purposes.

### 5.4.3 Discussion

The forest committees, both those that are formally instituted and those that are not registered but enjoy the support of their community, are playing active roles in negotiating the transaction of forest usufruct within and outside their communities. This often includes approving customary extractive methods to which villagers resort to fulfill various forest-based needs and creating 'zones of exclusion' where the forest becomes out of bounds for 'outsiders'. The working methods employed in informal activities and transactions are often independent of what is allowed as part of the JFM agreement. The practices are grounded in notions that the forest belongs to the entire village community, and, although rights to its land tenures rest with the government, the villagers cannot be alienated from the use of forest to fulfill their essential requirement: '*Sircar*, [the government] after all, cannot take forests away', one of the respondents challenged.

### 5.5 Records from Forest Committee Meetings

The final section of this chapter draws on the written records from the village meetings held in Vanadag and Ober in Jharkhand and the FPC meetings in Gopegarh in West Bengal. It is only in the case of Ober that the villagers, on Lahru Bediya's initiative, started to maintain records of meetings. In other cases, record-keeping was prompted by other institutions; the NGO, Ram Krishna Mission in the case of Vanadag, and the Forest Department in the case of Gopegarh FPCs in West Bengal. Nonetheless, the minutes from the meetings illustrate a common theme: as the forest forum evolves into a stable body, the villagers engage in non-forestry issues as well, and the sustainability of the forum depends on how successfully it can address these issues. Forestry is seldom treated by the villagers in isolation, and often various themes, including social, agricultural, and educational issues are discussed in what essentially were forest forums.

### 5.5.1 Constructing a Case for the Voluntary Forest Committee in Vanadag

Vanadag is the neighbouring village to Nawagarh and is composed predominantly of Oraon households. A relatively small village, it sits next to approximately 100 acres of good Sal forests. The voluntary forest protection committee in Vanadag has not been registered under the JFM agreement, although Mahadev Oraon, a resident of the village, had started protecting the forest as early as 1980. The initial phase of his protection initiatives was as troublesome as those in Ober; after each good phase of protection, the entire forest would be cut down, he remembers. Mahadev addressed the young men of his village saying that, 'It is a shame that outsiders can take away *our* forests'. By 1987, Mahadev was an accepted forest leader and, on 14 February of the same year, he named the village committee the *Van Raksha Samiti* (VRS), or the Forest Protection Committee. He started to hold regular meetings and initiated protection through forest patrols.

In an important turn of events, in March 1989, the NGO, Ram Krishna Mission (RKM) approached Vanadag to work on development schemes. As is typical of RKM, it constituted *Vivekanand Seva Sangh* (VSS), a self-help body to oversee its work in the village (see chapter 7). The NGO, unlike in Ober, retained Mahadev as the leader of the VSS.[14] Mahadev in turn merged his own committee with the VSS. This was crucial for Mahadev because, during the weekly meetings in Vanadag (about various NGO-initiated development work), he could continue to review the forest management and advocate penalties for defaulters of forest offences and non-attendance of meetings. He occasionally, with great caution, sanctioned cutting Sal poles for construction and repair of houses. There were cases when a piece of confiscated lumber would be sold to a villager for Rs. 50, and the money would go into the community fund. Mahadev's forest protection forum would not allow villagers from outside Vanadag to take out even shrubs and fuelwood. It would instead put great insistence on forest patrols; indeed the phrase that recurs the most in the minutes year-after-year is the reminder that 'we must not let the forest duty slip'.[15] Meetings frequently had 35 people (there are only 50 households in the village), and differences were easily ironed out. The minutes from meetings demonstrate that Mahadev Oraon used psychological warfare: in the

---

[14] Mahadev faced cynicism and opposition to his leadership, similar to the case of Ober's Lahru Bediya. In 1992, the second in command of VSS, Kishun Baraik, resigned and remained quite vocal about the hopelessness of VSS and its demise within six months. Mahadev instead got another member of the village elected, and Baraik's responsibilities were effortlessly passed on to him.

[15] Mahadev Oraon wanted five to ten people to patrol the forest in two shifts each day. In a few instances, it is recorded that forest guarding was extended to the morning and night (due to some timber theft). Although the records kept mentioning the names of forest offenders, there is, however, little indication that these names were ever reported to Forest Department personnel.

seven years of records, he does not even once let the villagers compliment themselves for protection of what had become an invaluable forest cover.

Mahadev Oraon was luckier than Lahru in his ability to combine forestry concerns with village development. By 1994, because of the involvement of the NGO, Vanadag had accumulated a number of assets sponsored by RKM: a community hall, hand pump, deep well, public lavatories, solar cells, water pipes, etc. Moreover, a number of activities were institutionalized, including the practices of holding meetings, daily night-schools, rental of agricultural implements, distribution of seeds, fertilizers, and hosting training on agricultural matters. The VSS was also an effective conduit for information on development projects and funds from Jawahar Rozgar Yojana (JRY) and the State government (discussed in chapter 7). Mahadev himself showed great credibility in balancing the dual interest of forest management with rural development issues. He insisted on transparency and held consensus for lower posts in the VSS. The support for Oraon had widened because the issues of forest protection, which not everyone approved (not with the same intensity at least), became part of village development programmes.[16]

### 5.5.2 The Meeting Records at Ober: Lahru Bediya's Forum

Lahru Bediya started to record the forest protection that he initiated in Ober on 12 March 1985. As a guiding principle, he identified the future of the village with the sustenance of forest wealth. He called the voluntary forest protection group *Van Bachao Samiti* (VBS) or Save the Forest Committee. Early on, Bediya suggested that an area in their adjacent forest be carved out where the resident and outsiders would not be allowed to cut forest. He proposed a Rs. 10 fine and use of force against the offenders. The villagers were required to make donations to the committee's funds. The record shows that people from other *tolis* of Ober came along to join the committee. However, Lahru Bediya was never on good terms with the villagers from *Upar toli* who do not figure in the meetings. As mentioned earlier, one year after inception, Lahru used the forum to address moral issues, such as drunkenness, thefts, and village morality. He also used the forest forum to hold many meetings on alleged rape, maltreatment of women, affairs, and so on and, in each case of conviction, he proposed a fine and/or excommunication.

Lahru Bediya occasionally contemplated village development during the meetings. He complained of an inactive *panchayat* and suggested digging a well on

---

[16] Like other forest leaders, Mahadev Oraon also shied away from addressing the women directly. However, in early 1992, in one of the largest meetings (62 residents, including women, attended), Mahadev asked the women of his village not to enter the *rakhat* forest to fetch firewood. He reasoned that there was no dry, fallen timber in the forest, and the only way they could get firewood would be by tearing apart the green poles. In the interview, Mahadev recognized the limited interaction he and indeed the VSS could manage directly with women. However, he pointed out that since 1996, an NGO, Anganbari, has started to work exclusively with women.

their own and discussed measures needed to save the crop from elephants (the Forest Department is normally responsible for compensation for damage caused by elephants). These initiatives seldom bore satisfactory results. Unfortunately, when the NGO, RKM, started to work in Ober in 1992 and selected young representatives from Lahru's rival *Upar toli*, they took away the development aspect from Lahru's patronage. On 15 February 1992, Lahru, comprehending the implications of his exclusion from the NGO's activities, wrote to RKM with the complaint that the NGO should reconsider its decision because the representative that it was supporting was not 'the right one'. He desisted from suggesting his own name and, instead, proposed that RKM should take a leader who had the consensus of the village. Little attention was paid to Lahru's protests. Lahru wrote again to the RKM's headquarters in Ranchi that they should not go on with their work unless they 'corrected the wrong they have done'. In his interview, Lahru said that by electing a leader from *Upar toli*, RKM had made him the 'bastard son' of the village. He said, 'You cannot marry off a younger son of a family and have a feast, while the older son is left a bachelor'. Indeed, by then the development project had given enough legitimacy to the NGO-run forum, *Vivekanand Seva Sangh* (VSS), and the young leaders were beginning to make decisions in forest matters as well. Lahru noted in frustration during a meeting in 1993:

> ... for eight years not even a sapling was harmed. However, in the last two years, 30 households have joined the Mission (RKM) and the forest is being secretively cut down. The women have started to sell timber in the market... hence RKM should oust the current leaders who don't care for the forest ... if not the VSS should go from the village. (Ober's meetings registers 1993, my translation).

Once the village was officially registered by the FD as a Village Forest Management and Protection Committee (VFMPC) under the leadership of Lahru Bediya, he tried to reinstate himself as an effective leader in the village. In 1993 and 1994, he continued to call for forest duties and penalties. In 1994, outsiders were caught in their *rakhat*, but villagers could not care less, so Lahru filed a case. As mentioned in chapter 3, Lahru continued to run to the lower-level officials from the Forest Department to complain of irregularities in the village. There was, however, little support from the FD. In 1996, the minutes note that the lower-level foresters had been informed that the government intended to take up cottage industries, digging wells, and bee-keeping in the villages. Lahru, as a leader of the VFMPC, used the occasion to issue a fresh call to the villagers to give their names and enjoin his efforts in forest management (in return for development projects). Little came of this.

### 5.5.3 West Bengal FPC General Meetings

In Gopegarh, villages have kept the minutes only for those meetings held at the all-FPC level. The annual general meetings are attended by the *sabhapati* (the head of *panchayat samiti*), *anchal pradhan*, beat officer, and the executive members of the FPCs. However, other topical meetings are also held at the behest of the beat office. The microplans demonstrate that villagers expressed interest in development microplans.[17]

The first meeting in 1991 recorded the names of the villages who were recommended for Joint Forest Management. The meetings that followed were concerned with routine matters, such as the list of beneficiaries in each village who were to be registered and information about committees that were not working well.[18] They also recommended other responsibilities that the FPCs had had, including protection of forest, holding meetings in the villages, and reporting forest offences. The meetings that followed discussed the work at hand, generally preparation of microplans concerning harvests and occasionally the villagers' demands for plantations, selection of species, and, on invitation of the FD, suggestions of development work, such as building culverts, earthen dams, roads (recorded mainly in the years 1992 and 1993) for the next five years.[19] In 1996, the meetings suggested the formalization of the remaining villages under the JFM agreement. In 1997, one village, Delua, was removed from the FPC list and an elephant scare was discussed. More importantly, the Forest Department, realizing that a number of villages had qualified for the timber harvest, had started drawing a list for harvest operations for the next five years.

### 5.5.4 Discussion

Using the records from meetings, this section has illustrated that villagers do not treat forest management in isolation from other rural issues. Indeed, in Vanadag, Mahadev Oraon was able to indulge in an intense form of forest protection over a long period of time only because he could combine forest protection with village development. The forum he led is responsible for bringing several development projects into the village. One of the meetings recorded an outburst from a fellow villager in Vanadag, '*Pahle gaon rakho, phir ban rakho*'. [First save the village, then the forests.] In the case of Ober, Lahru's style of protection was equally passionate but he failed to find an ally who could cater to other interests and

---

[17] Similar experience is reported in Haryana where the villagers utilized the majority of funds generated through JFM programmes for development activities and lesser amounts for forest development (Datta and Varalakshmi 1999).

[18] The JFM resolution in Bengal states, as part of the duties of an FPC member, 'The Forest Protection Committee shall maintain a minutes book wherein proceedings of the meetings of the Executive Committee held from time to time as well as the proceedings of the Annual General Meeting of the Forest Protection Committee will be recorded and such minutes duly attested shall be sent to the concerned Range Officer for record' (GOWB 1990, clause 2 [iii]).

[19] Actual development initiatives would be little. In 1997, Rs. 5,000 was, however, allotted for the beat to purchase a thresher and insecticide sprayer (*Source*: Gopegarh beat office records).

legitimize his forest management methods. The new leaders who were sponsored by the NGO, despite having little concern for forest conservation, have drawn more attention and loyalty among fellow villagers. In West Bengal, the records of meetings and microplans in Gopegarh betray that the villagers expressed interest in the FD's involvement with development schemes.[20]

### 5.6 The Gender Divide in Community Forestry

There seems to be an agreement that pre-JFM debates on women's crucial and unique relationship to forests has helped them with a formal representation in JFM (Locke 1999). On the other hand, it is noted that, despite the efforts to involve women in the JFM process, an actual participation that is based on women's needs and interests remains minimal (Sarin 1995, 1996b). Correa (1996) points out the dismal attitude of field-level staff who would neither register women on their rosters nor encourage them to join male members during FPC meetings. The following section considers the division of labour between men and women, communication patterns on management of local forests, and representation of women in forest committee meetings.

Division of labour in extraction of forest usufruct is sharp.[21] Women members of households carry out most of the fuelwood extractions, often on a per day basis. Also, women in areas of high male seasonal migration (in both Annagarha and Gopegarh area) are left 'behind' in the villages to scour the forests. Forests in some ways are their exclusive work-zone, so that men find it socially awkward to scrounge forest floors. The role switches when men have to cut trees for timber, construction of houses, and agricultural implements.

Despite women going into the forest more frequently, the control that men exercise over forestry practices is unmistakable.[22] Men believe they can keep

---

[20] That forest activities be integrated into larger management and economic activities has been recommended elsewhere too (see Poffenberger and Sarin 1995, for example).

[21] Das (1992) reports the strict code of division of labour that is followed in household and agricultural activities among Jharkhand tribals. Women, for example, face being excommunitcated if they take up tasks (such as ploughing or thatching of roof) that are meant to be performed exclusively by men. Rocheleau et al. (1996) note 'gendering of geographical spaces', where rural women are excluded from certain physical spaces at one instance and, at others, use the commons to socialize while collecting grass and fodder at a distance from menfolk.

[22] In chapter 4, we noted areas of success and failure for the all-woman VFMPC in Maheshpur, how it was artificially instituted by the Forest Department, and its dismal performance due to the lack of support from the FD, cohesion between the committee sub-units and understanding of forest needs and perception of the member households by the woman leader.

women from violating the rules set by forest forums. A standard explanation by women in Annagarha, Jharkhand, over extraction of fuelwood is, '*Pooch kar late hain*'. [We ask the men before we bring forest usufruct.][23] The case changes slightly in Bengal, where men do, at times, collect fuelwood and even barter it in markets in the nearby towns. However, they are men who invariably cut down trees for timber-related purposes. They reason that, '*Woh laa sakegi*'? [She afterall can't carry heavy logs.]   Despite a less profound role in collection of forest usufruct, men demonstrate considerable knowledge of time, species, and pathways that regulate choices in the forest on the part of their womenfolk (as shown by Sarah Jewitt [1996], and in contradiction of Vandana Shiva's [1989] ecofeminist arguments). Indeed, the familiarity of women with the forests, and hence their affinity towards them cannot be overemphasized. Although forests provide women with a *zenana* womb where they socialize with other female members of the community and *toli* to get essential forest usufruct and graze the livestock, they remain 'alien' quarters where familiarity is seldom beyond a point, never past a time: what with herds of elephants and, according to one respondent in Annagarha, even a 'small' tiger that are present in forests, women rarely venture out on their own.

Researchers with ecofeminist concerns have reported of disappointment about women not holding primary membership in JFM or not being invited to key activities such as meetings  (Correa 1996; Sarin 1996b). It is also noted that the forest community groups are represented to outsiders primarily by men and women are permitted to have little contact with external institutions (Brodt 1998). Indeed, representation by women in village meetings (including in self-initiated forest protection groups) is negligible. The protection of the forest is again considered to be a male bastion. As mentioned in chapter 4, the forest patrols, in practice, are informal and irregular. Although the women report the presence of outsiders or unwanted felling and, as in the case of Bhagwati Chowk, occasionally offer physical resistance, it is the men who are expected to act as the forest marshals. A few men responded that when they disobey, the women can be threatened with violence, '*Marenge nahin*'? [Won't we beat them if they disobey?] However, in practice, the men, like the FD officials, may be reluctant to accost and stop women in forests. The young respondents said they find it difficult to stop a woman. They are shy about doing so and also they can get rascally naughty: '*Nocch leti hai*'. [They scratch if we get near.] It is noteworthy that, although the complaints by Sarin (1995, 1996b) and Correa (1996) as noted earlier are true (that women do not get formal representation in formal FD-sponsored forest committees), that is the case even in voluntary forest committees that are formed and managed by villagers on their own. However, informal modes of communication ensure that women obtain the essential information in community-based forest management.

---

[23] In Lemha, however, where business-dependent women are intensively involved with the Sal- leaf plate making business, they may listen to menfolk but do not show submissiveness. Many men said that, 'They (the women) will do what they wish to'.

## 5.7 Conclusion

The first section of the chapter aimed to shift attention to an important attribute of participatory forest management in South Asia, namely the forest-directed influences on forestry practices. I addressed temporal and spatial facets of forest and how they influence community forestry practices. However, I pointed out that the approach has limitations and stopped short of proposing to dismantle the discipline of political ecology and create one that would better serve if it were renamed ecological polity.

I also argued that, although the state still maintains a strong hold over both tenure and forest land practices, the participatory paradigm has made inroads for unprecedented concessions that allow rural people greater control over the village and protected (community) forests. The villagers are using protection patterns similar to those used by the FD, albeit with different sensibilities about protected areas of forests that lie in proximity to their villages and on which they depend to fulfill their needs. Armed only with a limited knowledge of tenurial arrangement in JFM, the tribal population, in particular, has demonstrated various autogenous activities in the issues of forest management.

The forest forums are spearheaded by village leaders, often by those who demonstrate a passionate interest in forest resources. Chapters 4 and 5 noted how village leaders play a crucial role in the management of forests. In the case of the voluntary forest protection groups, the importance is so great that villagers often associate forest committees with their leaders' names.[24]   More sustainable leadership results, however, when the leaders are able to combine forestry issues with other facets of rural life, particularly development.  Ober's Lahru Bediya depended more on rules that were inhibitory than on facilitating development. Mahadev Oraon, on the other hand, was fortunate to lead the development reforms through the NGO-initiated projects and, as a result, could ensure support for his conservationist forest agenda. In Bengal, Poltu Singh similarly combines his role as forest leader with his access to *panchayat* and the Forest Department. These inherent characteristics (protection patterns, usufruct use, associations with village leaders), provide important lessons for participatory approaches to natural resource management.

---

[24] Panangatt (1983) mentions five kinds of leaders in the tribal villages in Santal Paragnas, Jharkhand: elected, educated unemployed, ex-military men, political leaders, and traditional leaders. In Ober, Lahru Bediya and Sanichar both embodied educated unemployed leaders who, at one point or the other, commanded village consensus (elected). Both leaders marginalized the traditional leadership: Lahru by challenging him, and Sanichar by taking over the important responsibilities of village development.

Chapter 6

# *Panchayat* and Community Forest Protection Groups: Equity and Institutional Compliance in Rural Development Forestry

## 6.1 Introduction

Chapter 6 compares the community-based forest protection groups with the traditional village institutions, the village councils or the *panchayats*. *Panchayats* are institutions meant for village-level governance with an all-round development focus. They are provided with constitutional rights, and their structural and functional network links them to the larger State politics. They have also been given responsibilities, mostly as a coordinator, in Joint Forest Management. The Forest Protection Committees (FPCs) and the voluntary forest protection groups, on the other hand, are newly established bodies meant for forest management alone. They have limited power to enforce their objectives and little autonomy to negotiate with other institutions.

In West Bengal, the *panchayats* are parallel to the civil administration and assume responsibilities in a range of activities that include health, education, administration, and environment. In Jharkhand, the *panchayats*, despite having been ascribed with similar, if not identical, roles, have achieved dismal results in rural administration. Moreover, in 1997, the *panchayats* were made non-functional by the State High Court because of overdue elections. Again, in Bengal, the Forest Committees have been sponsored and supported strongly by the Forest Department; in Jharkhand, on the other hand, the villagers have depended instead on their own recourse to secure local forest usufruct. *Panchayats*, nonetheless, loom above the overall village polity in both Jharkhand and Bengal. The formal responsibilities they have been entrusted in JFM make their presence felt in forest management as well.

While juxtaposing the village councils with the forest committees, this chapter tests the degree and nature of homogeneity of interests, opinions, and functions of these two key stake-holding institutions in Joint Forest Management. It analyzes the worthiness of the newly established issue-specific institution, the community-based forest management groups, against the traditional and larger body, the *panchayats*. It thus endeavours to answer whether decentralization of decision making over natural resources can effectively be fostered within the current institutional setup where forest committees hold specialized forest management responsibilities and the *panchayats* play the role of an overall coordinator.

It is argued that, despite a marginal status of the forest protection groups as compared with the established *panchayats*, these committees create a power base and legitimacy of their own. The forest protection groups have best been able to secure the forests for peasants who depend heavily on these resources; particularly so when they find little support from elsewhere. *Panchayat* leaders, on the other hand, are not averse to compromising the interests of the forest. Although the chapter commends the role of forest protection groups in forest management, it recommends that they work not in seclusion, but with support from the FD and *panchayats*.

## 6.2 Village Councils and FPCs: Composition and Structure

This section examines the structure of *panchayats* and the Forest Protection Committees and voluntary forestry groups. In comparing them, I explore the commonalties (dual membership, interests on welfare, organizational capacities) and the conflicts (area under jurisdiction under each institution, incentives to participate and defect) that JFM faces with respect to these two village-based institutions.

### 6.2.1 *Panchayati Raj*

*Panchayats* have existed in north Indian villages principally to serve as a judiciary body. A Hindu institution, *panchayats* have typically been represented by the elites. They also served to link the villages to the larger state economy (Bayly 1991). By supplying human and material resources, they provided a framework that held the Hindu-caste system together (Lal 1988) and served as an intermediary through which the larger state processes could interact with the rural systems. The institution was cherished by the Indian nationalist leaders as India's claim to village republicanism and the exercise of democratic norms at the grassroots level. After Independence, the Indian provinces established *panchayat* governance through legislative Acts. These Acts provided the framework under which the *panchayati* governance would be carried out. In Bihar (and Jharkhand), the State government, for example, was to 'establish in each village, or parts of villages, or for more than one village', these councils called *panchayats* (GOB 1964, 6). In 1992, the 73rd amendment to the Indian Constitution made it mandatory for each State to have *Panchayati Raj* governance in villages (Rajaraman et al. 1996).[1]

---

[1] On the other hand, researchers have noted the disappearance of a tribal system of governance, such as the *pargana* council (Panangatt 1983) and the *paharia* system (Jewitt 1996) that coincided with support for the *panchayati raj* institutions (PRIs).

*Panchayats* have also had the responsibility of managing the village commons, including those that have forests.

*Panchayats* follow an elective system as in the rest of India, in which representatives are elected for five years who in turn choose the *panchayat* leader. The members of a *panchayat* are elected for a term of five years by the villagers on the basis of universal adult franchise. *Panchayats* are provided with concrete powers to stake claims on land, fix rules and taxes in local markets, take loans from the government and banks and, importantly, as a repository and conduit for funds that are meant for rural work.[2] They possess *faujdari* or the policing powers that permit the leaders to arbitrate village conflicts and, on conviction, punish the offenders with fines and recommend imprisonment. The decisions taken at the *panchayat*-level are legally enforceable. Moreover, the level of representation (both formal and informal) ensures *panchayat* contacts with the villagers and the higher echelons in the bureaucracy and State politicians.

*Panchayats* are elaborately organized, have an all-round development focus and are provided with constitutional powers. In West Bengal, the *panchayats* are organized in a three-tier system: at village-, intermediate- and district- levels (*gram panchayat, panchayat samiti*, and *zilla parishad* respectively) and function through as many as nine departments.[3] In Bihar and Jharkhand, *panchayats* are to follow a two-tier system organized at village and district level.[4] *Panchayats* have been responsible for managing village forests, and since the onset of JFM, they are meant to supervise JFM efforts as well. In West Bengal, the FD continues to align its JFM efforts in the same way that the *panchayats* are structured and function. A

---

[2] In Bihar (and Jharkhand), for example, the 1963 Act states that *panchayats* should be allotted with not less than 6.25% of the revenue that the State collects from agricultural land. Moreover, the 73rd and 74th Constitutional Amendment Acts, 1992 provide for a decentralised public finance system and make the *panchayati raj* institutions (PRIs) responsible for fiscal devolution and finance management (see Rani 1999 for a discussion).

[3] The *panchayat* in West Bengal is headed by the *sabhadhipati* or the chief executive who represents the *panchayati raj* institutions (PRIs) at the district level. He is assisted by nine *karmadakshya*, or department heads, one each for finance, civil works, public health, education, relief, food and supplies, electricity and unconventional energy, fishery and husbandry, and *Ban-o-Bhumi* (forest and land). In Bengal, the bureaucrats work in tandem with the *panchayat*. For example, the district magistrate is in consultation with *sabhadhipati*, the *panchayat* leader at the district level, whereas the block development officer (BDO) coordinates with *sabhapati*, the *panchayat* leader at the block level.

[4] In Bihar (and Jharkhand), the *panchayat* leader, *mukhiya*, is assisted by eight executive members, six of whom are elected. *Mukhiya* heads the executive whereas the judiciary officer, the *sarpanch*, is responsible for judicial matters. *Mukhiya* is also responsible for advising the block development officer (BDO) on development work. A fully-fledged traditional *panchayat* has the following administrative elders: headman (*mukhiya*), deputy-headman, overseer and his assistant, village priest, and his assistant (Panangatt 1983).

post-JFM circular issued by the headquarters in West Bengal, for example, expressed,

> Forest officers of the district will be associated with p*anchayat* bodies, in addition to their own duties, for implementation of various afforestation schemes that are done by *panchayats* from their own funds (GOWB 1997b).

### 6.2.2 Community Forest Protection Groups

Forest committees were officially organized and recorded since 1988 in West Bengal and 1990 in the rest of the country. These committees are essentially non-statutory bodies and invested with little real budgetary (Sivaramakrishnan 1996) or executive power. They are not registered under society or cooperative acts that could allow them to function as autonomous bodies. Moreover, the JFM agreement between the Forest Department and the village community is a 'resolution' by the State governments which, in essence, is a statement of intention and not legally binding for the State or the Forest Department.

The organizational structure of FPCs too has limitations. Although States differ on how a village forest protection committee is to be constituted, many, as is the case in Jharkhand and West Bengal, have in practice adopted universal membership, i.e. all the households are registered as member beneficiaries. The committees are to be headed by an executive committee, with representation from the *panchayat* and the Forest Department. In doing so, JFM assumes homogeneity in composition of the village population and the level of dependence on forests, where the members would have a similar stake in forest conservation. The voluntary forest protection committees in Jharkhand, on the other hand, are obviously not subject to limitations from the JFM framework. As discussed earlier, these committees typically organize around a single leader, and membership principally comes from the villagers who have a strong interest in the forest products. It was also noted that these voluntary forest forums try to coax the non-participants – both within and outside their community – to comply with their forest management norms. Nonetheless, these bodies too, like FPCs in West Bengal, are limited in their reach and power as compared with *panchayats*.

### 6.2.3 Discussion

Unlike FPCs, *panchayats* are powerful entities because of their history, political networking, and statutory status. In the JFM framework, they are members of the executive committee that allows them to both monitor and control the functioning of FPCs. On the other hand, there is no provision that allows FPCs to negotiate with other institutions, nor are they given judiciary powers to resolve conflicts, nor an authority with which they can prevent forest offences. They do not have a complementary relationship with the *panchayats*; for example, they cannot use the *panchayat's* executive and judiciary powers for forestry or village development purposes. Hence, the FPCs must function within this constitutional and functional rigidity.

### 6.3 *Panchayats* and FPCs: Compliance Between Two Rural Institutions

In its policy guidelines on Joint Forest Management (JFM), the Indian Government called for cooperation between the forestry and non-forestry institutions. The GOI's letter on Joint Forest Management (GOI 1990) suggested that *panchayats* represent the village communities on participatory forest management. The letter stated that,

> ...access to forest land and usufructory benefits should [belong] only to the beneficiaries who get organized into a village institution, specifically for forest regeneration and protection. This *could be the panchayat* (my emphasis) or cooperative of the village, with no restriction on membership. It could also be a Village Forest Committee (GOI 1990, clause iv).

The letter, to be sure, had remained open to the manner in which village communities would be invited to manage forests (however, it restricted the State to allow access to forest by specific individuals). The GOI initiative, which was informed by the West Bengal experience in participatory forest management, ignored the more focused approach which the West Bengal Forest Department had taken in Arabari and subsequent endeavours in participatory forest management. Although the FD had involved the *panchayats* in forest management (through *Ban-o-bhumi Samiti*), it did so with a conservation interest. Appreciating the heterogeneity of interests and stakes that different population groups have in forests, it had invited only select groups for forest management. With the goal of raising forest cover in southwest Bengal, the FD had targeted the impoverished rural population, particularly the tribals. The 1989 resolution in West Bengal had reflected this sentiment.

> The beneficiaries shall be identified from amongst the economically backward people living in the vicinity of forests concerned (GOWB 1989).

Once the Government of India had asked the State governments to invite all the communities for JFM, the resolution in West Bengal was altered to one that invited all the households to membership in the JFM. The JFM resolution in Jharkhand that was made in response to the GOI's letter also heeded the universalization in forest committee formation and was clear in the guidelines about the constitution of VFMPCs.

> One representative from every family of the village will be member of the Village Forest Management and Protection Committee (GOB 1990).

The centre's resolve to replicate the success of Bengal and take up JFM in the entire country meant (particularly through grant of universal membership) that members who played only a small role in the management of forests were also entitled to shares in forest usufruct equal to those who were more dependent and invested greater time and energy in forests. The Forest Department also assumed that the executives who were to head each of these committees could bring about consensus on various forest management issues.

On the other hand, to promise equity and use democratic and decentralized means in forest management, the *panchayats* were not only to be members of the executive committees in the Forest Protection Committees, but also to be responsible for each of the three key stages of the JFM programme: registration, monitoring, and usufruct distribution (see GOWB 1990, GOB 1990). As a result, not only is the membership in JFM spread out to the population at large, the JFM is inextricably linked with the *panchayats*. However, what might appear to be a complementary relationship between two rural institutions is instead mired in situations in which the FPC and the *panchayats* are in contradiction, and even opposition to each other. For example, in giving executive membership to *panchayat* leaders, it is assumed that they can represent and understand well the forest needs of all the members of forest committees and act in a reliable, efficient, and just manner in the realm of forest management.

In practice, this is not always the case. For example, the leaders who represent *panchayat* are not averse to trading forest usufruct for gains in the *panchayat* electoral politics and otherwise. The *panchayat* leaders may not share the same FPC and, although they may represent a particular village in a *panchayat* on routine village matters, on forests, they can be members of another FPC, leaving the village with no real representation in forest management.[5] With respect to territorial configurations, the JFM arrangement presents a number of contradictory situations. The constitution of forest committees is, by default, limited to villages that lie in the vicinity of protected category forests. This jurisdiction of *panchayats*, on the other hand, characteristically depends on demographic factors (often on the count of heads, but also on the make up of the population; for example, tribes and members of certain castes in the scheduled list are to have their own *panchayat*). There is seldom a situation where one finds a one FPC-one *panchayat* situation. Moreover, the territorial jurisdiction of a community forest protection group over a forest often does not concur with that of the *panchayat* to which it belongs. For example, as is the most common case, more than one forest committee is located in one *panchayat*, and the forest that is put under the management of that FPC could, in practice, have a history of use (hence potential contestation) by villagers from

---

[5] For example, the leaders of Phulpahari reside in nearby Golabichowk who, though they share the same *panchayat*, are not members of Amratola-Phulpahari Forest Protection Committee.

another *panchayat* (for example, the residents of Maheshpur exploiting the forests in Nawagarh or Ober).

### 6.3.1 Discussion

Two processes occurred side by side when the Government of India recommended JFM as the principal manner in which the protected category forest be managed in the country. The participatory forest management initiative that had remained limited to select forest dependent groups in West Bengal was made open to everyone through universal membership of FPCs (and VFMPCs). *Panchayats* were invited in larger numbers than ever to participate with the state in Forest Management and were made responsible for forest management committees. However, this presented an asymmetrical relationship between the *panchayats* and FPCs because of the roles that are assigned to each institution, and the ways the executive (*panchayat*'s leaders) functions (sometimes to the detriment of forests and the interests of forest citizens) and the contradictions in territorial jurisdictions of the two institutions.

### 6.4 Case Studies

This section discusses the community forest protection groups and *panchayats* in Jharkhand and West Bengal. It is argued that the forest protection committees, despite several limitations, are best able to secure forest usufruct for their communities. Burman (1996) has argued that the non-statutory status of FPCs is a major limitation in their playing an effective and democratic role in forest management. In another paper, he has asserted that *panchayats* should, as is the case in Rajasthan and Uttaranchal, be entrusted with JFM (Burman 1997). This section, however, argues that one does not witness a proto-political institution in community forest protection committees. In these committees, villagers have ably negotiated with fellow residents and villagers from outside in regulating access to local forests. They also take help from the *panchayats*, the FD, and NGOs to establish forest protection norms and try to engage them in 'their' version of forest management and in rural development. *Panchayats*, particularly in West Bengal, continue to have the key role in the larger village polity and command enormous legitimacy among the rural population. In Jharkhand, the embeddedness of the *panchayati raj* institutions (PRIs) is less evident, and, since its dissolution, the presence of the *panchayat* is felt informally and mainly through the legacy of former *panchayat* leaders. It is suggested that forest committees should not be left subservient to the village polity and should instead get support from the *panchayats* in ways that they can negotiate as equals on forest management and other support activities.

### 6.4.1 West Bengal

The *panchayat* office for most of the villages in Gopegarh forest beat is located in Konkabati. The *panchayat* covers 32 villages in all and, as is typical in Bengal, function through the nine departments with the *sabhadhipati* as the head of the council. A number of villagers in recent years have benefited from *panchayat*-run projects, such as the Jawahar Rozgar Yojana (JRY), Indira Vikas Yojana, Integrated Rural Development Projects (IRDP),[6] and other welfare schemes. Villagers unanimously credit the *panchayat* for carrying out development work in villages, such as dug wells, ponds, and recent electrification. They also recognize the famous role it played in facilitating the distribution of vested land to the villagers.[7] Nonetheless, the *panchayats* have drawn several criticisms. Despite more than two decade of left politics, the role of *panchayats* has remained limited to managing funds that trickle down from the top and in several ways it has mimicked the bureaucratic administration it had set out to change. Although *panchayats* in West Bengal remain largely free of corruption and serve the target groups (Sengupta and Gazdar 1997), they are not immune to local pressures, limitations in funds, and the larger state polity.[8] Maity (1997), for example, reports bias in allocation of benefits in the Phulpahari *panchayat*. The leader, Dhiren Mallick, comes from the dominant clan of Lodha community, and other communities are at a disadvantage in getting benefits from *panchayat* schemes. As noted earlier, the *panchayat* leaders have used forests as incentives to get votes in elections. However, this seldom makes the leaders corrupt in the eyes of the villagers, who wish them to deliver goods on other more essential fronts.

In Amratola, *panchayat* politics plays a dominant role in the overall village polity. The population make-up is diverse and so is the dependency on forest. The caste-Hindu households are better off than the rest of the population, and their womenfolk do not go to the forest for collection of fuelwood. Even those respondents who depend substantially on forest produce and are against the *panchayat* representatives (they voted for the rival Trinamool Mamta Congress) complained little about the *panchayat* as far as forest management was concerned. As discussed in chapter 4, the blame was laid on the Forest Department, market pressures, and Phulpahari and Khairulla villages. *Panchayat* is seldom seen in

---

[6] See, however, Mathur (1995) who, although sceptical of the poverty alleviation programmes, agrees with other authors that Bengal has performed better than several other States in the country in the allocation of IRDP funds to rural poor.

[7] The *panchayat* recommends potential beneficiaries to the District Land and Land Reforms Office land distribution.

[8] *Panchayats* are used essentially for bookkeeping, subsistence-level work (seasonal employment, paltry loans) and as a political tool to create vote 'banks' for the State-level politicians.

competition with FPCs. A respondent said that other institutions such as the FD and NGOs 'come and go' but *panchayats* are there to stay.[9]

On the other hand, Poltu Singh in Bhagwati Chowk has been able to secure forest usufruct for the resident villagers. He had shown concerns about the protection of the forest adjacent to his village since the early 1980s. When the villagers started facing a shortage of fuelwood and fodder, he was a natural choice to head the forest protection forum. As discussed earlier, many conservation and extraction norms in Bhagwati Chowk FPC have since been established informally through village consensus. The use of forest is not limited to the prescriptions within the JFM concessions – i.e. fuelwood on a needs basis, and a share of usufruct at harvest. Villagers regularly take logs of wood for construction of houses and agricultural implements. The villagers have used the legitimacy derived from the FPC to safeguard their interests in the local forest. They have also had confrontations with infiltrators who are often from the same *panchayat*. Poltu Singh, a former *panchayat* leader, successfully negotiated with the FD and the *panchayat* that the residents of Bhagwati Chowk alone would exercise exclusive rights to fuelwood and Sal leaves in their forest.

Although no longer a member of *panchayat*, Poltu Singh remains the leader in the eyes of the residents of Bhagwati Chowk because of his formal control over a vital resource. Bhagwati Chowk residents are able to keep the villagers from the neighbouring village and often from the same *panchayat* at bay. This contrasts with Amratola where the dominant *panchayat* leaders compromise the forest interests. Bhagwati Chowk FPC's response to forest management is an example of how the villagers use their membership to build relationships with other institutions and secure the forest for themselves.

The villagers hold dual membership in the *panchayats* and Forest Protection Committees. However, in cases where the *panchayat* remains only nominally representative or indifferent to forest usufruct concerns of villagers, the FPCs provide an effective platform for managing forests to meet essential needs. The FD should endeavour to identify such committees and bolster their efforts instead of trying to align JFM with the *panchayat* design in a manner that would leave the principal representative of the forest citizens (the FPCs) subservient to these councils. However, this is not to suggest that the state should create a divisive strategy between FPCs and *panchayats*, but instead it should take FPCs more into confidence. In extending JFM membership to *panchayats*, the FD should strive to undo (through the partnership) what was achieved through colonial settlement operations; legal separation of the 'field from forests' (Sivaramakrishnan 1996, 465). Indeed, taking cognizance of the villagers expectations, the FD in West

---

[9] This is not to state that villagers do not complain about the *panchayat* or their leaders. The complaints that they mention concern the partisanship practices by their leaders; that 'they make you run a lot if you need something, and they are slow in finishing the projects they are entrusted with'.

Bengal has invited an integration, albeit limited, of forestry work into the larger development of villages.

> It is not possible for the FD to meet [the] support activities out of their own funds. There are many anti-poverty programmes implemented by the *panchayats*. The FPC members should benefit from these programmes (GOWB 1997, 112).[10]

### 6.4.2 Jharkhand

The niche that forest protection groups occupy is even clearer in the case of Jharkhand. Unlike West Bengal, Jharkhand has had a different history in terms of village-level governance and relationship with the Forest Department. Villages in Annagarha lack both support from the Forest Department and a formal *panchayati raj* system. As noted earlier, in Annagarha, the foresters have done little to foster a trustworthy relationship with the forest citizens. The *panchayats* too have had a patchy record in their ability to provide uniform access to development and agrarian reforms. Moreover, since 22 April 1997, the *panchayats* were dissolved by order of the State's High Court because of overdue elections. *Panchayats* continue to play informal roles through former *panchayat* leaders who, for example, are still associated with the development projects that are carried out by the block offices. They are invited to the meetings at the block office, called usually once a month (they get 20 Rupees for each attendance).[11]

Similar to Bengal, the Annagarha villagers comprehend the usefulness of forest protection groups as compared to *panchayats*, based on their experience of each institution. In Nawagarh, for example, many Munda villagers said that the *panchayat* is a 'benevolent force that protects us'. The village of Ober that falls within the jurisdiction of the Nawagarh *panchayat*, on the other hand, has received little help from *panchayat*. As the centre for local governance, the Munda community of Nawagarh has been better able to strengthen development (e.g. culverts, roads, school, tube-wells, etc.) and institutional base (e.g. police, post office, information network, respectability, etc.) in their village. The Bediyas in Ober village find themselves in isolation when it comes to their relationship with the Munda-dominated *panchayat*. Instead, through voluntary forest protection groups and the subsequent NGO-run forum, the villagers in Ober have tried not only to institutionalize their perceptions of rights over forest resources and methods of forest management, but also used the forum to invite development work. For communities with a minimal *panchayat* presence, these specialized forums can work not only to secure forest usufruct but also to initiate engagements

---

[10] The department's involvement with the *panchayat* is evident elsewhere too. Another letter from the FD (GOWB, 1997b), for example, requests the *sabhadhipati* of Midnapore to allocate 15% of the Jawahar Rozgar Yojana (JRY) share on afforestation programmes and the department would be happy to advise on the procedures.

[11] Since February 1998, the block development office (BDO) took over the *panchayat* work.

in other areas of rural life. Similarly, the *panchayat* leaders of Maheshpur *khas* dominate the politics, but forest interests, particularly of the tribal population, are little catered to.

### 6.4.3 Discussion

The case studies for Bengal and Jharkhand show that the forest committees in cases of high dependence and able leadership are able to articulate effectively within the structure and functional spaces that are available to them. However, the forest protection groups do not necessarily work in opposition to the *panchayats*. JFM provides a platform for the two rural institutions (through dual membership and common leadership) not only for an effective and equitable forest management but also rural development.

### 6.5 Conclusion

The juxtaposition of *panchayats* with forest protection committees provides a useful paradigm to gauge the worthiness of the newer, work-specific institution. In both Jharkhand and Bengal, the forest committees in several instances are working not merely as the 'sounding board for schemes that the department would wish to undertake in villages' (Sivaramakrishnan 1996) but have used the forum, both formally and informally, to secure forest usufruct. The *panchayats*, on the other hand, are not always sensitive to the forest-based needs of the villagers.

In the JFM programme, the state has provided the *panchayats* with a dominating managerial role. Nonetheless, the villagers in both Jharkhand and West Bengal have used JFM membership to secure forest usufruct often in opposition to fellow villagers from the same *panchayat*. It would be imperative, in such cases, that the Forest Department bolsters the initiatives that are made by the members of the FPC. To make forest committees subservient to the *panchayat* and the dominant village polity would not be an effective solution for forest management. Instead, the Forest Department should provide support to the community-based forest protection groups from which it draws its membership and ensure that the *panchayats* complement their needs and roles in Joint Forest Management.[12]

---

[12] Chapter 8 carries a discussion on how the recent guidelines issued by the Ministry of Environment and Forests (GOI 2000, 2002) have attempted to ensure the autonomy of JFM committees.

Chapter 7

# Putting Voluntarism to the Test: Case Studies of NGOs in Bengal and Jharkhand

## 7.1 Introduction

This chapter discusses the case studies of two NGOs, the Indian Institute of Bio-Social Research and Development (IBRAD) and Ram Krishna Mission (RKM) that work towards fostering participatory forest management and rural development in West Bengal and Jharkhand respectively. The objective of this chapter is to examine the working methods that are employed by the NGOs to promote Joint Forest Management (JFM). The ways in which they address rural development, either as part of a forest management initiative or otherwise, are also examined.

The Government of India invited the voluntary agencies (VAs)[1] to work at the 'interface between State Forest Departments and the local village communities for revival, restoration and development of degraded forests' (GOI 1990) to help the Joint Forest Management efforts. Referring to the classic tools which the NGOs use, I evaluate the effectiveness, efficiency, and impact of the projects taken up by IBRAD and RKM. This chapter also discusses the organizational structure, funding opportunities, and the work philosophy of the two organizations. The final section of the chapter examines the constraints that the NGOs face in their respective States.

IBRAD has been criticized on several counts. The organization, despite following the rhetoric of development work (rural appraisal, sensitization, capacity-building, a bottom-up approach) not only constantly undermines the sensibilities and needs of the rural community, but also fails to impart sustenance to its projects. The survey work and operating methods are patronizing and lack competence. There is a mismatch between the villagers' expectations and needs and what the NGO strives to do. Although IBRAD's partnership with the forest bureaucracy is commendable, it is argued that the NGO has essentially used this contact to gain access to the rural communities and failed to use it to the advantage

---

[1] The terms Voluntary Agency (VA) and Non Governmental Organization (NGO) have been used interchangeably.

of the villagers.  Even so, working with an extroverted attitude, IBRAD follows a formal plan of action and has published regularly. It has disseminated the results in workshops and training programmes.

In Jharkhand, the work of *Divyayan*, a wing of a large NGO, Ram Krishna Mission (RKM), is examined. *Divyayan* was conceived in 1969 and initially worked as a quasi-polytechnic institute to train farmers in modern agricultural technology. The NGO has subsequently shown sustained involvement in agriculture, health, education and development projects in the villages it has adopted. Although *Divyayan* has not addressed forest management in any explicit fashion, the strength that the NGO-run forum commands in the villages has nonetheless affected forest management.

## 7.2 NGOs and Joint Forest Management

The role that NGOs play in the field of rural development generates a mixture of lofty optimism and rhetoric (Hulme and Edwards 1995; Howes 1997). These voluntary agencies, with flexible organizational models (Heredia 1988) and methods, are credited with using innovation in experimentation and providing entry points for radical works (Faust 1996; Sethi 1982; Sarin 1996b; Warren 1995).[2] NGOs are expected to perform better than governments in promoting participation and converting aid money into development (Mathur 1997). Their contributions in development, particularly in the third-world context are both cherished and debated (Sundaram 1986). Indeed, the methods they have used to foster participation, raise awareness, and mobilize the local personnel and resources (Singh 1996) are parameters against which similar activities may be tested.

Although the Government of India (GOI) recommended that NGOs be invited to help promote Joint Forest Management, it permitted only a limited role for them. The JFM letter from the GOI stated that the NGOs are 'particularly well suited for motivating and organizing village communities for protection, afforestation and development of degraded forest land' (GOI 1990). However, the letter remained guarded about how the NGOs were to become involved on the forest land. It cautioned that 'no ownership or lease rights over the forest land should be given to NGOs' and the 'access to forest land and usufructory benefits should be given only to the beneficiaries who [became] organized into a village institution' (ibid., clause [ii] and [iv]). These directives initiated a qualified support by the FD for inclusion of NGOs in the JFM programme. The FD in West Bengal envisaged that the presence of a well-meaning NGO could be a helpful factor in cases where the 'villagers are poor and ignorant, and the FD, on the other hand, are subject to

---

[2] Sarin, for example, notes the work of the NGO, SAATHI (Social Action for Rural and Tribal Inhabitants of India) in central India, Warren of AKRSP (Aga Khan Rural Support Programme) in Gujarat.

bureaucratic tradition' (GOWB 1997). A similar role was seen in Jharkhand; it was perceived that NGOs could help facilitate a partnership between VFMPCs and the FD and provide feedback, training, and capacity building to help promote JFM in the State (GOB 1994, annex 9).

The West Bengal FD tried to facilitate avenues where voluntary agencies could promote the JFM programme. Understandably, the areas that the FD wanted the NGOs to tackle were linked with strengthening the FD's own initiatives on JFM: the formation of Forest Protection Committees, ensuring the sustenance of the committees, and 'orientation' of the FD's field staff and villagers towards the new participatory rhetoric. The NGOs were expected to work along with these traditional institutions that had taken up newer roles for themselves. The forest bureaucracy in Bengal could, however, not only claim to have more experience but also an established access to various aspects of forest management and rural life. Arguably, this would have required the NGOs to function in a way that allowed them to work in tandem with the official agencies, and remain in competition with these giants.

### 7.2.1 NGOs in Bengal and Jharkhand

There are three important NGOs working to foster Joint Forest Management in southwest Bengal: the Ram Krishna Mission Lokasiksha Parishad (RKM-LP),[3] the Rural Development Centre (RDC),[4] and the Indian Institute of Bio-Social Research

---

[3] Lokasiksha Parishad is a part of the parent NGO, Ram Krishna Mission in West Bengal. The NGO, like its counterpart in Jharkhand (see later section), is involved with rural development particularly in villages that are remotely located and poverty-ridden. The organization carries out such projects as 'fistful of rice saving scheme' and training programmes (in tasar cultivation, lac culture, fisheries, bee keeping, animal husbandry and Sal-leaf plate making). The NGO also employs qualified 'resource persons' from other organizations to provide support for its projects. With respect to its involvement in JFM, Ram Krishna Mission, in consultation with the FD, identifies clusters of villages in a forest range and then works there. The Ford Foundation is the main funding body of RKM-LP for the JFM work.

[4] Headed by Dr. R.N. Chattopadhay, RDC is a research-oriented centre affiliated with the Indian Institute of Technology (IIT), Kharagpur (West Bengal). Since 1993, the centre has focused on JFM efforts. The major concern of RDC is the processing and marketing of non-timber forest products (NTFPs) by the villagers. The NTFP collected by the villagers, Dr. Chattopadhay explained, are bought at a pittance by the town merchants and sold at a much higher price. 'If reasonable technology and knowledge are imparted in marketing and processing the NTFPs, the villagers could increase their earnings by multifold', he reasoned. RDC has assisted villagers with better technology in making Sal-leaf plates, processing medicinal plants (Indographis *snipoculata*, for example), mushroom plantation, and apiary training. The funds for forestry work come from the Ford Foundation, the IIT, and the Forest Department. The latter has, for example, granted experimental plots to the RDC to train the villagers on 'livelihood generation'.

and Development (IBRAD). IBRAD is, arguably, the most prominent NGO working on JFM in the State. The key methods that IBRAD uses to promote participatory forestry are the various rural appraisal techniques. These tools are now widely used to seek voluntary interventions. Chambers (1983) describes Participatory Rural Appraisal (PRA) as 'a family of approaches and methods to enable rural people to share, enhance, and analyze their knowledge of life and conditions, to plan, and act'. It is in this sense that IBRAD purports to make use of them.[5] It is argued that the rhetoric that the NGO employs is in line with the current progressive thinking in development circles. Nevertheless, there is a considerable lack of effectiveness and sustenance in the projects that IBRAD undertakes.

In Jharkhand, on the other hand, there is a large number of NGOs. In Annagarha alone, there are three NGOs that are working with the villagers: the Agrarian Assistance Association Trust run by a local villager from Maheshpur, Abdul Aspand Yar Khan,[6] the Society for Rural Industrialization (SRI),[7] and *Divyayan*, a wing of the NGO, Ram Krishna Mission (RKM). *Divyayan* has had considerable influence on agriculture and development in the tribal villages in Annagarha and, obliquely, also on forest management. *Divyayan* provides a

---

[5] Chambers, however, warns that the PRA methods can easily become an excuse for sloppy and hurried field work, over-adoption, and misuse of techniques (Chambers 1983).

[6] The Agrarian Assistance Association Trust has had a chequered history. Earlier, it worked in the Santhal Paraganas district (south Bihar, now Jharkhand) as an unregistered body but, in 1988, Mr. Khan shifted to his native village, Maheshpur and got the organization registered as a Trust under India's Society Act. Mr. Khan has organized awareness festivals on the Environment Day (5 June) where amid cultural activities and festivities, group discussions are held to promote conservation of forest. In 1998, he was in conversation with the rival faction in Ober (led by Lahru Bediya against the *Divyayan*-run forum) to bring development projects from the Block Office. Mr. Khan has also worked off and on in the nearby villages of Benti, Gandhigram, Sirka, and Bisa. The trust is, however, a marginal force as a promoter of participatory forest management in Annagarha.

[7] SRI was established in 1985 with its head office in Ranchi and since has functioned as a 'technology resource centre' for rural population. On 13 October 1995, the 'technology demonstration centre' was inaugurated at Chamghatti in Annagarha block to promote rural development by training villagers in procuring alternative sources of energy (through solar panels, gassifiers, smokeless stoves), agroprocessing (of mushrooms and tomatos) and low cost construction of houses (from the funds provided through Indira Vikas Yojana). Although SRI is not directly involved in promoting JFM in Annagarha region, it seeks to play an important role in rural development. The field office at Chamghatti covers 92 villages and 19 *panchayats* of Annagarha block. The Department of Science and Technology in New Delhi and the Department of Electronics (Government of India) are SRI's main funding bodies. SRI has also received funds from the Ministry of Environment and Forest in New Delhi to train staff from Jharkhand's Forest Department (GOB 1994, Annex 9, 25).

contrast to the working principles of IBRAD. RKM's choice of methods is fairly conventional in that it engages with villagers over a long period of time to intensively cover a range of issues from agriculture and health to education. RKM has proved more sustainable in obtaining results.

## 7.3 IBRAD and Participatory Forest Management

S.B. Roy founded the Indian Institute of Bio-Social Research and Development (IBRAD) in 1985 after giving up a government job with the Geological Survey of India. The NGO became operational in 1987 and initially worked in health[8] and soon expanded to other areas including tribal development, joint irrigation management, and participatory forestry. IBRAD opened three field offices in West Bengal, one each in Kharagpur, Vishnupur, and Jalpaiguri, with its head office at Kolkata. The members of staff at IBRAD grew from four in 1989, to thirty-two in 1997. Each of the field offices has a programme officer and graduate field-workers on short-term contracts. A range of donors fund IBRAD, of which the Ford Foundation (India) remains the biggest donor. Other donors are the Department for International Development (DFID), the Swedish International Development Agency (SIDA), Euro-consult, and the World Bank. The Government of India and the State of West Bengal, too, have financed IBRAD for carrying out training programmes for the forest officers.

IBRAD is one of the two best-known NGOs working on participatory forestry in West Bengal (another is the monastic Ram Krishna Mission). Being based in Kolkata has been advantageous for the NGO. During the initial phases of JFM, IBRAD was invited by the Forest Department to become a member of the 'apex body' committee.[9] The interaction with the high profile bureaucrats in Kolkata provided the organization with introductions to key people and permission to work in the forest villages of southwest Bengal. My field experience at Bhagwati Chowk (Midnapore) and Jhantiboni (Vishnupur) illustrated that IBRAD introduces itself in the village through village leaders who are usually also influential in *panchayat* politics. Again, the 'entry' is mediated by forestry and civil bureaucrats. This is, however, not to suggest that the process creates mistrust among the villagers or that it has adversely affected the distribution of any of the benefits that the NGOs might bring into the villages. However, the top-down disposition taken by the NGO while initiating the contact has affected the perceptions of both the villagers and the

---

[8] For example, IBRAD took up a project on impact assessment of immunization. As part of the project, IBRAD encouraged the members of target communities to participate in a government-run immunization programme.

[9] As noted in chapter 2, the 'apex body' meetings were started at the initiative of the Forest Department in West Bengal. Key NGOs were invited to discuss areas that needed to be addressed to promote JFM in the State.

NGO: on the one hand, the villagers usually expect only their leaders to know about the NGO's activities in their village and do not find themselves involved, and second, it is difficult for the NGO to understand the processes that they cannot learn from leaders and lower-level FD officials. Nonetheless, the extroverted outlook provides IBRAD with an edge over those voluntary organizations that are working in remote areas in seeking funded projects[10] for rural development, organizing a network of resource personnel, and publishing and disseminating results.

### 7.3.1 Succession of Goals

After 1989, IBRAD diversified its activities into forestry, agriculture, training, ethno-botanical studies, microplanning, research, and various other facets of participatory development, such as health, watershed management, irrigation, rural and tribal development, forestry, and gender studies. IBRAD terms its activities 'need-based and action-oriented research and training in the field of development' that 'aims to develop human resources through a holistic approach capable of evolving solutions to both particular and special problems' (IBRAD undated, g). In essence, IBRAD has never specialized or worked intensively in one field, and instead has used its field experience and contacts from one project to venture out into another. Whereas this might invite innovations from a voluntary agency, a closer scrutiny, however, indicates that IBRAD's activities are guided by the availability of funds and opportunities. IBRAD depends heavily on external funds. This not only weakens its ideological bases, but the grounds on which it can bargain with the donors.[11] It is true that there are few avenues for acquiring voluntary income or opportunities for local funding. However, when judging an institution that is dependent on external support, one must respect the rationale for its viability (Hulme and Edwards 1995) and remain guarded when the *means* of an NGO start dictating its *ends*. The ability to keep one's operations solvent has to be distinguished from an organization whose sole purpose becomes self-perpetuation.

The organizational culture of IBRAD is determined in its entirety by its director, S. B. Roy. Roy admits to have fashioned IBRAD based on his visions of

---

[10] For example, IBRAD was able to clinch a World Bank project to prepare microplans for village development and enhancement of employment opportunities in the Buxa tiger reserve region (to last from March 1998 until September 2001). Interestingly, due to lack of information, few NGOs applied to the public-tender notice that was put up by the Forest Department on behalf of the World Bank. IBRAD has also received corpus funding from the Ford Foundation for projects on participatory forest management.

[11] NGOs frequently use the methods and goals to which donors subscribe. As a solution, it has been suggested that funding bodies insist that the NGOs produce a matching grant from the target population, which can be a percentage of what the donors are going to offer (Sundaram 1986, 127). The voluntary bodies would then feel obliged to work closely and responsibly at the grassroots level and over a longer period of time.

development and voluntarism. As the organization has grown, it has increasingly become procedural, and the hierarchy within is two-tier: one occupied by the director, S.B. Roy, the other by the rest of the members. The NGO, whose entire dictas and dogmas are fashioned by one man, faces a near absence of intraorganizational democratic processes and is run like what Chandra (1985) calls a 'privately owned shop'.

### 7.3.2 The Work-strategy of IBRAD

This section discusses the field practices of IBRAD by examining each of the categories in which IBRAD has stated that it works to nurture participatory forestry (see IBRAD undated, g).[12] The working plan that IBRAD follows can be broken down into a number of stages (see Figure 7.1).[13] A project typically involves consultation with the senior-level forest officers to help select the sites where the NGO will work. This is followed by visits to the villages where introductions are made with resource personnel in the villages, and background reports are drafted. The NGO then draws out its working plans and decides on the nature of the work it will take up in the village. IBRAD has worked under three broad categories to promote Joint Forest Management in West Bengal: institutional strengthening, social action, and ecological research activities (IBRAD undated, g).

### 7.3.2.1 Institutional Strengthening: Bilateral Matching of Institutions

The failures of Social Forestry indicated that there was a need for social engineering through processes such as group formation, innovative leadership, villagers' participation in decision making, introduction of incentives and penalties (Mitra 1995, 105) to bring the Forest Department and the villagers to the same place. These two key stakeholders in Joint Forest Management indeed need to arrive on a common working ground for the JFM to succeed. IBRAD suggests a need for 'bilateral matching of institutions' and resolution of conflicts between the FPCs and the Department.[14] The NGO proposes that both institutions need to agree

---

[12] The facilitation of participatory forestry, to IBRAD, hinges on rural appraisal methods and open-ended discussions. These methods had originally evolved in the late 1970s as rapid and effective information gathering techniques (Anonymous 1987). The key to these techniques is their *flexibility* and thus there is no definitive description of approaches.

[13] The organization has published what can pass as 'do-it-yourself' manuals that advise its staff members on methods that need to be followed for seeking participatory results in villages.

[14] The theoretical framework that IBRAD has designed to advise its field officers to work on participatory issues is discussed in its publications. The working paper on 'Strengthening Institution' (IBRAD undated, a), for example, discusses how people can consent to participation. Amongst the identified 'causes' for poor functioning of a FPC, IBRAD identifies 'lack of clear values and norms'. As a remedy, IBRAD proposes 'inculcation of

on procedures and plans of action to enable fruitful forest management (Roy et al. undated). However, the way IBRAD has done this shows a unilateral approach to the issue. The level at which IBRAD intercepts is mainly at the village (FPC)-level. For example, when IBRAD interacts with the senior bureaucrats (during the training sessions or during the 'apex body' meetings [the latter are defunct now]), it uses bureaucratic-level leverage to gain access to the rural communities or carry out a project on behalf of the Forest Department. However, it does not use this advantage to challenge the FD on various issues where JFM has fallen short or further the goals situated at the village-levels.   On the other hand, IBRAD has

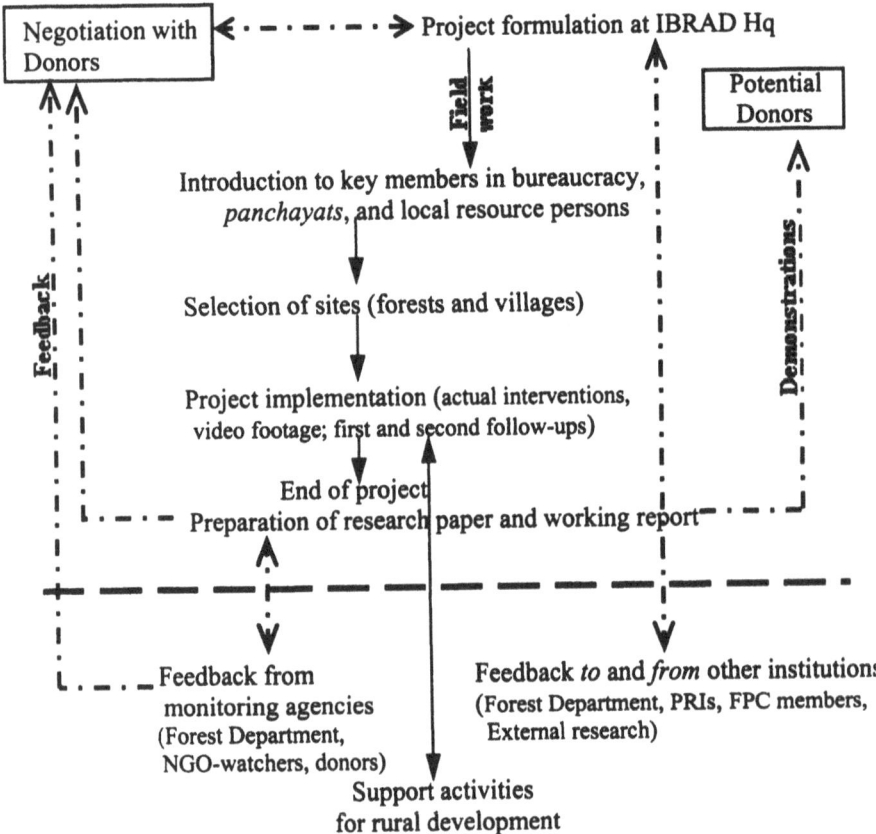

*Note*: IBRAD's work-plan (above the line, ▬ ▬)
    Facets that are largely ignored (below the line)

**Figure 7.1 The Work-strategy of IBRAD: Emphases and Omissions**

values through social functions, ritual, and other traditional devices as well as through collective pressures' (ibid.).

worked with the villagers advocating that they make adjustments to accommodate the tenets of the JFM agreement (for example, hold mandatory committee meetings and guard forests).[15] IBRAD seldom addresses the failures of the FD or the complexities (historical, constitutional, and temporal and spatial factors) while playing match-maker between the FD and FPCs. There is, for example, no case study report in which IBRAD challenges the department or the state on the JFM framework or the implementation of the programme. The village Forest Protection Committees alone are left to adapt to the norms set up by the bureaucracy. In doing so, IBRAD has effectively pronounced the Joint Forest Management in its current form an ideal paradigm in which forests should be managed.

### 7.3.2.1.1 Conflict Resolution

In one of its publications, IBRAD states that 'behind any conflict there is a lack of communication and information, and the presence of illogical value systems' (Roy et al. undated). The conflicts, IBRAD states, arise from inequalities in the areas of gender, religion, race, political ethos, occupation, and the distribution of resources. However, IBRAD tries to ease animosities through village-level meetings, where attempts are made to create a network of communication between the two rival groups. The work it did in Ghugimura-Vinodbari FPC in Bankura is a case in point. The field workers from IBRAD started to get the members of the two communities to meet in the village courtyard and discuss their problems. IBRAD could elicit a promise from the villagers that they would protect their forests and maintain a log-book on meetings and forest guard-duties. IBRAD followed up the meetings with a few more visits, but soon the workers stopped coming to the villages. As a result, the practice of holding meetings became non-existent in Ghugimura-Vinodbari FPC. Apparently, the reason the agreement between the two factions occurred was that, because of the incentives, the villagers felt they had to cooperate with an organization that, for them, has sanctions from the State and the Forest Department. It was perceived that an amiable partnership with the NGO might bring in development work. As a result, in the absence of a regular presence of IBRAD, the temporary truce was broken and the essential differences between the two villages were never resolved. The narrow focus that IBRAD kept for resolving the conflict between the villages excluded the possibility that there could be wider social, political, and economic reasons for the poor functioning of the FPCs. Also, the method did not take into account the fact that villagers could put up a united front for the short term, while all fissures remained underneath such an agreement.

---

[15] S.B.Roy reasoned that 'it is necessary to work with the forest bureaucracy to be able to change the system'. It is, however, not to imply that IBRAD's attitude towards bureaucracy is that of complete cooption. On the contrary, Mr. Roy, for example, has criticized the bureaucracy over the methods that the FD follows to solicit participation (see below).

### 7.3.2.2 Capacity Building and Social Intervention

The process of capacity building is based on the premises that IBRAD has established for resolving conflicts between FPCs. IBRAD suggests that the poor functioning of rural institutions is because of a lack of leadership, the absence of roles and responsibilities, a dearth of values and norms, and the inadequacy of reward and punishment (IBRAD undated, e). As a cure, IBRAD proposes 'sensitization' of the target village communities in which the villagers are made aware (sensitized) of the existing physical and human resources and their potential (IBRAD undated, c).[16] In a field situation, the staff members from IBRAD, using PRA techniques, identify people who can take responsibilities for the forest resource. IBRAD also proposes identification of leaders (including the training of old ones), rituals (plantation ceremonies, quizzes in the village) that can assist in forest management. IBRAD expects that the villagers will take on unique roles and responsibilities among themselves to manage the forest resource. During the village meetings, the staff members of IBRAD enlist actions that need to be encouraged by the villagers, and those that are harmful to the forests are discouraged. IBRAD hopes that the process will create opportunities for duties and norms to become institutionalized, and the villagers will have their 'capacity built' for an efficient forest management.

In the case of Bhagwati Chowk village, the process of sensitization involved having the villagers do vegetation monitoring and wealth ranking. The villagers mapped the local forest by transect walking and later discussed the findings in the village meeting. IBRAD proposed that through these activities and discussions, villagers not only were able to identify the problems they faced in protecting the forests, but also gained a sense of 'belongingness' towards the forest resource. IBRAD, in its report on a similar exercise, noted that, after one such meeting, 'the villagers felt assured, the process of belongingness started and the doubts at the back of their mind that the forest really belonged to the government, not the community, were lessened' (IBRAD undated, a). Shivanand Bhagat at Bhagwati Chowk, however, narrated a different story. He said that, as the secretary to the FPC, he considered it his duty to show the people from IBRAD around. He often accompanied the staff members from IBRAD with two or three villagers while 'they looked around in the forest'. When asked if the visits by IBRAD had helped to motivate the villagers for forest conservation, another respondent replied, 'Our jungle was good and standing before IBRAD came in'. In its publications, IBRAD frequently asserts that the villagers are not 'aware of their own problems' (or capacity) or that the Forest Department staff displayed 'utter ignorance about the

---

[16] Sensitization has been defined as, 'A process of educating the people by feeding them with adequate information and knowledge. Its effect lies in the fact that after sensitization, a person can make decisions based on realistic, dependable, and complete information' (IBRAD undated, c).

people whom they had to deal with'.[17] These views are not only not constructive, but they are almost certainly untrue and call into question the credibility of IBRAD's approach and judgement of the situation.

The methods and level of interception (at the FPC-level) that IBRAD employs for 'social action' are similar to those used for 'strengthening the institutions' (IBRAD undated, a). Although rural appraisal and sensitization form the core methods, IBRAD occasionally takes up support activities (such as the 'fistful of rice'[18] or 'money-saving' schemes) to bolster the participatory social capital. The 'fistful of rice' scheme that IBRAD had carried out in Ghugimura-Vinodbari villages met, in fact, with enthusiasm. The villagers maintained a log book, and many households diligently saved rice for the scheme. Although this project yielded some money for the village-pool fund, the villagers, in the long run, were disappointed to find the scheme was limited to collection of money and, for example, no other activity followed the NGO's visits. The project soon ceased to exist. Although this case points to the importance of support activities in lending stability to participatory initiatives, in the case of IBRAD's 'fistful of rice' scheme, both the support activity and the main body of work were largely misnomers.

### 7.3.2.3 Ecological Activities and Research

IBRAD does not carry out its ecological activities with a strict ecologist or conservationist point-of-view. The NGO instead uses appraisal tools to collect data on forest and, based on them, makes suggestions to the FPC members on how to manage their forests. IBRAD suggests that villagers adopt 'scientific' methods for vegetation monitoring, such as the use of quadrats and estimation of vegetation biomass to manage their forests. The NGO suggests that this would 'develop scientific skills and attitude among the villagers' and result in a 'trained manpower to conduct certain types of vegetation studies on their own' (IBRAD undated, b). It also speculates that vegetation monitoring will provide an 'avenue for using indigenous knowledge in combination with scientific knowledge for better

---

[17] A publication from IBRAD explains, 'The villagers were found to be a disorganised lot, and it is unfortunate that these poor people were neither aware of their own problems nor about the bad consequences of the felling of forest trees. They were totally oblivious about their own capacity to solve their own problems through discussion and cooperation. On the other hand, even the Forest Department staff [...] were a discontented lot, and victims of their own inhibitions, false values, judgements and above all, utter ignorance about the people whom they had to deal with' (IBRAD undated, j).

[18] The fistful of rice scheme requires that the villagers put aside a fistful of rice in a container and, after a period (typically a month), sell the collection at market price. This money can then be used either for personal use or put aside as a community emergency fund.

management of the forest' (ibid.),[19] although how this is to be accomplished is not made clear.

The work carried out by IBRAD on vegetation monitoring in Bhagwati Chowk has, however, left bitter memories. The villagers complained that the exercise was a waste of time for which they were not compensated. Shivanand Bhagat stated that,

> We accompanied the people from IBRAD with the expectation that a project or some benefit was going to come down to the villagers, and hence the survey. Instead, we are not even paid Rs. 10 for the *job* (my emphasis).

The villagers reported that on IBRAD's subsequent visits they hid and did not show up. Villagers well-acquainted with their forests saw their input as unnecessary work. Many villagers, including women, argued that they know the forest too well to be introduced to it through formal training. Although measuring the growth in height and width of the trees made little sense to them (because they can make an instinctive approximation), they were particularly vexed at IBRAD for not paying them for the investment of time and labour in exchange for the PRA exercises the villagers carried out for their team.

IBRAD has published its results in the form of working reports and research papers. Many of the papers are instructive about background information on villages, vegetation, and people. The research papers discuss useful areas, such as gender roles in JFM. Mitali Chatterjee, IBRAD's secretary, has reported on ecological knowledge and forestry practices of men and women in the area (Chatterjee undated; McGean et al. 1996). In addition, occasional collaboration with researchers from the Indian Institute of Forest Management, Bhopal, the Indian Institute of Technology, Kharagpur, and the Ford Foundation have resulted in research papers on ethnobotanical issues. However, IBRAD's research methodology and analysis lack scientific rigour and are characterized by populist and over-simplified results.[20] The bibliography is either missing or, if there is one, it is more often than not incestuous, citing mainly the previous publications of IBRAD. IBRAD's assessment of its own achievements is less than self-effacing. Working paper 35, for example, asserts that 'IBRAD, a professional organization [...] has initiated the programme of forestry development through people's participation... and [it] does not stop at revolutionizing the FPC alone' (IBRAD undated, f). Although which programme of forestry development is being referred to is unclear, the implication is that the role of IBRAD has been critical in fostering participatory forest management in West Bengal.

---

[19] Such speculation probably reflects a need to satisfy donor demands rather than a genuine belief that this is likely to occur.

[20] For example, the working paper number 4 (p 17), reports that the vegetation profile of a forest was *'fairly* good' (my emphasis) and concludes that 'after protection for 5 years, the forest started to regenerate *considerably'* (my emphasis) (IBRAD undated, k). Such studies serve little purpose in understanding the true nature of forest management.

The propagandist and self-promotional assessment of IBRAD shows a hard-sell attitude, which has little grounding in reality. Two senior forest officers, Ajit Banerjee and Narendra Pandey, opined that IBRAD, or for that matter NGOs in general, were not the 'big players' during the initial growth of JFM, and that participatory forest management was entirely an initiative on the part of the Forest Department with assistance from the *panchayats* and the villagers. Amitabh Singh Deb, the beat officer at Gopegarh Beat, compared IBRAD with the high priest in Hindu rituals; one who appears in the end and daintily puts the ceremonial banana topping on the preparation that has already been made by the *lower* priests.

### 7.3.3 Discussion

The rationale and working methods that IBRAD has developed are highly simplistic and patronizing, if not impractical. The field visits are brief and often done through key people. The 'hit-and-run' principle that IBRAD follows affects the sustenance of the activities and issues taken up in the villages. The implementation of projects by IBRAD consumes a small amount of time, and instead a good amount of resources is used up during the deliberation period (with the donors and also the bureaucrats and resource people) (see Figure 7.1).

Many of the approaches that IBRAD takes often go against the very grain of development efforts. S.B.Roy, for example, states that it is a 'myth that unless some material or financial incentive is offered to the villagers they will never join the programme of forest conservation' (IBRAD undated, h). This, for example, contrasts with Rangan (1993, 1997) who argues that the reason behind the contest between forest citizens and the state bureaucracy is the need for greater access to development.[21] IBRAD goes further, suggesting that material or financial support can actually be detrimental to institution-building objectives because material demands become the focus of the relationship with the villagers. There is little evidence of this.

### 7.4 The Case Study of the NGO, Ram Krishna Mission

This section discusses the case study of *Divyayan*, a wing of a large NGO, Ram Krishna Mission (RKM). RKM was established in Kolkata by the Hindu monk, Vivekanand on his return from the United States of America in 1897 (RKM 1998). Later, in 1909, the organization was registered under the Society Registration Act XXI of 1860 and grew into a relatively large organization with 135 centres in India and 34 abroad.

---

[21] IBRAD's viewpoint is contradicted also by Sahu who argues in one of IBRAD's Working Papers,'the poorest of the poor will continue to plunder nature for survival' (IBRAD undated, i).

### 7.4.1 Ram Krishna Mission (*Divyayan*): A Background

Ram Krishna Mission began to work in Bihar in 1899 initially to provide flood relief. Subsequently, it carried out relief provision in incidents of fire, cholera, famine, drought, and riots (these were limited to northern Bihar). The RKM centre at Ranchi was established in 1927. In March 1969, a specialized wing, *Divyayan*, was conceived within the larger body of RKM, mainly to train people in agriculture and development activities (RKM 1997, 2). In 1977, the *Krishi Vikas Kendra* (KVK) or the Centre for Agriculture Development was added to *Divyayan*. KVK has worked as a quasi-polytechnic institute to transfer modern agricultural technologies to farmers and carry out support activities in the villages (RKM 1994).

During the early years, RKM received funding from the Unitarian Service Committee of Canada, and some funding came from the GOI's Ministry of Welfare. In 1977, the Indian Council for Agricultural Research (ICAR) recognized *Divyayan* as a centre for agriculture research (*Krishi Vigyan Kendra*) and since has provided its major assistance.

### 7.4.2 Working Methods of *Divyayan*

The Mission is headed by Hindu monks who employ several assistants and volunteers to run the various departments in the NGO. RKM in Jharkhand works fairly autonomously from the RKM headquarters in Kolkata. For example, both the nature of interventions and generation and management of revenue are carried out independent of the Kolkata branch. In villages, the NGO (*Divyayan*) works through key leaders and communicators. Although the working method of *Divyayan* is fairly standard, it allows a latitude for the villagers to shape the NGO forums according to their visions and initiatives. *Divyayan* works usually in tribal villages on invitation from the villagers. First, *Divyayan* invites groups of young farmers for training in a variety of farming and vocation skills for six weeks at its headquarters in Ranchi. Later, these men return to the villages and lead the NGO-run forum in their villages.[22] *Divyayan* additionally takes up construction projects that are financed by the state's welfare programmes and also follows up the activities in the villages it adopts with information, development projects, and support activities.

---

[22] The six-week training is in areas such as agronomy, horticulture, poultry, dairy, farm machinery, carpentry, welding, lathe work, bee-keeping, and mushroom production. There are shorter courses of three weeks for farmers who wish to specialize in one of the above-mentioned areas. The former trainees often return to the Ranchi centre for follow-up meetings and get-togethers.

### 7.4.2.1 Vivekanand Seva Sangh (VSS)

The young men who are trained at the *Divyayan* centre at Ranchi are responsible for running the NGO forums, called *Vivekanand Seva Sangh* (VSS). *Divyayan* considers VSS the most important of its activities, where the villagers are asked to build self-help groups that can bring in development 'without seeking help from outside' (RKM 1997, 16). The VSS leaders nevertheless maintain strong links with *Divyayan*.

Once a village has been registered as a VSS, *Divyayan* requires that the members contribute a nominal amount of money that goes to the all-VSS revolving account and is used by all the member villages.[23] Next, the villagers are required to contribute labour in building a clubhouse on the village commons where the activity of the *Vivekanand Seva Sangh* (VSS) can be coordinated. This building houses materials (seeds, fertilizers, pipes, and records), serves as a night school location and hosts village meetings and one-day workshops conducted by *Divyayan*.[24] The role of the leader is usually a permanent one and he is responsible for bringing information to and from the headquarters, carrying out routine jobs, such as night schools (see Table 7.1), and attending the monthly meetings at Ranchi. The representative is paid a token sum of money to run these errands on behalf of the NGO. He ensures that NGO-run projects are carried out, the membership is kept to an optimum level, and new members are sent to the *Divyayan* centre at Ranchi for training.

**Table 7.1 Activities of *Divyayan* in Select Villages in Annagarha (1995-96) (RKM 1997)**

| Villages | Registered members | Students in night school | Cash with VSS (in Rs.) |
|---|---|---|---|
| Maheshpur (in Lemha toli) | 20 | 48 | 9,243 |
| Ober | 59 | 76 | 36,322 |
| Vanadag | 60 | 67 | 22,500 |

---

[23] Revolving Fund of VSS: The total collection from all the member villagers is in the order of Rs. 1.24 million, with an average of Rs. 20,780 per VSS (RKM 1997, 22). This fund is meant to 'meet the agricultural requirement of the member villages' (ibid.). Using this fund, *Divyayan* purchases agricultural raw material, such as seeds and fertilizer from the market in bulk and at a lower rate and sells them as per the demand to members of the VSS (see Table 7.1).

[24] *Divyayan* conducts one-day audio visual training programmes in villages and covers such areas as farm research extension, social forestry, orchard development, tube well construction, lift irrigation, watershed management, community centre construction, control of diarrhoeal diseases, water sanitation, installment of biogas plants, and solar lanterns.

The work of *Divyayan* in agricultural support is noteworthy. Beyond the training that the NGO imparts at its town centre, it continues with support activity through the supply of agriculture-related material, such as high-yield variety (HYV) seeds, fertilizers, and irrigation pipes, and conducts frequent workshops to advise member farmers on methods to improve agricultural productivity.

### 7.4.2.2 The Role of *Divyayan* in Rural Development and Forestry

Apart from the fairly routine support activities that the NGO carries out in the registered villages (VSS), *Divyayan* also takes up a number of development projects, mainly construction work, such as digging wells, construction of roads, houses, and culverts. The projects are funded by state-run welfare programmes, such as the Jawahar Rozgar Yojana (JRY) and Integrated Rural Development Programme (IRDP). The NGO essentially works as a contractor, which receives the funds to carry out the construction in the village. The key way in which the NGO has made a departure from other contractors in the area is to ensure efficient and timely completion of the projects. Second, the villagers are asked not to hire labourers but contribute labour for construction and thus earn money from the employment. One of the large-scale undertakings that *Divyayan* has carried out is in *Jaladhara* (literally, water-stream) schemes (RKM 1991). The NGO got more than 800 wells dug in the period from 1987 to 1996 in the villages it had 'adopted' (RKM 1997).

However, *Divyayan* has had limited opportunities to become directly involved in forest management or the promotion of JFM. On the one hand, the officials of RKM excuse themselves on the basis that the Forest Department has made no efforts to invite the NGO to help foster JFM. (RKM was involved in occasional plantations and forest research under the Social Forestry schemes [RKM 1994b]). On the other hand, the popularity and strength that the VSS has gained in the village has produced definite impacts on the way local forests are managed. In Ober, the VSS leader, Pahlu Bediya, has displaced the forest leader Lahru not only in village development but also on issues of forest management and extraction of timber. The villagers reason, 'Pahlu *ka baat manne se fayda hota hai*'. [It profits to follow the NGO leader, Pahlu]. In Vanadag, on the other hand, the veteran forest leader, Mahadev Oraon, has usefully combined the roles of forest management with those supported by *Divyayan* (the impact of the presence of *Divyayan* in Ober and Vanadag villages is discussed at length in chapter 5).

### 7.4.3 Criticisms

The Muslim residents in Maheshpur claimed that *Divyayan* works only in those villages that have tribal populations because the tribals are gullible. They challenged the NGO to do development work in their villages instead.[25] Indeed,

---

[25] The antagonism from the Mahespur residents is also because of the Hindu background (of the founder and the current managers) with whom the NGO is associated. For its part, the

the VSS that have been registered are predominantly in villages that are composed of scheduled tribes (60%) and scheduled caste (20%) (RKM 1997, 5). The monk who heads the *Divyayan* reasoned that their mission is for the destitute and the illiterate peasantry, and only after 'everything has been done for them and there is spare time and resource that the RKM would work for the gentry'. Another distinct fact is that women are conspicuous by their absence in VSS activities. Not only are they not invited to be trained at the *Divyayan* centre in Ranchi, they find little space for themselves in the leadership of *Vivekanand Seva Sangh* (VSS) and are seldom invited to the meetings. Although *Divyayan* could hardly be blamed for intravillage activities, a senior monk reasoned that it was not possible for celibates to have women trainees on the *Divyayan* campus in Ranchi.[26]

A few villagers complained that too much demand is made on their time. There is, for example, an obligation to attend the meetings, which is an obsession with the leaders of the NGO-run forums. Finally, the limited involvement of *Divyayan* in forest management is a matter of concern. (Villagers, however, seldom criticized the absence of the NGO in forest management.) It is likely that *Divyayan* would be able to bolster forest conservation and equitable use of forest usufruct if it were invited by the Forest Department to combine its rural development initiatives with the management of local forests.

### 7.4.4 Discussion

The section argued that a large and specialized organization such as *Divyayan* has created a sustainable presence and impact in the villages. Where IBRAD fails, *Divyayan* succeeds; it creates agents in people, buildings, and projects that have a constant presence in the villages. Moreover, it addresses the essential needs of the villagers, such as agriculture, health, and education. In Jharkhand, in the absence of *panchayats*, *Divyayan* has played an important role as a conduit of information and in bringing in development projects from the bureaucracy that is notorious for red-tape and a patronizing attitude. For the villagers who were earlier plagued by dishonest contractors, *Divyayan*'s approach to construction work has come as a welcome change. *Divyayan* has also helped put the villagers in touch with officials in civil and forest administration.

*Divyayan*, however, has not addressed forest management in any direct manner. The increased membership and popularity of the *Divyayan*-run VSS in Ober

---

NGO makes it clear that it does not work to 'convert religious beliefs' (RKM 1997). Nonetheless, the material that the NGO distributes to children in night schools contains Hindu texts. On the other hand, and to RKM's credit, it remains secular in all its other core activities.

[26] A few cloth-spinning stations that were being managed by women and had been only newly installed by *Divyayan* as part of its support activity were observed.

villages has, however, brought the forestry issues into their purview. In Ober, the VSS has had a detrimental effect in that the new leadership is careless about forest management; in Vanadag, Mahadev Oraon has used the VSS to strengthen the management of forests in his village (discussed in chapter 5).

## 7.5 Constraints Faced by NGOs

There are several constraints that IBRAD and RKM (*Divyayan*) face while working in rural development forestry. There is an obvious limiting factor in the numerical strength of the organizations. For example, with less than forty staff members, it is physically impossible for IBRAD to address the more than three thousand FPCs scattered throughout the State of West Bengal. Although this may not ideally limit the work philosophy and successful models an NGO might generate for villagers to replicate, IBRAD finds itself small in comparison to the Forest Department. This often entails an unequal relationship with the department and prevents it from being radical in its approach. *Divyayan* overcomes this problem somewhat by building human resource capital in the villages it adopts. By training villagers at its centre in Ranchi and subsequently having them work for routine agricultural purposes and development projects, *Divyayan* ensures a long-lasting presence in these villages.

Second, the villages in southwest Bengal are grouped into political camps (the two important political parties are the Communist Party of India (Marxist), and the Trinamool Mamta Congress), and, not surprisingly, an NGO like IBRAD remains an 'outsider' as far as the core functioning of such ideologically committed village *panchayats* are concerned. Although the chapter has criticized IBRAD for taking a sheepish attitude towards bureaucracy, it is noteworthy that it is difficult to make progress in a rural set up without the support of senior officials. For example, despite all the antagonism at the village level, IBRAD still receives cooperation from junior forest officers because it holds a 'letter from the Principal Chief Conservator of Forests (PCCF)'.[27] In Jharkhand, RKM too has used its reputation and contacts to muscle its way into getting contracts from the government and the facilitation of funds to work in tribal villages.

The unlikely situation of NGOs being funded locally often places these bodies in a contractual relationships with the donors. This not only weakens the ideological bases but also the grounds on which the voluntary bodies may bargain with donors. For example, the Ford Foundation (India), IBRAD's major funding body, provides IBRAD with a wide latitude to work in, and there is little scrutiny of the NGO's works and policies. On the other hand, the voluntary agencies that are located in remote areas are unlikely to be recruited for such funded projects.

---

[27] N.K.Pandey, Divisional Forest Officer, suggested that IBRAD actually gains legitimacy in the eyes of the villagers through this introduction from the forest officers.

Last, the Forest Departments too have maintained a cynical distance from the day-to-day working of the NGOs. Although they have constitutionally facilitated the work of the voluntary agencies, they do not take a formal account of the activities which NGOs carry out.


## 7.6 Conclusion

The role of non-governmental organizations in rural development forestry has been noted with substantial optimism by academics and practitioners alike. Forest Departments have been asked to include NGOs in the JFM system. As a result, new NGOs have stepped in to work on forest management issues and the older established NGOs have begun to put the 'forest' component on their agendas.

IBRAD, while fostering participatory forestry, essentially proposes various participatory rural appraisal (PRA) exercises in the target villages. There are, however, limits to what can be achieved through PRA exercises by small voluntary bodies. Villagers, for example, want a multisectoral and integrated rural development and, as a result, often perceive their inputs in an NGO's initiatives as unproductive. Moreover, IBRAD seems to be using the PRA techniques less as initiators in a genuine and well-supported programme for forest management or development, but more as an extractor of information. PRA is used instead as an excuse to legitimize a superficially worked out project and information gathering for records and publications. IBRAD does not recognize the wider social and economic processes that underscore the predicaments in forest management, such as conflicts between two neighbouring FPCs over the local forest. Both the methods that the NGO adopts and the results that are published are simplistic. In effect, I question the very premises that inform the goals, methods, and results of IBRAD-run projects. On the other hand, I have suggested that a large and specialized organization has created a more sustainable presence in the villages. *Divyayan*, with its fairly large size, standard rigourous structure, and even patronizing attitude, has performed better through addressing basic needs, working as a conduit of development, and creating a strong base in the village.

Both NGOs, however, remain limited in fostering Joint Forest Management. The areas where the NGO could work include debates on equitable access and distribution of usufruct benefits from forests, the framework of JFM, promotion of autogenous activities (instead of undermining the traditional rural and institutional practices), and engagement of forestry institutions in rural development. There are also 'hard' challenges of development where NGOs need to intervene. The downward accountability (Hulme and Edwards 1995) should be encouraged where the target population is aware of the sources of income of NGOs and, these voluntary agencies do not appear as an enigma to the villagers. This would reduce the patronizing relationships between voluntary bodies and village institutions. The Forest Departments need to be more imaginative in opening areas where the NGOs can fruitfully participate in forest management. An end to the current isolated approach could initiate more meaningful roles from the voluntary agencies in resource management.

To conclude, the chapter states that IBRAD performs less well than it claims. This is not to say that IBRAD has worked less potently than other voluntary bodies (the report is, perhaps, a pointer to the general trend for several NGOs working in rural development forestry). I have argued that although IBRAD has been useful with some of its experimental models, *Divyayan* has proved more useful with conventional goals and methods. The chapter also states that villagers, on involvement with institutions from outside, strongly demonstrate expectations for multisectoral and integrated rural development agendas to be included in the NGOs' work plan. For an NGO to have an impact, a mere populist agenda will have to give way to readjustments that take into consideration a more strenuous regime and one that seeks new allies and a new legitimacy.

Chapter 8

# Conclusion:
# The Role of Ecological Institutions
# in Participatory Forest Management

## 8.1 Introduction

The concluding chapter summarizes the key findings in this monograph. It is also conscious of the research issues that were set out in chapter 2. Several lacunae are recognized in the JFM programme, and recommendations are made to render the programme more effective and lucrative for both the Forest Department and the forest citizens. The final section of the chapter suggests possible directions for Indian forestry and points out areas for further research.

Four institutions – village-based forest protection groups, the Forest Departments, *panchayats* (village councils), and non-governmental organizations (NGOs) – were examined across the States of Jharkhand and West Bengal. The focus of the research has been to study the various characteristics that mark community forestry and the relationships that village-based forestry forums share with their own members and other JFM institutions. The discourses that remain informed by a strict state-citizen dichotomy were criticized. The forest management nexus is perforated and diverse at just about every level. Any 'unique' categorization of forests, bureaucracy, citizens, forest use, and practice of forest policies in the current Joint Forest Management policy is misleading. It was argued that the shift in management paradigm was as much a consequence of the popular rhetoric on equity and welfare as it was the realization that forests next to habitation cannot be protected without seeking participation from villagers who live nearby. The impact of Joint Forest Management is evident in several ways. It is demonstrated that the members of Forest Protection Committees (FPCs), an institution formed on the JFM initiative, and the self-initiated forest protection groups are playing active roles in negotiating transactions of forest usufruct within and outside their communities. This includes creating 'zones of exclusion' where local forests become out of bounds for outsiders and approving customary extractive methods of resident villagers. On the other hand, JFM is primarily offered for protected category forests, and the Forest Department continues to exercise a strong hold both on the tenure of forest land and the managerial aspects of Joint Forest Management. *Panchayats* in their supervisory roles are not always found to be playing supportive roles in safeguarding forest cover or in securing usufruct for the forest-dependent population. The role of non-governmental organizations is found to be less clear. A standard, albeit superficial, participatory rural appraisal (PRA) method, that seeks participation is less helpful than those NGOs who are involved in village development and use the forum to bolster forest management initiatives.

It is suggested that the *participation* from forest citizens cannot be limited to soliciting their involvement and initiatives. Rather, it must provide a conducive atmosphere where these village-based forums can form linkages with other institutions and actors and bargain on a variety of issues pertaining to rural development forestry in a symmetrically located fashion. More autonomy is recommended for village-based forest committees and the lower-level staff of the Forest Department. The former should be able to determine working methods (while keeping to goals mutually agreed with the FD) that suit their interests and management methods and best uses opportunities available in exchange for the labour expended in forest management and building institutional relationships. The lower-level forester, on the other hand, should be equipped to involve itself in an independent dialogue with the villagers over methods of forest management. They should have access to senior offices and the decision-making systems to enable them to make periodic recommendations for adjustments in methods of management and changes in the Forest Department's goals in forest land.

## 8.2 Village-based Committees and the Forest Department: Key Stakeholders in Joint Forest Management

This section discusses the findings with reference to the village-based forest protection committees and the Forest Department. Features that are inherent to community forestry are noted. For example, the self-initiated forest protection groups work in ways that are remarkably similar to the villages that are registered under the JFM agreement. These usefully contrast with those features that are not recognized in the JFM resolution. Adjustment in the JFM framework that takes into account inherent elements in community forestry practices and better work environment for beat officials are recommended.

It is suggested that, paradigmatically, Joint Forest Management provides a most useful structure for allotting patches of state-owned forests to local villagers for management purposes. In allowing territorialization of the forest resource, the method of the state is close to what villagers inherently devise for local forest management. One of the most important strategies and analogous forestry practices used by villagers in both Jharkhand and West Bengal is the creation of 'zones of exclusion' in local forests to exclude outsiders from using their forest. However, the area of forest land that has been allotted by the Forest Department for JFM purposes may not necessarily be the area which the villagers identify for protection. The villagers' choice is usually influenced by factors such as the history of use and dependence by local population and even such spatial coordinates as proximity of the forests to their homestead and agricultural lands. The villages that are not situated next to forest, despite having similar needs from forest land, are typically left out of registration under the JFM agreement.

It was argued that the government's goal to universalize the formation of village forest committees around protected forests with a universal membership has not proved effective in every case. Often, a uniform, small group of villagers with members having high incentive to save forests performs well. However, this is not to suggest that smaller groups necessarily need to be ethnically homogeneous. Rather there is a need for a homogeneity of interest in the population that is supposed to manage a forest resource. Indeed, several non-tribal villages and different groups of population in the same village are engaged in similar practices of forest protection across the States. JFM has attempted to make room for participation by women by adding the 'women component' (Anonymous 1996). Although they remain absent in formal activities of JFM (in West Bengal), what is equally noteworthy is that women are absent in meetings and in the decision-making process in self-initiated committees in Jharkhand. On the other hand, it was found that women are usually knowledgeable about the protection rules that the community forest protection committee adopts and are often active partners in monitoring and even apprehending forest offenders.

Joint Forest Management recommends that the representation of forest protection groups is made through a number of executive committee members who are to be elected regularly. However, in practice, such egalitarianism and democratic attitudes are seldom the case. Instead, a handful of villagers (indeed, often only one), and particularly those who have a dependence on forests, a passion for forest conservation, and inter-institutional skills, can override differences within the community. They are able to combine forestry concerns with other facets of rural life and are best able to sustain the community's interests and achieve unity in forest management. These leaders play a crucial role in representing community interests and building relationships with external institutions. They are the chief contact persons for the Forest Department and crucial in determining protection methods, arbitration in instances of contestation within the village or from outside, and in distribution of forest usufruct.

The duties that are asked of the forest citizens in JFM are similar in both States: protection of forests, apprehension and reporting of offenders, and assisting the Forest Department with forestry works. However, village forest protection committees, including those who show positive indicators about forest management, do not necessarily follow the formal requisites of JFM, such as regular patrolling, reporting forest offences to the Forest Department officials, or extracting only those forest usufructs that are permitted in the JFM framework. The monitoring and patrolling of forest, for example, is seldom carried out in any formal manner or on a sustained year-round basis. When they do so, the villagers typically resort to policing techniques of the Forest Department in trying to safeguard their forest from outsiders. This involves exclusion of outsiders, violent confrontations, and penalizing those (with fines and detainment, for example) who are caught by the resident villagers. However, villagers hardly ever report petty forest offenses to the Forest Department. The extraction of forest usufruct too does not adhere to what is allowed in the JFM. Clear felling of trees for household and agricultural purposes is routinely practised. Nonetheless, many of these committees have demonstrated that they are capable of fostering forest protection, maintaining restraint from destruction, and indeed in several instances, their efforts have led to better forest cover.[1]

The research finds that one of the key incentives that was provided in the JFM programme – a cash share from harvest – although an attractive proposition, is often a paltry sum, and is made available by the Forest Department at irregular intervals, if at all. In the case of Jharkhand, because of past unfair harvest practices, villagers are not convinced that the harvest would yield fair shares for them. Instead, securing forest usufruct for routine use and petty business is the most potent incentive for villagers to get involved in forest management.[2] The silvicultural decisions are controlled by the Forest Department and rarely take cognizance of market opportunities or ways villagers may want to carry out the operation. The usufruct arrangement in JFM also fails to appreciate the contribution from individuals or households in forest management duties. Instead, a uniform set of rights and duties is assigned to all the members of the forest management committee, and the benefits are to be equally divided among the members.

The village-based forest management committees need to be given more autonomy so that they can partake in forest management in ways that are in consonance with the inherent community practices as mentioned above. The FD should provide room for villagers to decide on forest management duties and harvest options that best reflect their labour input, dependence on the forest, and larger market opportunities. However, left to itself, this specialized institution remains inherently unstable. Support from the Forest Department on forestry and rural development is crucial in bolstering the initiatives that are taken by the village-based committees. Outside institutions would need to ensure that their affiliations do not cause detrimental effects in the way the committees function.

---

[1] Figures that could prove conclusively that JFM has helped to increase the forest cover in India are wanting. The forest survey of India (FSI), for example, reported that in the years between 1991 and 1993 there was an increase of 171 sq. km. in the total forest cover in West Bengal (FSI 1991; FSI 1993; also Raha et al. 1997). However, of this, only 41 sq. km of forest was located in the southwestern (JFM) districts of Bankura, Purulia and Midnapore. In Bihar (and Jharkhand), the forest cover had lowered by 81 sq. km. in these two years (FSI 1993). The loss of forest was, however, not localized to one place but was spread throughout the State.

[2] This finding is in contradiction to a key attribute of Social Forestry, where income generation was found to be the prime incentive for villagers to participate in afforestation programmes on private land and village commons (see chapter 1).

It is not surprising that JFM has crystallized differently in the States of Jharkhand and West Bengal. To foster participatory forest management in southwest Bengal, the Forest Department in West Bengal has taken several innovative steps, such as registration of several thousand villagers under the Joint Forest Management agreement, monitoring the FPCs, conducting all-FPC meetings, carrying out harvest in FPCs that complete the mandatory five-year period after registration, distribution of usufruct, and preparing development microplans when funds are available. It has also made efforts to restructure the department and align itself with the *panchayats* to better suit the participatory rhetoric. It was argued, however, that a certain conservationist and target-oriented bias continues to underscore the work style and focus of West Bengal's forest bureaucracy. Jharkhand's Forest Department, on the other hand, needs to remedy its infrastructure failings. The department faces the challenge of revamping the ethics and work style to gain the trust of forest citizens. The lackadaisical attitude with which it has added the 'participatory' clause in its forestry project reflects no less than a doublespeak by the Forest Department, where top-down management and the older paradigm of scientific forestry continue to dominate management plans. However, I am not of the opinion that the Forest Department should only pursue the community goals of making forest usufruct available to the dependent citizenry. Instead the FD could pursue a number of goals that are in line with the participatory principles. The bureaucracy could, for example, solicit and support participation and equity goals in forestry that could be put under community management and, in other instances where community dependence and management characteristics are less visible, pursue conservationist, even revenue-generation goals.

The forest bureaucracy is not a solid and unified entity. For lack of explicit instructions, the lower-level officers make several departures from JFM provisions in their day-to-day functions. In both Jharkhand and West Bengal, there is a certain withdrawal in policing of forest resources by the Forest Department. On the other hand, the lower-level officials acknowledge the community management of forests and trust villagers with carrying out forest protection responsibilities, including dealing with petty offences. The lower-levels officials are instrumental in providing support and legitimacy to methods that are chosen by the community for forest management (including looking away from petty offences), resolving intervillage contestations over access and use of forest land, and providing vital support through recommendations for earmarking an FPC 'ready for harvest', and provision of infrastructural support in carrying out harvest and usufruct distribution. However, the beat officials have limited power to negotiate profitably with the villagers. Many of their formal work styles, such as patrol duties, the manner in which they interact with the villagers and book-keeping, are replete with methods that have been in existence since the colonial period.

I pointed out that senior bureaucrats have continued to retain a hold over the forest management machinery. Decentralization may not, however, necessarily mean tearing down the current management structure. In the interinstitutional atmosphere it could well be that a solid and disciplined Forest Department can negotiate with other rural agencies such as FPCs, *panchayats*, and NGOs more effectively without compromising the safety of the staff or the managerial stakes in participatory forestry. A central unit could efficiently combine the feedback from the decentralized and empowered forest management units and make more effective decisions about forest management policies.

The beat-level office needs to be strengthened in numbers, have better-trained and orientated officers, and offer an attractive remuneration package and fair promotions to staff at this level (issues such as non-participatory attitude towards villagers, practice of partisanship and corruption will also need to be addressed). Not unlike the village-based forest management committees, there needs to be provision of autonomy where lower-level officials can respond more independently to the field situations. Each responsibility for the lower-level officials may not need to be put in black and white; indeed, their unique approach in deciphering the histories of local forest land, nature of villagers' dependence on forests, and other ground truths are key to the success of participatory forest management.

## 8.3 JFM Promoters and Rural Development Forestry

This section sums up the impressions of the two JFM-promoting institutions: *panchayats*, and NGOs. Forest Protection Committees with limited powers are found to be in an asymmetrical relationship with the traditional village institution, the *panchayat*. With respect to NGOs, it is argued that those NGOs that include rural development agendas in their work plans and maintain a sustained presence in villages provide strong forums that can be used for forestry management as well.

As members of the executive committee, the members from the *panchayat* are to play a supervisory role. This provision, however, assumes that the *panchayat* leaders can represent and understand well the forest needs of all the members of forest committees and act in a reliable, efficient, and just manner in the realm of forest management. It was argued that the village polity (represented by the *panchayats*) is not always sympathetic to forest management. The *panchayat* leaders have bartered forests in order to strengthen electoral positions in their villages. In other instances, the management of forests holds little interest for many *panchayat* leaders. *Panchayats* continue to hold an indispensable position in rural life and are seldom held responsible by the villagers for mismanagement of the forest. I argued that the members of Forest Protection Committees (FPCs) are in the best position to secure forest usufruct and should be provided with support that bolsters their initiatives. FPCs should be encouraged to maintain a symmetrical relationship with the *panchayats*, particularly over the issue of forest management. The FPCs can also be useful to the FD as a formal point of contact that the forest bureaucracy can use to approach the villagers for forest conservation, harvest work, and microplans without necessarily having to fall back on the *panchayat* to act as the 'go-between'. Indeed, to make forest committees a complete subsidiary of the *panchayat* would not be an effective solution to forest management. Instead, the Forest Department should recognize those community-based forest protection groups that need support and ensure that the *panchayats* complement their needs and roles in Joint Forest Management.

Although the Forest Departments have invited non-governmental organizations to play supporting roles, their role remains unclear, or limited at best. They cannot work on forest land, and their efforts are not coordinated with the Forest Department or *panchayats* on any regular basis or with a definite agenda. Findings from this research indicate that the NGOs that specialize only in *fostering* 'participation and institution building' are held in lesser esteem than those that are involved in development projects or are insinuators of development.[3] The development NGOs that remain involved with the villages on a sustained basis are likely to produce powerful forums that can also be used to bolster forest management initiatives. Indeed, the fact that village-based forest committees can combine forest concerns with development issues is one of the most optimistic signs to emerge from the village-NGOs relationship.

The history of the participatory paradigm warns us of the disjunction between the goals set by the planners and the actual product. Although Joint Forest Management has addressed many criticisms that Social Forestry faced, it would do well to approach the current informal practices among villagers with sympathy and make needed adjustments. Until such accommodations are made, the villagers will continue to play 'hide and seek' in forest land.

### 8.4 Future Directions for Indian Forestry

This section extrapolates on the key findings and recommendations that were made in the dissertation and suggests the possible directions that forest management and related policies might take in the future in India. It also discusses the recent guidelines issued by the Ministry of Environment and Forests to bolster JFM efforts and redress some of the criticisms the programme has faced. I maintain optimism for the state's engagement in forest villages where citizens can benefit equitably from forest resources, and be involved in development, and a number of institutions can participate in rural development forestry to cover a number of goals.

In 2000, the Ministry of Environment and Forests issued guidelines to strengthen Joint Forest Management efforts in the country (GOI 2000). Accordingly, JFM was proposed, also in forests that have good canopy (GOI

---

[3] This is not to undermine the role played by the genuine efforts of those NGOs who have used participatory rural appraisal tools to make the target population aware of and create formats of participation, dispute resolution and institutional building, and which can be used as a model to be replicated elsewhere.

2000). It was also proposed that self-initiated forest groups be identified and registered as JFM committees, and that the period of their existence and duties performed for protection and regeneration be taken into account while allotting benefits under the JFM programme (ibid. 2000). In another set of guidelines issued in 2002, the Ministry reasoned,

> the relationship between *panchayats* and JFM Committees should be such that the JFM Committees take advantage of the administrative and financial position and organisational capacity of the *panchayats* for management of the forest resources. However, the unique and separate non-political identity of the JFM Committees as 'guardian of forests' should be maintained and ensured (GOI 2002).

The Ministry of Environment and Forests looks eager to consolidate the gains that were made in the past 10 years and convert JFM into an all-India phenomenon. To extend JFM in forests with good canopy and rich vegetation diversity will mean an important paradigmatic shift in how Forest Departments tend to function: FDs will no longer be looking to involve people only in degraded forests and taking a target-oriented approach to JFM (as discussed in chapter 3).[4] Similarly, it is significant that the Forest Department has recognized the importance of autonomy for JFM committees in the overall village polity (as recommended in chapter 6). These guidelines and the policy pronouncements in the 10th five-year plan (for the period 2002-2007) make it clear that Joint Forest Management has become the mainstay of forest policies and projects in India and that the JFM is not going to meet the fate that the now near-redundant social and farm forestry programmes met, after a decade or two of inception.

However, the policy makers are yet to address many other core issues surrounding JFM. It has been proposed that a number of Joint Forest Management committees (JFMC) will form the Forest Development Agency (FDA) which will be responsible for a variety of forestry works including afforestation and regeneration of degraded forests, watersheds and CPRs. All the funds for the JFM programme will be channeled through the Forest Development Agencies. Again, most of the funded projects will come through the National Afforestation Programme (NAP), a '100% centrally sponsored scheme' (GOI 2003). A memorandum of understanding (MOU) is proposed to be signed between the Forest Department and the JFM committees, where roles and responsibilities, implementation of work programme, pattern of sharing of usufructs and conflict resolution will be put into black and white.[5] In claiming to be more efficient, one

---

[4] However, the Ministry clarified that the activities would be limited to NTFP management and no alternation should be permitted in the basic silvicultural prescription in the working plan. (GOI 2000). Also, the sharing percentage should be limited to a maximum of 20% of the revenue from the final harvest (ibid. 2000). Also, JFM is not extended to forest lands that are under reserved category (RFs).

[5] On the positive side, FDAs will be registered under the Societies Registration Act, 1860 thus giving the JFM members legal recognition (GOI 2000).

suspects there is a tighter center-state arrangement being planned over the JFM projects. These new provisions do not show an understanding of how local forests are managed, intra- and inter- village communication is carried out, and the incentives villagers need to be involved in participatory forest management. For example, to encourage participation of women in JFM, all that the guidelines have suggested is having more women on committees and meetings (GOI 2000). In suggesting that 'no less than 25% of the share of village community should be deposited in the village development fund for meeting the conservation and development needs of the forests' (ibid. 2000), the forest bureaucracy has overestimated the general cash returns from harvests and shown poor appreciation of the dynamics of cash returns as an incentive to participate in JFM. Also the emphasis to place several afforestation responsibilities on village forest committees may elicit poor enthusiasm.

On the other hand, the decision-making apparatus at the village and beat level have not been sufficiently empowered, nor the incentives to be party to JFM (equity, access, development) been given a firmer footing, nor all the problems in the interinstitutional set-up (except the autonomy aspect of JFM committees vis-à-vis *panchayats)* addressed and resolved. The forest bureaucracy cannot expect to micro-manage JFM projects from the headquarters and senior bureaucrats' offices. Merely viewing the country's forest policies with a JFM-tinted glass without effective decentralizatioin or recognition of the nature of the immense variety in actors, forest lands and goals that form the basis to the participatory principles of forest management, will not allow honest forest management solutions.

Nonetheless, Joint Forest Management has provided an important opportunity to take stock of the forestry infrastructure and the principles behind it. It would be necessary to identify contradictions at the policies level and to analyze how forest decision making and executive systems are set up. Vis-à-vis participatory forest management, there is a need for the Forest Department to take into account the context-specific variables in forests and be able to respond in a timely and efficient fashion to the ever-evolving local forestry situations. For example, the management should be able to take into account that community forestry practices can be vastly different in a relatively small area.[6] It will also be important to recognize that just as the history of local forests and related forestry practices is important, community behaviour and practices in forests change over time. A group that is at one time actively and fruitfully involved in forest management may disengage from forest activities. In such cases, the Forest Department, for example, might assign management responsibilities to a more dependent and responsible group or, if such cannot be found, alter the goals that are affixed on the land. Indeed, on the other hand, the villagers who do not live next to the forest but are dependent on the forest or show promise for managing the forest should be considered by the Forest Department for partnership.

---

[6] Similarly, local institutions and actors that engage with the state and villagers are different.

Forest management in India calls for provisions that can allow new surveys and reclassification of forest lands. Many forest lands that are under reserved category no longer have the pristine characteristics of reserved forests, and several communities live and depend on them. On the other hand, several cases of protected category forest are not used by village communities and can be used to achieve goals that are oriented more towards conservation, research and/or revenue generation. Working plans that form the basis for timber operations and other forest works have several limitations, such as the long gestation periods to prepare them, delays, and even absence. These working plans are prepared at the senior bureaucratic levels and are guided by central government rules that take little congnizance of microsituations. Although certain overall principles may remain in place, JFM forests need to be guided by microplans prepared locally by the lower-level officials in consultation with the concerned villagers and local institutions. The silvicultural decisions and harvest operations should acknowledge the immediate goals of the villagers while recognizing market realities and opportunities, and returns for the individual labour that is put into the management of forest.[7] An ideal participatory forest management should be able to maintain a symmetrical dialogue with local actors and institutions and keep an eye on the equitable distribution of forest usufruct, generation of revenue, conservation, and overall development, although each goal is not necessarily to be fulfilled from the same patch of forest land.

Further research is, however, needed to examine the role of the state in different forest management situations and purposes that are intended from forests and forest lands. Research is also needed to understand the unsatisfactory performance of the Forest Department in particular, and the state in general in rural development forestry. Case studies that are located in different situations are required to more rigorously scrutinize the facets of the evolving involvement of the rural population in forest management. These might include studies of the hierarchy that is built up between ecological institutions, their linkages, and resultant efficacy. Equally important would be the need to examine the detrimental affiliations in intra- and inter-institutional set ups. Research is also needed to explore potentials for enhancing rural livelihood opportunities from forest resources and gauge how villagers utilize the ecological institutions and microplanning situations to push agendas according to their own priorities.

To sum up, romanticizing community characteristics or representing the state and Forest Department essentially at loggerheads with poor communities is misleading. To simply hand over forest lands to forest citizens with assumed virtues of being the rightful owners and sustainable managers smacks of populism.

---

[7] The 2000 GOI guidelines have given guarded support to microplans prepared in consultation with JFM members. Once prepared and submitted, the 'senior bureaucrats will dovetail the requirements of microplans with the working plans' (GOI 2000).

The land tenurial rights can continue to be held by the state where a set of management systems is devised to serve subsistence and development needs in forest land with community interests while the Forest Department is free to pursue pure conservation and commercial interests on other lands. However, piecemeal solutions, as we have seen before (from strict custodial to *social* to *joint* forestry) will not achieve this aim. The state will need to be more sure-footed than ever before in pursuing new legislations and a bureaucratic framework that allow recategorization of forest land, overhaul working plan systems, stress on microplans and ensure efficient decision-making systems at the ground level.[8] *Panchayats* and NGOs should be given more defined, even autonomous roles, albeit without making village-based forest committees subservient to them. Specific forests should also be opened to partnership from outside institutions including private entrepreneurs. I believe that these provisions will also help foster the normative ethical principles that cater to the needs of forest citizens and help evolve forest management regimes in India that are more participatory.

Considering the conservative framework in which the forest bureaucracy tends to operate, some suggestions that are made here are ambitious. However, I am optimistic about the role of the state in forest management, which alone has the infrastructure and legitimacy (and the mandate for welfare) to make the most compelling paradigmatic changes in forest management over time, take initiatives for rural development and monitor involvement of external institutions and individuals.

---

[8] The state will need to reevaluate those constitutional and institutional provisions that have accumulated from the past and are impediments to dynamic and modern forest management in India.

# Bibliography

Acharya, P. (1999) End of the Congress: New Turn in Bengal Politics. Economic and Political Weekly, Vol. 34, No. 33, 2298-2299.

Adams, W. (1990) Green Development: Environment and Sustainability in The Third World. Routledge, London.

Adhikari, N., Yadav, G., and Roy, S. (1991) Process Documentation of Women Involvement in Forest Management at Maheshpur, Ranchi District. Paper Presented at the National Workshop on Managing Commons (15-16 December), Organized by the Indian Institute of Forest Management, Bhopal.

Agarwal, B. (1986) Cold Hearths and Barren Slopes: The Woodfuel Crisis in the Third World. Zed Books, London.

Agarwal, B. (1992) The Gender and Environment Debate: Lessons from India. Feminist Studies, Vol. 18, No.1, 119-158.

Agarwal, B. (1994) A Field of One's Own: Gender and Land Rights in South Asia. Cambridge University Press, U.K.

Agrawal, A. (1995) Dismantling the Divide between Indigenous and Scientific Knowledge. Development and Change, Vol. 26, 413-489.

Agrawal, A. (1999) Community-in-Conservation: Tracing the Outlines of an Enchanting Concept, p 92-108 in Jeffery, R. and Sundar, N. (eds.) (1999) New Moral Economy for India's Forests? Discourses of Community and Participation. Sage Publications, New Delhi.

Agrawal, A. (2001) Common Property Institutions and Sustainable Governance of Resources. Forthcoming: World Development.

Agrawal, A. and Sivaramakrishnan, K. (2000) Agrarian Environments: Resources, Representation, and Rule in India. Duke University Press, Durham.

Agrawal, V. (1985) Forests in India: Environmental and Production Frontiers. Oxford and IBH Publications, New Delhi.

Anonymous (1987) Proceedings of the 1985 International Conference on Rapid Rural Appraisal. Khon Kaen University Publication, Thailand.

Anonymous (1990) Forest Management Partnerships: Regenerating India's Forests. Executive Summary of the Workshop on Sustainable Forestry (10-12 September), New Delhi.

Anonymous (1994) Proceedings of JFM Workshop in Bihar, Ranchi. Society for Promotion of Wastelands Development, New Delhi.

Anonymous (1996) Gender and Forestry: Conclusions and Recommendations. Society for Promotion of Wastelands Development, New Delhi.

Arora, D. (1994) From State Regulation to People's Participation: Case of Forest Management in India. Economic and Political Weekly, Vol. 29, No. 12, 691-698.

Bagchi, A. (1998) Studies on the Economy of West Bengal since Independence. Economic and Political Weekly, Vol. 33, No. 47-48, 2973-2978.

Bagchi, S. and Phillip, M. (1993) Wastelands in India: An Updated Potential. Society for Promotion of Wastelands Development, New Delhi.

Balachander, G. (1995) Fire Grazing, and Extraction of Non-Timber Forest Products in the Nilgiris Biosphere Reserve, Southern India: Implications for Forest Policy, Sustainable Use and Local Economies. Unpublished Ph.D. Dissertation, The State University of Rutgers, U.S.A.

Baland, J. and Platteau, J. (1996) Halting Degradation of Natural Resources: Is There a Role for Rural Communities? Clarendon Press, Oxford.

Banerjee, D. (1998) Indian Industrial Growth and Corporate Sector Behaviour in West Bengal, 1947-97. Economic and Political Weekly, Vol. 28, No. 47-48, 3067-3074.

Bannerjee, A. (1996) Some Observations on Community Forestry. Wasteland News (February-April). Society for Promotion of Wastelands Development, New Delhi.

Baumann, P. (1997) Decentralizing Forest Management in India: The Case of *Van Panchayats* in Kumaun. Unpublished Ph.D. Dissertation, University of Cambridge, U.K.

Bayly, C. (1991) Rulers, Townsmen and Bazaars: North Indian Society in the Age of British Expansion, 1770-1870. Oxford University Press, New Delhi.

Beck, T. and Ghosh, M. (2000) Common Property Resources and the Poor: Findings from West Bengal. Economic and Political Weekly, Vol. 35, No. 3, 147-153.

Bharti, I. (1989) The Decay of *Gram Panchayats* in Bihar. Economic and Political Weekly, Vol. 24, No.1, 18-19.

Bharti, I. (1990) Bihar, Most Wretched. Economic and Political Weekly, Vol. 25, No.38, 2124-2125.

Bharti, I. (1992) Bihar Bane: Slow Progress on Land Reforms. Economic and Political Weekly, Vol. 27, No.13, 628-630.

Bhatia, B. (1998) After the Bathe Massacre. Economic and Political Weekly, Vol. 33, No. 14, 751-752.

Biehl, J. (1991) Finding Our Way. Rethinking Ecofeminist Politics. Black Rose Books, Montreal.

Blair, H. (1969) Caste, Politics and Democracy in Bihar State, India: The Elections of 1967. Unpublished Ph.D. Dissertation, Duke University, U.S.A.

Blaikie, P. and Brookfield, H. (ed.) (1987) Defining and Debating the Problem in Land Degradation and Society. Methuen, London.

Blomley, T. (1996) Tree Committees Protect a Forest in Kenya. Wasteland News (February - April). Society for Promotion of Wastelands Development, New Delhi.

Brodt, S. (1998) Learning from the Land: Local Knowledge Systems of Tree Management in Central India. Unpublished Ph.D. Dissertation, University of Hawaii, U.S.A.

Brown, V. (1997) Landcare in Australia: Talking Local Sustainability in Policy, Practice and Place. ODI Rural Development and Forestry Network Paper (Winter 1996/97; 20e).

Bryant, R. (1992) Political Ecology: An Emerging Research Agenda in Third-World Studies. Political Geography, Vol. 11, No. 1, 12-36.

Burman, J. (1996) Joint Forest Management in West Bengal: Issues to Ponder. Journal of the Indian Anthropological Society. Vol. 31, 257-264.

Burman, J. (1997) Community Participation in Indian Forestry. Journal of the Indian Anthropological Society. Vol.32, 173-183.

Byres, T. (ed.) (1994) The State and Development Planning in India. Oxford University Press, Delhi.

Campbell, J. (1997) Emerging Federations in JFM and Community Forestry in India and Nepal. Wasteland News (November-January), Society for Promotion of Wastelands Development, New Delhi.

Carter, J., Connelly, S. and Wilson, N. (1994) Participatory Forestry in Sril Lanka: Why So Limited Change on the Horizon? ODI Community Forestry Network Paper (17b).

Castells, M. (1997) The Power of Identity. The Information Age: Economy, Society and Culture, Volume II. Blackwell, Oxford.

Chadha, Y. (1997) Rediscovering Gandhi. Century, London.

Chaitanya, K. (1996) Opportunistic Alliances and Shifting Party Loyalties. Economic and Political Weekly, Vol. 31, No. 16-17, 993-994.

Chakrabarty, B. (1998) 1998 Elections in West Bengal: Dwindling of the Left Front? Economic and Political Weekly, Vol. 33, No. 50, 3214-3220.

Chakraborty, R., Freir, I., Kegel, F. and Mascher, M. (1997) Community Forestry in the Terai Region of Nepal: Policy Issues, Experience and Potential. Report and Working Paper Series 5, German Development Institute, Berlin.

Chambers, R. (1983) Rural Development: Putting the Last First. Longman, Harlow.

Chambers, R., Pacey, A. and Ann Thrupp, L. (ed.) (1989) Farmer First: Farmer Innovation and Agricultural Research. Intermediate Technology Publications, London.

Chandra, S. (1985) Limitation of Voluntarism. Mainstream (New Delhi), Vol. 23, No. 38, 11-12.

Chatterjee, M. (undated) Women in Joint Forest Management: A Case-study from West Bengal. An IBRAD Publication, Kolkata.

Chatterjee, N. (1995) Social Forestry in Environmentally Degraded Regions of India: Case-study of Mayurakshi Basin. Journal of Environmental Conservation, Vol. 22, No. 1, 20-30.

Chatterjee, P. and Finger, M. (1994) The Earth Brokers: Power, Politics and World Development. Routledge, London.

Chatterji, A. (1996) Community Forest Management in Arabari: Understanding Sociocultural and Subsistence Issues. Society for Promotion of Wastelands Development, New Delhi.

Chaudhuri, N. (1965) The Continent of Circe. Chatto and Windus, London.

Corbridge, S. (1986) State Tribe and Religion: Policy and Politics in India's Jharkhand. Unpublished Ph.D. Dissertation, University of Cambridge, U.K.

Corbridge, S. (1993) Ousting Sinabonga: The Struggle for India's Jharkhand in Robb, P. (ed.) (1993) Dalit Movements and the Meaning of Labour in India. Oxford University Press, Delhi.

Corbridge, S. and Jewitt, S. (1997) From Forest Struggles to Forest Citizens? Joint Forest Management in the Unquiet Woods of India's Jharkhand. Environment and Planning A, Vol. 29, 2145-2164.

Correa, M. (1996) No Role for Women: Karnataka's Joint Forest Management Programmes. Economic and Political Weekly (June 8), 1382-1384.

Das, A. (1986) Bihar: Landowners Armies Take Over Law and Order. Economic and Political Weekly, Vol. 21, No. 1, 15.

Das, A. (1989) Bihar: A Lost Cause. Economic and Political Weekly, Vol. 22, No. 17, 736-737.

Das, A. (1992) The State of Bihar: An Economic History without Footnotes. Centre for Asian Studies (VU University Press), Amsterdam.

Das, A. (1998) Jharkhand Aborted Once Again. Economic and Political Weekly, Vol. 33, No. 45, 2827-2829.

Das, V. (1992b) Jharkhand: Castle over the Graves. Inter-India Publications, New Delhi.

Dasgupta, S. (1998) West Bengal and Industry: A Regional Perspective. Economic and Political Weekly, Vol. 33, No. 47-48, 3049-3060.

Datta, S. and Varalakshmi, V. (1999) Decentralization: An Effective Method of Financial Management at the Grassroots (Evidence from India). Sustainable Development, Vol. 7, No. 3, 113-120.

Disilva, E., Appanah, S. and Kariyawasam, D. (1994) Sustainable Forestry Management in Developing Countries: Experiences from Asia. Natural Resources Forum Journal, Vol. 18, No. 4, 251-262.

Dodson Gray, E. (1979) Green Paradise Lost. Roundtable Press, Massachusetts.

Dove, M. (1992) Foresters' Beliefs About Farmers: A Priority for Social Science Research in Social Forestry. Agroforestry Systems, Vol. 17, 13-41.

Dove, M. (1994) The Existential Status of the Pakistani Farmer: Studying Official Constructions of Social Reality. Environmental Series No. 2, East West Center, Honolulu.

Dréze, J. and Sen, A. (ed.) (1997) Indian Development: Selected Regional Perspectives. Oxford University Press, Delhi.

Ehrlich, P. (1968) The Population Bomb. Ballantine, New York.

Farmer, A. and Bates, R. (1996) Community versus Market. Comparative Political Studies, Vol. 29, No. 4, 379-400.

Faust, D. (1996) Ecological Restoration in Rural India: The Contribution of NGOs to Participatory Natural Resource Management. Unpublished Ph.D. Dissertation, University of Minnesota, U.S.A.

Fortmann, L. (1988) Great Planning Disasters: Pitfalls in Technical Assistance in Forestry. Agriculture and Human Values, Vol. 5, 49-60.

FSI (1991) The State of Forest Report. Government of India, Ministry of Environment and Forests, Dehra Dun.

FSI (1993) The State of Forest Report. Government of India, Ministry of Environment and Forests, Dehra Dun.

Gadgil, M. (1985) Towards an Ecological History of India. Economic and Political Weekly, Vol. 20, No. 45-47, 1909-1913.

Gadgil, M. and Guha, R. (1993) This Fissured Land: An Ecological History of India. Oxford University Press, Oxford.

Gadgil, M., and Guha, R. (1995) Ecology and Equity: The Use and Abuse of Nature in Contemporary India. Routledge, London.

Gangopadhyay, S. (1991) West Bengal in Agro Climatic Zone Specific Research - Indian Perspective Under NARP (ed. S.P.Ghosh). ICAR, New Delhi.

Gauld, R. (2000) Maintaining Centralized Control in Community-based Forestry: Policy Construction in the Phillippines. Development and Change, Vol. 31, No.1, 229-254.

Ghai, D. and Vivian, J. (ed.) (1995) Grassroots Environmental Action: People's Participation in Sustainable Development. Routledge, London.

Ghosh, M. (1998) Agricultural Development, Agrarian Structure and Rural Poverty in West Bengal. Economic and Political Weekly, Vol. 33, No. 47-48, 2987-2995.

Gillan, M. (1998) BJP in 1998 Lok Sabha Elections in West Bengal: Transformation of Opposition Politics. Economic and Political Weekly, Vol. 33, No. 36-37, 2391-2395.

GOB (1964) Bihar *Panchayati Raj* Act, 1947 (and Amendment, 1963). Government of Bihar Press, Ranchi.

GOB (1986-1998) Forest Offence Registers. Records held at Annagarha Forest Beat, Forest Department, Bihar.

GOB (1988) Annual Administrative Report and Statistical Glimpses, 1987-88. Compiled by Forest Research Division, Department of Forest and Environment, Bihar.

GOB (1990) Government of Bihar Resolution and Forest Department Letter on Joint Forest Management (Resolution No. 5244, dated November 8). Department of Forest and Environment, Bihar.

GOB (1994) Bihar Forestry Project: Preparation Report (No. 10/94 CP-IND 105). Submitted to the Investment Centre, FAO/World Bank Cooperative Centre. Prepared by the Forest Department of Bihar. Department of Forest and Environment, Bihar.

GOB (1996) *Pratiwedan*: Annual Report, 1995-1996. Department of Forest and Environment, Bihar.

GOB (1998) *Pratiwedan*: Annual Report, 1997-1998. Department of Forest and Environment, Bihar.

GOB (1999) *Pratiwedan*: Annual Report, 1998-1999. Department of Forest and Environment, Bihar.

GOI (1927) The Indian Forest Act, 1927 (Act XVI of 1927). Central Publication Branch, Government of India, Kolkata.

GOI (1980) Agricultural Statistics, 1978-79. Central Forestry Commission, Government of India, New Delhi.

GOI (1988) National Forest Policy. Ministry of Environment and Forests, New Delhi.

GOI (1990) Involvement of Village Communities and VAs in Regeneration of Degraded Forests. Circular on Joint Forest Management. Ministry of Environment and Forests, New Delhi.

GOI (2000) Guidelines for Strengthening of Joint Forest Management Programme. Circular no. 22-8/2000-JFM (FPD), Issued on 21 February 2000. Ministry of Environment and Forests, New Delhi.

GOI (2002). (Additional) Guidelines for Strengthening of Joint Forest Management Programme. Circular no. 22-8/2000-JFM (FPD), Issued on 24 December 2002. Ministry of Environment and Forests, New Delhi.

GOI (2003) National Afforestation Programme: Compendium of Operational Guidelines and Circulars. National Afforestation and Eco-Development Board, Ministry of Environment and Forests, New Delhi.

GOWB (undated) Joint Forest Management in East Midnapore Forest Division. Forest Department, Government of West Bengal.

GOWB (1966) West Bengal Forests. Directorate of Forests, Government of West Bengal, Kolkata.

GOWB (1986-1998) Records on Forest Offence, Minutes from FPC Meeting and Harvest Operations. Records held at Gopegarh Beat and Midnapore Range Offices.

GOWB (1989) JFM Resolution No. 4461 Covering Southwest Bengal. Forest Directorate, West Bengal.

GOWB (1990) Modified JFM Resolution No. 5062, Covering Southwest Bengal. Forest Directorate, West Bengal.

GOWB (1991) JFM Resolution No. 8554 and 8555 Covering North Bengal and Darjeeling Gorkha Hill Areas Respectively. Forest Directorate, West Bengal.

GOWB (1993) Various Letters from the Divisional Forest Officers (DFOs) in Reply to the Proposal from the Forest Directorate (Kolkata) to 'Restructure' the Department.

GOWB (1993b) West Bengal Forestry Project: Annual Report (1992-93). Monitoring and Evaluation Wing, Forest Directorate, West Bengal.

GOWB (1993c) Status Report on Arabari Socioeconomic Project. Forest Directorate, Silvicultural Division, West Bengal.

GOWB (1994) Role of Forest Protection Committees in West Bengal, West Bengal.

GOWB (1995) Letters from the Officer on Special Duty and the DFO, Midnapore East to the PCCF of Forest, West Bengal on Reorganization of the Directorate of Forest and Creation of Posts. Midnapore Forest East Department File No. 2655 - For/ FR/O/D/4E-2/95).

GOWB (1995b) Greening the Waste. East Midnapore Forest Division. Forest Directorate, West Bengal.

GOWB (1996) Proceedings of Regional Workshop on Joint Forest Management (February). West Midnapore Division, West Bengal.

GOWB (1996b) West Bengal Forestry Project: Annual Report, 1995-1996. Monitoring and Evaluation Wing, Forest Directorate, Government of West Bengal.

GOWB (1997) Recent Trends in JFM: Proceedings of National Workshop, Forest Department, Bankura, West Bengal.

GOWB (1997b) West Bengal Forestry Project: Survey Monitory Report, 1996-1997. Monitoring and Evaluation Wing, Forest Directorate, West Bengal.

Grove, R. (1995) Green Imperialism: Colonial Expansion, Tropical Island Edens, and the Origins of Environmentalism, 1600-1860. Cambridge University Press, Cambridge.

Guha, R. (1983) Forestry in British and Post British India: A Historical Analysis. Economic and Political Weekly, Vol. 18, No.44, 1882-1896.

Guha, R. (1989) The Unquiet Woods: Ecological Change and Peasant Resistance in the Himalaya. Oxford University Press, Bombay.

Guha, R. (1994) Forestry Debate and Draft Forest Act: Who Wins, Who Loses? Economic and Political Weekly, Vol. 29, No. 34, 2192-2196.

Guha, R. and Martinez-Alier, J. (1997) Varieties of Environmentalism: Essays North and South. Earthscan, London.

Gupta, A. (1998) Ecology and Development in the Third World. Second Edition. Routledge, London.

Gupta, A. and Ferguson, J. (ed.) (1997) Anthropological Locations: Boundaries and Grounds of a Field-Science. University of California Press, London.

Gupta, J. (1995) Evolution of a Legal Agreement for Joint Forest Management in Haryana. Wasteland News (August-October). Society for Promotion of Wastelands Development, New Delhi.

Gupta, S. (1981) Non-Development in Bihar: A Case of Retarded Sub-Nationalism. Economic and Political Weekly, Vol. 16, No. 37, 1496-1502.

Gupta, T. (1992) Yadav Ascendancy in Bihar Politics. Economic and Political Weekly, Vol. 27, No. 26, 1304-1306.

Haeuber, R. (1991) Development and Deforestation: Indian Forestry since Independence. Unpublished Ph.D. Dissertation, University of South Carolina, U.S.A.

Hall, J. (1997) Canada's Model Forest Programme: Bringing Community Forest Values into the Development of Sustainable Forest Management in the Canadian Context. ODI Rural Development and Forestry Network Paper (Winter 1996/97; 20e).

Haque, M. (1996) Revitalizing Forest Development Corporations for Reclaiming Wastelands with Institutional Finance. Wasteland News (May-July). Society for Promotion of Wastelands Development, New Delhi.

Hardin (1968) The Tragedy of Commons. Science, Vol. 162, 1243-1248.

Hauser, W. (1997) General Elections 1996 in Bihar: Politics, Administrative Atrophy and Anarchy. Economic and Political Weekly, Vol. 32, No. 41, 2599-2607.

Heredia, R. (1988) Voluntary Action and Development Towards a Praxis for Non-Governmental Agencies. Concept Publishing Company, New Delhi.

Hiremath, S., Kanawalli, S. and Kulkarni, S. (1995) All About Draft Forest Bill and Forest Lands: Towards Policies and Practices as if People Mattered (Third Edition). Akhil Graphics, Dharawad, India.

Hobley, M. (1996) Participatory Forestry: The Process of Change in India and Nepal. Rural Development Forestry Study Guide 3. Rural Development Forestry Network. Overseas Development Institute, London.

Howes, M. (1997) NGOs and the Institutional Development of Membership Organizations: The Evidence from Six Cases. Journal of International Development, Vol. 9, No.4, 597-604.

Hulme, D. and Edwards, M. (ed.) (1995) Non Governmental Organizations-Performance and Accountability: Beyond the Magic Bullet. Earthscan, London.

IBRAD (undated, a) Strengthening Institutions: An Experience from Joint Forest Management. An IBRAD Publication, Kolkata.
IBRAD (undated, b) Vegetation Monitoring by the People. An IBRAD Publication, Kolkata.
IBRAD (undated, c) Steps in Sensitization: A Manual. An IBRAD Publication, Kolkata.
IBRAD (undated, d) Participatory Vegetation Monitoring: A Case-study in Midnapore. An IBRAD Publication, Kolkata.
IBRAD (undated, e) Identification of Leadership: A Quantitative Approach. Working Paper No. 33. An IBRAD Publication, Kolkata.
IBRAD (undated, f) Facilitating Institutional Change for JFM. IBRAD. Working Paper No. 35. An IBRAD Publication, Kolkata.
IBRAD (undated, g) Activities of IBRAD in the Field of Joint Forest Management. An IBRAD Publication, Kolkata.
IBRAD (undated, h) Bilateral Matching of Institutions: An Illustration in Forest Conservation. Working Paper 22. An IBRAD Publication, Kolkata.
IBRAD (undated, i) Problems and Prospects of Participatory Community Development. Working Paper 15. An IBRAD Publication, Kolkata.
IBRAD (undated, j) Comparative Study of the Functioning of Forest Protection Committees of the Villages Dahi and Lengamara, Midnapore, West Bengal. Working Paper No. 26.
IBRAD (undated, k) Working Paper 4. An IBRAD Publication, Kolkata.
Inoue, M. (undated) Scope of Research in Participatory Forest Management. Unpublished paper. University of Tokyo, Japan.
Jeffery, R. and Sundar, N. (eds.) (1999) New Moral Economy for India's Forests? Discourses of Community and Participation. Sage Publications, New Delhi.
Jewitt, S. (1995) Voluntary and 'Official' Forest Protection Committees in Bihar: Solutions to India's Deforestation? Journal of Biogeography, Vol. 22, No. 6, 1003-1021.
Jewitt, S. (1996) Agro-ecological Knowledge and Forest Management in the Jharkhand India: Tribal Development or Tribal Impasse? Unpublished Ph.D. Dissertation, University of Cambridge, U.K.
Jodha, N. (1986) Common Property Resources and Rural Poor in Dry Regions of India. Economic and Political Weekly, Vol. 21, No.27, 1169-1181.
Joseph, K. (1997) Lessons from Bihar Fodder Scam. Economic and Political Weekly, Vol. 32, No. 28, 1686-1687.
Kant, S. (1996) The Economic Welfare of Local Communities and Optimal Resource Regimes for Sustainable Forest Management. Unpublished Ph.D. Dissertation, University of Toronto, Canada.
Kant, S. and Nautiyal, J. (1994) Sustainable Joint Forest Management through Bargaining: A Bilateral Monopoly Gaming Approach. Journal of Forest Ecology and Management. Vol. 65, No. 2-3, 251-264.
Khan, I. (1995) Forest Policy and Institutional Framework. Wasteland News (May-July). Society for Promotion of Wastelands Development, New Delhi.
Khan, N. (1998) Land Tenurial Dynamics and Participatory Forestry Management in Bangladesh. Journal of Public Administration and Development, Vol. 18, No.4, 335-347.
Khare, A. (1992) Profile of Activities. Society for Promotion of Wastelands Development, New Delhi.
Khare, A., Singh, S., Saigal, S. and Dutta, A. (1995) Participatory Forest Management in West Bengal: A Case-study. A Report Prepared for World Wide Fund for Nature-India and Society for Promotion of Wastelands Development, New Delhi.
Khator, R. (1991) Environment, Development and Politics in India. University Press of America, Lanham.

Khilnani, S. (1997) The Idea of India, Hamish Hamilton, London.

Kolavalli, S. (1995) Joint Forest Management: Superior Property Rights? Economic and Political Weekly, Vol. 30, No. 30, 1933-38.

Krishnaswamy, A. (1995) Sustainable Development and Community Forest Management in Bihar, India. Journal of Society and Natural Resources, Vol. 8. No. 4, 339-350.

Kumar, S. (1996) Forest Use Customs, Tenurial Law and Joint Forest Management in Bihar, India. Unpublished Fellowship Report, University of Cambridge, U.K.

Kumar, S. (1997) Forest Tenure and Joint Forest Management in Bihar, in GOWB (1997) Recent Trends in JFM: Proceedings of National Workshop, Forest Department, Bankura, West Bengal.

Kurian, M. and Bhatia, J. (1997) Forest Guards as Partners in Joint Forest Management. Ambio, Vol. 26, No. 8, 553.

Kurup, V. (ed.) (1996) New Voices in Indian Forestry. Society for Promotion of Wastelands Development, New Delhi.

Lal, D. (1988) Hindu Equilibrium (I): Cultural Stability and Economic Stagnation. Clarendon Press, Oxford.

Lieten, G. (1992) Continuity and Change in Rural West Bengal. Sage, New Delhi.

Ligon, E. and Narain, U. (1999) Government Management of Village Commons: Comparing Two Forest Institutions. Journal of Environmental Economics and Management, Vol. 37, No. 3, 272-289.

Locke, C. (1999) Constructing a Gender Policy for Joint Forest Management in India. Development and Change, 1999, Vol. 30, No. 2, 265-285.

Locke, C. (1999b) Women's Representation and Roles in 'Gender' Policy in Joint Forest Management, pp. 235-253 in Jeffery, R. and Sundar, N. (eds.) (1999) New Moral Economy for India's Forests? Discourses of Community and Participation,.Sage Publications, New Delhi.

Luthra, V. (1994) Lack of People's Involvement in Forest Management: Are Foresters the Villains? Wasteland News (February-April). Society for Promotion of Wastelands Development, New Delhi.

Maity, A. (1997) A Study of *Gram panchayat* in Midnapore, West Bengal. Unpublished M.Sc. Thesis, Vidyasagar University, Midnapore.

Malhotra, K.C., Deb, D., Dutta M., Vasulu, T.S., Yadav, G. and Adhikari. M. (1993) The Role of Non Timber Forest Products in Village Economies of South West Bengal. ODI, Community Forestry Network Paper (15d).

Mathur, H. (1997) Participatory Development: Some Areas of Current Concern. Sociological Bulletin, Vol. 46, No.1, 53-95.

Mathur, K. (1995) Politics and Implementation of Integrated Rural Development Programme. Economic and Political Weekly, Vol. 30, No. 41-42, 2703-2708.

Mawdsley, E. (1997) Nonsecessionist Regionalism in India: The Demand for a Separate State of Uttarakhand. Unpublished Ph.D. Dissertation, University of Cambridge, U.K.

McGean, B. (ed.) (1991) NGO Support Groups in Joint Forest Management: Emerging Lessons. Sustainable Forest Management Working Paper Series No. 13. Ford Foundation, New Delhi.

McGean, B., Roy, S.B. and Chatterjee, M. (1996) Learning to Learn: Training and Gender Sensitization in Indian Forest Departments, p 230-255, in Poffenberger, M. and McGean, B. (ed.) (1996) Village Choices, Forest Choices: Joint Forest Management in India. Oxford University Press, Delhi.

Mehta, V. and Verdhan, R. (1996) Microplanning in Joint Forest Management. Proceedings of the National Workshop on Microplanning in JFM. Tata Energy Research Institute, New Delhi.

Mitra,  K. (1995) Dynamics of Forest Product Consumption: The Role of Economic Development and Forest Policies in West Bengal, India. Unpublished Ph.D. Dissertation, University of Florida, U.S.A.

Moench, M. (undated) Training and Planning for Joint Forest Management. Working Paper Series No. 8. Ford Foundation, New Delhi.

Mukherjee, N. (1995) Forest Management and Survival Needs: Community Experience in West Bengal. Economic and Political Weekly, Vol. 30, No. 49, 3130-3132.

Munro, W. A. (1998) The Moral Economy of the State: Conservation, Community Development, and State Making in Zimbabwe. Ohio University Center for International Studies, Athens.

Naik, G. (1997) Joint Forest Management: Factors Influencing Household Participation. Economic and Political Weekly, Vol. 32, No. 48, 3084-3089.

Naipaul, V.S. (1964) India: An Area of Darkness. Picador, London.

Nanang, M. and Inoue, M. (2000) Local Forest Management in Indonesia: A Contradiction between National Forestry Policy and Reality. International Review for Environmental Strategies. Vol 1, No. 1, 175-191.

Nautiyal, J. and Chowdhary, R. (1982) Forest Planning Process in India. The English Book Depot, Dehra Dun, India.

Nesmith, C. (1991) People and Trees: Gender Relations and Participation in Social Forestry in West Bengal, India. Unpublished Ph.D. Dissertation, University of Cambridge, U.K.

Nesmith, C. (1994) Trees for Rural Development. Journal of Applied Geography, Vol. 14, No. 2, 135-152.

Nygren, A. (2000) Development Discourses and Peasant-Forest Relations: Natural Resource Utilization as Social Process. Development and Change, Vol. 31, No. 1, 11-34.

Olivelle, P. (1993) The *Asrama* System:  The History of Hermeneutics of a Religious Institution. Oxford University Press, Oxford.

Ostrom, E. (1990) Governing the Commons: The Evolution of Institutions for Collective Action. Cambridge University Press, U.S.A.

Pachauri, R. (undated) Sal Plate Processing and Marketing in West Bengal. Working Paper No. 12. Ford Foundation, New Delhi.

Palit, S. (1993) The Future of Indian Forest Management: Into the Twenty First Century. Working Paper No. 15. Society for Promotion of Wastelands Development, New Delhi.

Panangatt, V. (1983) Indigenous Leadership and Tribal Development: A Case-study of 3 Villages in District of Santhal Parganas, Bihar, India. Unpublished Ph.D. Dissertation, Cornell University, U.S.A.

Pandey, D. N. (1999) International Network on Ethnoforestry for Indigenous Knowledge on Forest Management. IIFM Newsletter, Vol. 2, No. 3, 3-4.

Pandey, D. N. and Singh, S. (1995) Traditions of Sacred Groves in Aravallis. Wastelands News (in Hindi), April-June, 3-6.

Pathak, A. (1994) Contested Domains: The State, Peasants and Forests in Contemporary India. Sage Publications, New Delhi.

Pathak, A. (1995) Law, Private Forestry and Markets, in Saxena, N.C. and Ballabh, V. (1995) Farm Forestry in South Asia. Sage Publications, New Delhi.

Pattnaik, B. and Dutta, S. (1997) JFM in South-west Bengal: A Study in Participatory Development. Economic and Political Weekly. Vol, 32, No. 50, 3225-3232.

Peet, R. and Watts, M. (ed.) (1996) Liberation Ecologies: Environment, Development, and Social Movements. Routledge, London.

Peluso, N. (1992) Rich Forests, Poor People: Resource Control and Resistance in Java. University of California Press, Berkeley.

Pieterse, J. (1998) My Paradigm or Yours? Alternative Development, Post-Development, Reflexive Development. Development and Change, Vol. 29, 343-373.

Poffenberger, M. (1995) Transition in Forest Management: Shifting Community Forestry from Project to Process. Asia Forest Network.

Poffenberger, M. (1996) Grassroots Forest Protection: Eastern Indian Experiences. Asia Forest Network.

Poffenberger, M. and McGean, B. (ed.) (1996) Village Choices, Forest Choices: Joint Forest Management in India. Oxford University Press, Delhi.

Poffenberger, M. and Sarin, M. (1995) Fiber Grass from Forest Land. Journal of Society and Natural Resources. Vol. 8, No. 3. 219-230.

Powelson, J.P. (1998) The Moral Economy. The University of Michigan Press, Ann Arbor, U.S.A.

Prasad, B. (1997) General Elections of 1996: Major Role of Caste and Social factions in Bihar. Economic and Political Weekly, Vol. 32, No. 47, 3021-3028.

Raha, A. Sudhakar, S. and Prithviraj, M. (1997). Forest Change Detection Studies and Wetland Mapping in West Bengal through Digital Image Processing of Indian Remote Sensing Satellite Data. Regional Remote Sensing Centre Kharagpur, Indian Space Research Organization, Department of Space, Government of India.

Rajaraman, I., Bohra, O. and Renganathan, V. (1996) Augmentation of *Panchayat* Resources. Economic and Political Weekly, Vol. 31, No. 18, 1071-1083.

Ram Krishna Mission (RKM) (1991) *Jaldhara*: Report on the Activities of *Divyayan* and *Krishi Vikas Kendra*. Ram Krishna Mission *Asram* Publication, Ranchi, Bihar.

Ram Krishna Mission (RKM) (1994) Impact of *Divyayan* and *Krishi Vikas Kendra*: An Evaluative Study. Research and Evaluation Cell, Ram Krishna Mission, Kolkata.

Ram Krishna Mission (RKM) (1994b) Vision and Mission: a Souvenir on Silver Jubilee of Divyayan. Ram Krishna Mission *Asram* Publication, Ranchi, Bihar.

Ram Krishna Mission (RKM) (1997) Annual Report of Activities. Ram Krishna Mission *Asram* Publication, Ranchi, Bihar.

Ram Krishna Mission (RKM) (1998). Souvenir released on Centenary of Swami Vivekanand's Return from the U.S. Ram Krishna Mission *Asram* Publication, Ranchi, Bihar.

Rangan, H. (1993) Of Myths and Movements: Forestry and Regional Development in the Garhwal Himalayas. Unpublished Ph.D. Dissertation, University of California at Los Angeles, U.S.A.

Rangan, H. (1996) Development, Environment, and Social Protest in the Garhwal Himalayas, India, p 205-226, in Peet, R. and Watts, M. (eds.) (1996) Liberation Ecologies: Environment, Development, and Social Movements. Routledge, London.

Rangan, H. (1997) Indian Environmentalism and the Question of the State: Problems and Prospects for Sustainable Development. Environment and Planning A, Vol. 29, 2129-2143.

Rangarajan, M. (1996) Fencing the Forest: Conservation and Ecological Change in India's Central Provinces, 1860-1914. Oxford University Press, Delhi.

Rani, P. (1999) State Finance Commissions and Rural Local Bodies: Devolution of Resources. Economic and Political Weekly, Vol. 34, No. 25, 1632-1639.

Raustiala, K. (1997) States, NGOs, and International Environmental Institutions. Journal of International Studies Quarterly, Vol. 41, No.4, 719-740.

Rawat, A. (1991) History of Forestry in India. Indus Publishing House, New Delhi.

Raychaudhuri, A. and Chatterjee, B. (1998) Pattern of Industrial Growth in West Bengal during Last Two Decades: Some Policy Suggestions. Economic and Political Weekly, Vol. 33, No. 47-48, 3061-3065.

Reddy, V. R. (1999) Valuation of Renewable Natural Resources: User Perspective. Economic and Political Weekly Special Articles. Vol. 34, No. 23, 1435-1444.

Rego, S. (1995) Further Dispossessing the Tribals: Implications of Draft Forest Bill. Economic and Political Weekly, Vol. 30, No. 47, 2983-2984.

Ribbentrop, B. (1900) Forestry in British India. Government of India Press, Kolkata.

Rocheleau, D., Thomas-Slayter, B. and Wangari, E. (1996) Feminist Political Ecology. Routledge, London.

Roy, A. (1997) Can Courts Run the Country? Economic and Political Weekly, Vol. 32, No. 41, 2579-2581.

Roy, A. (2001) Community, Women Citizens, and Women's Politics. Economic and Political Weekly. Review of Women Studies, Vol. 36, No. 17, 1441-47.

Roy, B. (1994) Human Rights Abuse Continues Unchecked. Economic and Political Weekly, Vol. 29, No. 49, 3071-3072.

Roy, S.B., Yadav, G. and Mukherjee, R. (undated) Process of Conflict Resolution in Participatory Forest Management: A Case-study from Sarungarh Range, North Bengal, India. An IBRAD Publication, Kolkata.

Saberwal, V. (1997) Pastoral Politics: Bureaucratic Agendas, Shepherd Land-use Practices, and Conservation Policies in Himachal Pradesh, India, 1865-1994. Unpublished Ph.D. Dissertation, Yale University, U.S.A.

Sanyal, M., Biswas, P. and Bardhan, S. (1998) Institutional Change and Output Growth in West Bengal Agriculture: End of Impasse. Economic and Political Weekly, Vol. 33, No. 47-48, 2979-2986.

Sarin, M. (1995) Regenerating Indian Forests: Reconciling Gender Equity with Joint Forest Management. IDS Bulletin, Vol. 26, No. 1, 83-91. Institute of Development Studies, Sussex, U.K.

Sarin, M. (1996) The View from the Ground: Community Perspectives on Joint Forestry Management in Gujarat, India. International Institute for Environment and Development, London.

Sarin, M. (1996b) Latent Gender-Based Conflicts in Community Forestry Institutions. Wasteland News (May-July). Society for Promotion of Wastelands Development, New Delhi.

Sarin, M. (1998) Joint Forest Management: The Haryana Experiment. Centre for Environment Education, New Delhi.

Saxena, N. (1994) Leasing of Forest Lands to Industries. Wasteland News (February-April). Society for Promotion of Wastelands Development, New Delhi.

Saxena, N. (1996) Forests under People's Management in Orissa. Wasteland News (May-July). Society for Promotion of Wastelands Development, New Delhi.

Saxena, N. and Ballabh, V. (1995) Farm Forestry in South Asia. Sage, New Delhi.

Scott, J. (1976) The Moral Economy of the Peasant. Yale University Press, New Haven.

Scott, J. (1998) Seeing Like a State: How Certain Schemes to Improve the Human Condition Have Failed. Yale University Press, New Haven.

Sen, G. (ed.) (1992) Indigenous Vision: People of India and Attitudes to the Environment. Sage Publications, New Delhi.

Sengupta, S. and Gazdar, H. (1997) Agrarian Politics and Rural Development in West Bengal, p 129-204, in Dreze, J. and Sen, A. (ed.) (1997) Indian Development: Selected Regional Perspectives. Oxford University Press, Delhi.

Sengupta, U. (1999) Elections 1999: Bihar-Too Hasty a Requiem for Laloo Yadav. Economic and Political Weekly, Vol. 34, No. 44, 3106-3107.

Sethi, H. (1982) Voluntary Agencies and Social Change: An Analytical Study of Action Groups, Madras Development Seminar Series, Madras.

Shepherd, G. (1985) Social Forestry in 1985: Lessons Learnt and Topics to be Addressed. ODI Community Forestry Network Paper.

Shepherd, G. (1990) Forestry, Social Forestry, Fuelwood and The Environment: A Tour of the Horizon. ODI Community Forestry Network Paper.

Shepherd, G. (1997) Managing Africa's Tropical Dry Forests: A Review of Indigenous Methods. ODI Publications, London.

Shiva, V. (1989) Staying Alive: Women, Ecology and Development. Zed Books, London.

Shiva, V. (1992) Biodiversity: A Third World Perspective. Third World Network.

Shiva, V. (1993) Monocultures of the Mind: Perspectives on Biodiversity and Biotechnology. Third World Network, Zed Books, London.

Singh, A. and Mohanty, M. (ed.) (1996) Foreign Aid and NGOs. Voluntary Action Network, New Delhi.

Singh, R. (1997) Evolution of Forest Tenure in India: Implications for Sustainable Forest Management (c. 1500 B.C.-1997 A.D.). Unpublished Ph.D. Dissertation, the University of British Columbia, Canada.

Sivaramakrishnan, K. (1996) Forests, Politics and Governance in Bengal, 1794-1994. Unpublished Ph.D. Dissertation, Yale University, U.S.A.

Sivaramakrishnan, K. (1998) Comanaged Forests in West Bengal: Historical Perspectives on Community and Control. Journal of Sustainable Forestry, Vol. 7, No. 3-4, 23-51.

Snyder, M. (1995) Transforming Development: Women, Poverty and Politics. IT Publications, U.S.A.

Sontheimer, S. (ed.) (1991) Women and the Environment: A Reader. Crisis and Development in the Third World Monthly Review Press, New York.

Stebbing, E. (1921) The Forests of India: Volume I. London.

Sundar, N. (2000) Unpacking the 'Joint' in Joint Forest Management. Development and Change, Vol.31, No.1, 255-280.

Sundaram, I. (1986) Voluntary Agencies and Rural Development. B.R. Publishing Corporation, Delhi.

Thakur, S. (2000) The Making of Laloo Yadav: The Unmaking of Bihar. Harper Collins, New Delhi.

Thompson, D. (ed. ) (2001) The Essential E. P. Thompson. The New Press, New York.

Tiwary, M. (2003) NGOs in Joint Forest Management and Rural Development: Case Study in Jharkhand and West Bengal, Economic and Political Weekly, Vol. 38, Nos. 51-52, 5382-5390.

Vasan, S. (2000) Contested Categories, Blurred Boundaries: Rural Society, Forest Bureaucracy, and Timber Rights in Himachal Pradesh, India. Unpublished Ph.D. Dissertation, Yale University, U.S.A.

Verma, R. (1991) Caste and Bihar Politics. Economic and Political Weekly, Vol. 26, No. 18, 1142-1144.

Vira, B. (1995) Institutional Change in India's Forest Sector, 1976-1994: Reflections on State Policy. OCEES Research Paper No. 5, Oxford.

Voelcker, J. (1897) Report on Improvement of Indian Agriculture. Government Press, Kolkata.

Wade, R. (1994) Village Republics: Economic Conditions for Collective Action in South India. ICS Press, Oakland.

Warren, S. (1995) The Political Ecology of Rural Development Forestry: Land Use and Species Choice in Gujarat, India. Unpublished Ph.D. Dissertation, Yale University, U.S.A.

Westoby, J. (1987) The Purpose of Forests: Follies of Development. Basil Blackwell, London.

Wilde, V. and Vainio-Mattilla, A. (1995) How Forests can Benefit from Gender Analysis. Gender Analysis and Forestry Series. Food and Agriculture Organization Publication, Rome.

Williams, G. (1997) State, Discourse, and Development in India: The Case of West Bengal's *Panchayati Raj*. Environment and Planning A, Vol. 29, 2099-2112.
Yin, R. (1989) Case Study Research: Design and Methods. Sage, California.

# Appendix I

# Key Phases in Indian Forestry[1]

## Table I.a: Ancient Indian Forestry

| Year | Description |
|---|---|
| 1000 B.C. | Cleaning of forests by the Aryans for settlement and agriculture. |
| 320 B.C. | Reign of Chandragupt Maurya (Mauya Dynasty): Tax remission for cleaning forest is announced. |
| 269-232 B.C. | Reign of Ashok (Maurya Dynasty): *Vanpals* (guards) are appointed to enforce forest rules and catch elephants for the emperor's army. |
| 320-550 A.D. | Gupta Dynasty: Aryans push the tribal population farther into the forests. |

## Table I.b: Key Events in Colonial Forestry

| Year | Description |
|---|---|
| 1806 | Royalty rights over teak proclaimed in south India. Unauthorized felling of teak is prohibited in Madras Presidency. |
| 1846 | First forest service is established in Bombay Presidency. In 1870, the forest service is separated from the revenue department. The forest service is, however, not truly effective until 1920. |
| 1858 | India Act is passed. Following the Sepoy mutiny or the first war for Independence, the rule of East India Company is abolished; the British-ruled territories come directly under the control of the Crown. |
| 1864 | Indian Forest Services (IFS) is constituted by the Government of India; Dietrich Brandis is appointed the first Inspector General of Forests of India. |
| 1865 | Government Forests Act. Allows for demarcation and survey of forests. |

---

[1] Adapted from Warren (1995), Nesmith (1991), and GOWB (1966).

| | |
|---|---|
| 1878 | Forests Act of 1878 (revision of 1865 Act). Provides for the constitution of reserved and protected category of forests. The forest settlements that follow determine 'rights' and 'privileges' of the public. Forests officers gain greater power. |
| 1884 | Working plans branch of IFS is established to aid in carrying out systematic forestry. |
| 1891 | Provincial Forest Service is established to recruit officers from native India. |
| 1894 | Forest Policy of 1894. Upholding the interest of public is declared as one of the objectives of the forest administration. Agriculture is given preference over forestry. Forests are, on the other hand, to be managed for revenue generation. |
| 1920 | Native Indian offices are recruited into the Indian Forest Services. |
| 1921 | Forest management is transferred to the provinces. |
| 1927 | India Forest Act. Classifies forests into reserved, protected, unclassified, and village forests: 'in reserved forests any act not specifically permitted or authorized is an offence; in protected forest no act not specifically prohibited is an offence'. |

**Table I.c: Summary of Forest Acts, Policies and Orders**

| | |
|---|---|
| 1947 | Independence. |
| 1950s | *Zamindari* is abolished around the country. Adds large areas of forest to forest lands. |
| 1952 | National Forest Policy: Introduces concepts of balanced land use, protection of environment, need for establishing plantations, to increase grazing and wood product availability, maintain sustainable timber flow, and maximize forest revenues. Classifies forests into protection, national, village and tree lands. |
| 1966 | Indian Forest Services is reconstituted. |
| 1973 | Wildlife Protection Act. Provides for protection of certain species. Those without valid game licences are disallowed within forest areas, national parks and sanctuaries. |
| 1973 | Acquisition of Private Forest Act. Provides for compensatory transfer of mismanaged private forests to government. |
| 1974 | Private contractors in forests are discouraged. Forest Development Corporation established. |
| 1975-77 | State of Emergency. The central government under Indira Gandhi suspends citizens' fundamental rights. |
| 1976 | Agriculture commission recommandations. Forest becomes a concurrent subject between the States and the central government. |
| 1980 | Forest Conservation Act. Provides for protection of forest tracts, so that no forest area can be diverted for any purpose other than forestry without prior concurrence of the GOI. |
| 1988 | National Forest policy is declared. |
| 1990 | Joint Forest Management order. |

**Table I.d: Forestry Issues in Five-Year Plans**

| Five-year Interval | Description |
|---|---|
| 2nd plan (1952-1957) | One third of the country is to be put under forest cover (modeled on U.S.S.R. and U.S.A.). |
| 3rd plan (1961-1966) | Identifies role of community in enhancing forest cover, such as through sponsored tree-growing programmes. |
| 4th plan (1969-1974) | Plantation of quick growing species (eucalyptus) and vigilance on illegal activities. |
| 5th plan (1974-1979) | 'Social justice' call by Indira Gandhi. Social Forestry is introduced. |
| 6th plan (1980-1985) | Detailed plans about forestry. Support from people is sought, specially from the tribal community. |
| 7th plan (1985-1990) | The emphasis shifts from commercial forestry to social forestry where subsistence needs are to be met on a priority basis (National Forest Policy, 1988). |
| 8th plan (1992-97) | Commends decentralization of control over natural resources, albeit announces a stricter implementation of the Forest Conservation Act, 1980 and National Forest Policy 1988. Proposes an area-specific approach to fuelwood and fodder. Grants to NGOs for afforestation projects. |
| 9th plan (1997-2002) | Joint Forest Management made integral to all 'plantation' projects; emphasis on microplanning and special focus on the tribals and other weaker sections, including women living in and around forests. Proposals for technology and database development and survey and demarcation of forest lands (to compare with land records of revenue department and determine cases of civil encroachments). |
| 10th plan (2002-2007) | JFM becomes the mainstay of forest policies and projects. Formulation of National Afforestation Programme (NAP) at the centre and set up of Forest Development Agency (FDA) at the state level. Proposes to balance a number of 'forests and people' goals: give legal recognition to Joint Forest Management Committees (JFMCs), involve JFM members in microplanning and 'food for work' schemes, ensure involvement of women and tribals, find better market-value for forest products, better coordinate with NGOs and *panchayats*, and, also bring 25% of the country's landmass under forest cover, regenerate degraded forests & CPRs and promote agroforestry. |

Note: The 8th Five Year Plan could not take off in 1990 due to several crises, including a changed government at the centre.

# The Ownership of Forests in India

**Table II.a: Ownership of Forest Lands in India**

| Type of Ownership | Total Forest Area (million hectare) | Percentage of the Total Area |
|---|---|---|
| State Government | 71.33 | 95.2 |
| • Forest Department | 69.19 | 92.3 |
| • Other Departments | 2.14 | 2.9 |
| Corporate Bodies | 2.34 | 3.1 |
| Private | 1.29 | 1.7 |
| Total | 74.96 | 100 |

**Table II.b: Forest Categories**

| Forest Category | Area (million hectare) | Percentage of Total Forest Area |
|---|---|---|
| Reserved Forest | 38.07 | 50.8 |
| Protected Forest | 24.19 | 32.3 |
| Unclassed Forest | 12.70 | 16.9 |
| Total | 74.96 | 100 |

*Source*: GOI (1980)

**Table II.c: The Acquisition Pattern of Forest Land in Bihar (in sq. km)**

| Year | Reserved Forest | Protected Forest | Unclassed Forest | Total |
|---|---|---|---|---|
| 1945-46 | 3,637 | 2,091 | 9 | 5,737 |
| 1952-53 | 3,853 | 3,153 | 423 | 17,399 |
| 1954-55 | 3,864 | 21,338 | 444 | 25,646 |
| 1955-56 | 3,863 | 25,930 | 440 | 30,233 |
| 1987-88 | 5,051 | 24,069 | 7 | 29,226[a] |

Note: [a] Of this area, 15, 939 sq. km is made up of dry peninsular Sal forests (GOB 1994).

*Source*: (GOB 1988, 1994)

# Questionnaire and Interview Formats

## Questionnaire for Household Survey

**1. Demographic Data:**

Name:

| | |
|---|---|
| Age: | Gender: |
| Address (*Tola*): | JFM Membership Capacity: |
| Size of the family: | Number of adults: |
| Number of years in residence in the village: | Literacy (yes/no): |

Community Leaders (JFM and *panchayat*):

**2. Economic Indicators:**

a. Do you have a clear *title* for your land (area)?
b. Do you have land next to the forest?
c. Occupation (farmer/self-employed/service):
d. Daily wage/annual income (source):
e. Other income for family (source):

**3. Villagers' Use and Perceptions of Forests:**

**History**

1. How has forest cover changed in last
   a. 5 years
   b. 10 years
   c. 15 years
   d. 20 years
   e. 30 years?
2. Has the forest cover:
   a. Increased
   b. Decreased
   c. Remained the same
3. Have your living conditions changed over the past five years?
   a. Much better
   b. Better
   c. No change
   d. Worse

e.    Much worse
4.    If the extent of forest is reduced, will it effect you economically? How?
5.    What should be done to maintain forests for long-term use?
6.    Have the forest practices and dependence changed over years? How are they reflected in  practices such as collection, felling, and incidents of thefts?
7.    What has been the nature of your relationship in the past with:
      a.    Senior Forest Department Officials
      b.    Junior officials (beat officer/ guards)
      c.    *Panchayat* members
      d.    Block development officials?

## Functions

1.    The nature of the village forest management committee:
      a.    When was it formed? On whose initiative?
      b.    Who are actively involved in the work of the committee? Who are against the committee?
      c.    How do you identify your forest?  Is it contested by other villagers? Are other forests easily accessible?
      d.    Whom do you ask before you bring forest usufruct? (no one, head of the household, leader, committee members)
2.    Which forest do you go to? How often do you go to the forest?
      a.    Regularly
      b.    During certain months, seasons
      c.    For particular needs
3.    On your gathering trips, do you encounter other people collecting produce? How frequently?
      a.    If so, are they from your own village or are they outsiders?
      b.    Are there any rules in the village that regulate how much you can collect?
      c.    What do you think of these rules?
4.    Forest Duties and Offences:
      a.    Do you go for forest-guarding duty? If so, how often? What do you do? Do you mind losing time? What else could you have done in this time? Does your family agree to the voluntary guarding of forests?
      b.    Is it compulsory? Who assigns duty? Who monitors? What are the fines for negligence? How do you handle forest offences?
      c.    How is your relationship with the Forest Guard/officers? Do forest officials matter?
      d.    Have there been fights over forest? If so, what were the reasons behind them?
      e.    How do you find the new arrangement? a. approve strongly, b. mildly, c. disapprove strongly.
5.    Village meetings:
      a.    How often are meetings held? Where? Who summons the meetings?
      b.    Who attends the meetings: which groups from the village/forest officials/NGOs? Who do not attend? Are there penalties for those who don't come to meetings?

c. What issues are discussed? Have you expressed your opinions in village meetings?

d. What purpose do these meetings serve?

6. How is your relationship with villagers in neighbouring villages/*tolis*? What do you think of their use of forest? Do members of other communities or the opposite sex use forest differently?

7. What roles have the Forest Department, *panchayats*, and NGOs played in aiding the forest management in the village and resolving disputes?

### Usufruct

1. How do you use the trees: those on homestead, those in the forest?

2. What are your various forest-based requirements for household-, agricultural-, and business- purposes?

3. Do you keep trees as an asset for emergency?

4. What do you collect? Do fallen twigs and branches adequately meet your needs? If not, what do you do?

5. Who of your family members collect fuelwood, NTFP, poles?

6. If fuelwood depots provided wood, will you buy and stop collecting?

7. Do you use forest usufruct for trade? If yes, what do you sell? Where is the local market? How much money do you make from the sale?

8. Usufruct arrangement with the Forest Department:

a. Has there been timber harvest?

b. What role did you play?

c. What was your share in the usufruct? How did you use it?

d. What is the nature of support you get from the Forest Department?

e. Had there been projects that were undertaken by the Forest Department?

f. Are you happy with forestry work that is carried out by the Forest Department?

8. Have the *panchayats* and NGOs helped or worsened the management of forest and distribution of forest usufruct?

9. What is the nature of welfare projects undertaken by the *panchayats* and NGOs in your village, and in the vicinity?

Place:                                         Date:

# Format for Standard Data Collection on Village Forest Protection Committees

Range:                                                    Beat:
Name of the Forest Protection Committee:
Date of Formation and Registration (informal/official):
Villages and *tolis* included in the FPC:                 *Panchayat*:
Names of FPC leaders:
Types of lands (*usar/ dahi/* vested)
Adjacent FPCs and villages:

Total Number of Households involved in JFM:
Scheduled Caste:_____, Scheduled Tribe:_____, Others: _____
Landless families: ___ Small farmers (< 2ha)___ *Patta* (vested land holders): __
Women participation:

## Infrastructural Availability

Metal road: _____ kilometres (kms)        Bus service: _____kms
Railway service: _____kms                Veterinary/ fisheries/ health: ___ kms
Primary health centre: ____ kms            Primary school: ____ kms
Secondary school: _____ kms               Post office: _____ kms
Hospital: _____ kms                       Bank: _____ kms;
Weekly *haat* (local market): ___ kms      Principal market: ____km
*Panchayat samiti*: _____ kms             *Panchayat*: _____ kms

## Forest Resources

Forest area allotted: _____ hectares

| Sal Area | Plantation Area | Blank Area |
|---|---|---|
| 1- 5 years old: | 1- 5 years old: | |
| 5- 10 years old: | 5- 10 years old: | |
| >10 years old: | >10 years old: | |

Nature of boundary of the forest area:
If demarcated:

Other commons available to FPCs for use:
  a.  Private
  b.  Homestead
  c.  Strip plantations

Forest use history:                         Beat officer's remarks:

# Format for Discussions with Leading Members of Village-based Forest Protection Committees

Name:                          Age:                          Sex:

Village:                              Membership capacity:

1.  Demand and availability of forest products:
    a.  Fuelwood:
    b.  Fodder:
    c.  Small timber and Poles:
    d.  Bamboo:
    e.  Tasar host:
    f.  NTFP (names):

2.  History of forest land:
3.  Economic activities related to forest products (if any):
4.  If in possession of JFM agreement documents:
5.  Awareness of forest tenurial arrangement, usufruct rights, forest boundary:
6.  Recognition of rights of other villages on the forests:
7.  Condition of forest (Good/ Medium/ Poor):
8.  Harvest history and methods employed:
9.  Meetings details (date started, subsequent meetings, attendance, women attendance, agenda discussed):
10. Forest-guard Duties
11. Dealing with offences:
12. Work by NGOs (if any):
13. Demand for development works (microplanning, if any):

Place:                              Date:

# Index